Program Assessment

Timothy R. Cline
College of Notre Dame of Maryland

An imprint of Addison Wesley Longman, Inc.

Reading, Massachusetts • Menlo Park, California • New York • Harlow, England
Don Mills, Ontario • Sydney • Mexico City • Madrid • Amsterdam

Executive Editor: Michael Roche
Assistant Editor: Ruth Berry
Editorial Assistant: Adam Hamel
Production Supervisor: Louis C. Bruno, Jr.
Senior Marketing Manager: Julia Downs
Senior Marketing Coordinator: Joyce Cosentino
Cover Designer: Regina Hagen
Cover Illustration: Dick Hannus
Print Buyer: Sheila Spinney
Composition and Prepress Services: Pre-Press Company, Inc.
Printer and Binder: Courier Westford
Cover Printer: Phoenix Taunton
Cartoon drawings by Mr. Steve Gill, Outrageous Art Productions, 1924 Barrington Drive West, Clearwater, FL 34625.
Cartoon themes and captions by Tim Cline.

This book is in the Addison-Wesley Series on Human Resource Management.
Consulting Editor: John Parcher Wanous

Library of Congress Cataloging-in-Publication Data

Cline, Timothy R.
Program assessment / Timothy R. Cline.
288p. cm.
Includes bibliographical references.
ISBN 0-201-32259-5
1. Management—Evaluation. I. Title.
HD31.C566 1998
658.4'032—dc21 98-21988
CIP

1 2 3 4 5 6 7 8 9 10—CRW—0201009998

Series Foreword

The publication of Tim Cline's book, *Program Assessment,* marks the beginning of a new phase of productivity for the Addison-Wesley Series on Managing Human Resources. As we approach the twenty-first century, several new titles will be added to the series. The Arvey and Faley book, *Fairness in Selecting Employees* (1988), will soon appear in its third edition. This is ample testimony to the quality and popularity of this work, which was originally written by Arvey in 1979 as the very first title in the HRM series. Wexley and Latham's *Developing and Training Human Resources in Organizations, 2nd Edition,* is currently being revised for the series, as is *Globalizing People Through International Assignments* by Black, Gregersen, and Mendenhall. Finally, I expect to revise my own work, *Organizational Entry* (1980, 1992), in time for the next millennium. Still available are the classic works by Heneman (*Merit Pay,* 1992), Thornton (*Assessment Centers in Human Resource Management,* 1992), and Latham/Wexley (*Increasing Productivity Through Performance Appraisal,* 1994).

As always, this series is dedicated to the articulation of new solutions to human resource problems. My charge to the authors continues to be twofold. First, present your topic so that it will be recognized for its intellectual leadership among your peers at universities around the world. Second, make sure that your presentation is sufficiently readable for both college students and human resource professionals. These are challenging but necessary standards if the best academic knowledge is to be translated into human resources practice.

Series Editor
John Parcher Wanous
The Ohio State University

Other Titles in the Series on Managing Human Resources

Globalizing People Through International Assignments
J. Stewart Black, Hal B. Gregersen, Mark Mendenhall, and Linda K. Stroh
(1999) 0-201-43389-3

Gary P. Latham and Kenneth N. Wexley
Increasing Productivity Through Performance Appraisal, 2nd Edition
(1994) 0-201-51400-1

Merit Pay: Linking Pay Increases to Performance Ratings
Robert L. Heneman
(1992) 0-201-52504-6

Assessment Centers in Human Resource Management
George C. Thornton III
(1992) 0-201-55403-8

Organizational Entry: Recruitment, Selection, and Socialization of Newcomers
John P. Wanous
(1992) 0-201-51480-X

Developing and Training Human Resources in Organizations, 2nd Edition
Kenneth N. Wexley and Gary P. Latham
(1991) 0-673-46160-2

Fairness in Selecting Employees, Second Edition
Richard D. Arvey and Robert H. Faley
(1988) 0-201-00078-4

Preface

Organizations pursue effectiveness—perhaps via different strategies and with varying understandings of what constitutes effectiveness—but pursue effectiveness they do. Many managers initiate organizational programs to effect desired outcomes, but few managers entrust success to fate. Instead, they monitor organizational programs, noting what works and what doesn't. Organizational success turns on the quality of managerial decisions that continue, modify, or end organizational programs.

This book presents knowledge and skills basic to assessing organizational effectiveness: the degree to which employee orientation programs inform, training programs instruct, incentive programs motivate, safety campaigns safeguard, and quality programs assure quality. This book holds that the central function of assessment is to serve organizational decision making. Sound decisions, however, require sound information. Toward that end, this book identifies the types of error that can occur during program assessment and provides strategies that control or reduce each type of error. The premise is that these strategies will likely produce sound information; and in turn, decisions based on sound information are more likely to produce organizational success.

The cornerstone of the book is the author's model of program assessment. The model identifies four influences that can produce an apparent program impact: measurement error, extraneous error, sampling error, and the program itself. The model also makes clear the underlying logic of program assessment; namely, that only after the first three influences have been addressed in succession can an observed impact be attributed to the effectiveness of a program. No other book gives equal coverage to these important influences or shows that they are logical, successive issues to address in assessment.

This theme—that managers should address each influence in succession—structures the book as a whole and guides the content of chapters. At the beginning of each chapter, the model is reintroduced and the component that reflects that chapter's topic is highlighted. This visual technique helps students know the relevance of that chapter's topic. Students can cogently articulate this important theme after reading the book. They know why and how program assessments are completed, and they can ask pertinent questions about each stage of the process.

The current books on program assessment focus on large, social programs, such as a government job training program. Such assessments are usually conducted by trained evaluators. In contrast, this book emphasizes knowledge and skills basic to the assessment of programs within organizations, a common and vital managerial responsibility. Increasingly, managers assess internal programs where they work to ensure organizational effectiveness. This book pursues two goals: to enable readers to help plan program assessments where they work, and to equip readers to be educated consumers of assessment reports that cross their desks.

The approach is quantitative, emphasizing the use of questionnaires to gather data. Focus is also limited to summative assessments, in which the effectiveness of an existing program is assessed to decide whether it should be continued, modified, or ended.

I would like to extend my appreciation to the artistry of Steve Gill for transforming my cartoon ideas into his unique brand of "Outrageous Art," as he calls it. Thanks also go to Sandy Stack for helping clarify several topics and for her support and good humor.

I wish to thank the College of Notre Dame of Maryland for granting me a sabbatical to initiate work on this book. I also wish to acknowledge the Council for Faculty Research and Development at the college for its support of the project. Finally, I thank the following colleagues who reviewed the manuscript and offered many useful suggestions: Gonzalo Garcia, from Texas A&M University; John Kervin, from the University of Toronto; and David Williams, from Brigham Young University. I hope students find *Program Assessment* as useful to read as I found it enjoyable to prepare.

Baltimore, Maryland *Timothy R. Cline*

Credits

Figure 1.1 B. R. Bugelski and D. A. Alampay, The role of frequency in developing perceptual sets. *Canadian Journal of Psychology*. 1961, *15*, 205–211. Copyright © 1961 by the Canadian Psychological Association. Reprinted by permission of The Canadian Psychological Association.

Table 3.2 John P. Campbell, On the nature of organizational effectiveness. In Paul S. Goodman, Johannes M. Pennings & Associates, *New Perspectives on Organizational Effectiveness*. pp 36–39. Copyright © 1977 by Jossey-Bass Inc., Publishers. Reprinted by permission of Jossey-Bass Inc.

Figure 4.1 Earl Babbie, *The Practice of Social Research*. 7th ed. p. 128. Copyright © 1995 by Wadsworth Publishing Company. Reprinted by permission of Wadsworth Publishing Company.

Learning Module 4.1, Example 1 Delbert C. Miller, *Handbook of Research Design and Social Measurement*. 3rd ed. New York: David McKay, 1977, pp 368–370. Copyright © 1977. Reprinted by permission of Addison-Wesley Publishing Company, Inc.

Learning Module 4.1, Example 2 John P. Robinson and Phillip R. Shaver. *Measures of Social Psychological Attitudes*. Rev. ed. Ann Arbor, MI: Survey Research Center, Institute for Social Research, The University of Michigan. Copyright © 1973 by Academic Press. Reprinted by permission of Academic Press.

Table 6.1 Earl Babbie, *The Practice of Social Research*. 7th ed. p. 187. Copyright © 1995 by Wadsworth Publishing Company. Reprinted by permission of Wadsworth Publishing Company.

Appendix 1 D. B. Owen, *Handbook of Statistical Tables* (adapted from pages 519–520). Copyright © 1962 by Addison–Wesley Publishing Company, Inc. Reprinted by permission of Addison Wesley Longman, Inc.

Appendix 2 Sir Ronald A. Fisher and Frank Yates, Table III, *Statistical Tables for Biological, Agricultural, and Medical Research*. Copyright © 1963 by Addison-Wesley Publishing Company, Inc. Reprinted by permission of Addison Wesley Longman Ltd.

Appendix 4 Jacob Cohen, *Statistical Power Analysis for the Behavioral Sciences*, p. 53. Copyright © 1969 by Academic Press. Reprinted by permission of Academic Press, Inc.

Appendix 8 D. B. Owen, *Handbook of Statistical Tables* (adapted from pages 64–87). Copyright © 1962 by Addison-Wesley Publishing Company, Inc. Reprinted by permission of Addison Wesley Longman, Inc.

Contents

Chapter 1 An Introduction to Program Assessment
Chapter Preview and Learning Objectives 1
Sources of Pressure to Assess Programs 3
The Nature of Program Assessment 4
Scope of Program Assessment 6
Methods of Decision Making 7
The Metaphysical Method of Decision Making 7
Learning Module 1.1 Exploring Common Sense 11
The Empirical Method of Decision Making 13
The Scientific Method of Decision Making 21
Main Points of Chapter 1 25
Answers to Learning Module 1.1 26
Notes 26

Chapter 2 An Overview of Program Assessment
Chapter Preview and Learning Objectives 29
The Steps of Program Assessment 30
Involve the Stakeholders 31
Specify the Expected Program Outcome 31
Establish a Measure of the Program Outcome 32
Plan a Method of Gathering Data 33
Collect the Data 35

Analyze the Data 35
Communicate the Results 36
Make Program Decisions 36
The Scientific Model of Program Assessment 37
The Components of the Scientific Model 38
The Logic of the Scientific Model 42
Combining the Model and the Steps 45
Main Points of Chapter 2 48

Chapter 3 Constructing Program Theories
Chapter Preview and Learning Objectives 49
Focus of Chapter 3 50
Program Theories 52
Components of a Theory 52
The Program 53
Expectation 56
Explanation 57
Moderators 59
Boundaries 60
Defining Theoretical Concepts 62
Constructing a Program Theory 66
Learning Module 3.1 Constructing Program Theories 69
Qualities of Useful Theories 70
Main Points of Chapter 3 73
Answers to Learning Module 3.1 74

Chapter 4 Controlling Measurement Error
Chapter Preview and Learning Objectives 77
Focus of Chapter 4 78
Forms of Measurement Error 82
Sources of Measurement Error 83
Effects of Measurement Error 85
Correlation 86
Measurement Reliability 92
Stability 92
Internal Consistency 94
Increasing Measurement Reliability 96
Measurement Validity 96
Content Validation 97
Construct Validation 98
Predictive Validation 102

Learning Module 4.1 Assessing Measurement Reliability and Validity 102
Main Points of Chapter 4 107
Answers to Learning Module 4.1 108
Notes 111

Chapter 5 Controlling Extraneous Error
Chapter Preview and Learning Objectives 113
Focus of Chapter 5 114
Sources of Extraneous Error 115
Effects of Extraneous Error 116
Assessment Designs 117
Deficient Assessment Designs 119
One-Group Observation Design 120
One-Group Pre-and Post-Observation Design 121
Nonequivalent Groups Observation Design 124
Learning Module 5.1 Assessment Design Exercise I 125
True Assessment Designs 126
Equivalent Groups Observation Design 126
Equivalent Groups Pre- and Post-Observation 128
Quasi-Assessment Designs 129
Nonequivalent Groups Pre- and Post-Observation Design 129
One-Group Multiobservation Design 130
Two-Group Multiobservation Design 132
Learning Module 5.2 Assessment Design Exercise II 134
Main Points of Chapter 5 136
Answers to Learning Module 5.1 137
Answers to Learning Module 5.2 139
Note 140

Chapter 6 Sampling Target Audiences
Chapter Preview and Learning Objectives 141
Focus of Chapter 6 142
Sampling 144
Random Sampling 147
Learning Module 6.1 Exploring Random Samples 147
Forming Random Samples 150
Learning Module 6.2 Forming Random Samples 153

Random Assignment to Groups 157
Learning Module 6.3 Random Assignment of Employees to Groups 158
Non Random Sampling 161
Generalizing Sample Results 162
Sample Size 164
Descriptive Surveys 164
Program Assessment 168
Main Points of Chapter 6 172
Notes 173

Chapter 7 Controlling Sampling Error
Chapter Preview and Learning Objectives 176
Focus of Chapter 7 177
Sources of Random Sampling Error 178
Visualizing Random Error 179
The Effects of Random Sampling Error 180
The Mean 182
The Standard Deviation 183
Learning Module 7.1 The Standard Deviation 185
Degrees of Freedom 186
The t test 189
Comparing the Program Group to a Control Group 189
Learning Module 7.2 Conducting the t test 202
Comparing the Program Group to a Norm 213
Main Points of Chapter 7 215
Notes 216

Chapter 8 Matching Tests and Designs
Chapter Preview and Learning Objectives 219
Focus of Chapter 8 220
True Assessment Designs 223
Equivalent Groups Observation Design 223
Equivalent Groups Pre- and Post-Observation Design 223
Quasi-Assessment Designs 225
Nonequivalent Groups Pre- and Post-Observation Design 226
One-Group Multiobservation Design 227
Two-Group Multiobservation Design 230
Additional Designs 232

Multiple Programs 232
Multiple Program Outcomes 237
Main Points of Chapter 8 239
Notes 240

Chapter 9 Communicating Assessment Results and Making Program Decisions
Chapter Preview and Learning Objectives 243
Focus of Chapter 9 244
Communicating Assessment Results 245
Communication Goals 246
Preparing Oral Assessment Reports 248
Introduction 249
What Was Found? 251
Question and Answer Period 251
Preparing Written Assessment Reports 253
Summary 253
Background 254
Conclusions and Recommendations 255
Methods 255
Analysis of the Data 256
Appendix 258
Making Program Decisions 258
Level of Approval 259
Resources 260
Politics 261
Culture 262
Conclusion of the Book 263
Main Points of Chapter 9 263
Chapter Note 264

Appendices
1. Table of Random Numbers 265
2. Table of t Values 268
3. Survey Sample Sizes for **95 Percent (Boldfaced)** and 99 Percent Confidence Levels 269
4. Per Group Sample Sizes for **95 Percent (Boldfaced)** and 99 Percent Confidence Levels 270
5. One-Group Sample Sizes for **95 Percent (Boldfaced)** and 99 Percent Confidence Levels 271

6. Compilations of Research Measures 272
7. Journals That Publish Assessment Reports 273
8. Table of F Values 275
9. World Wide Web Sites Related to Evaluation 277
10. Guidelines for Academic Reports 278

Index 287

1

An Introduction to Program Assessment

Chapter Preview

In this initial chapter, we will review some of the reasons managers conduct program assessments, and we will explore several ways managers typically make program decisions. Our aim is to find an optimum method managers can use to make decisions about the effectiveness of programs within their organizations.

Learning Objectives

After reading Chapter 1, you should be able to:

- identify several sources of pressure for managers to conduct program assessment
- define the terms program and assessment
- distinguish between explicit and implicit programs
- appreciate that programs exist in, and thus program assessment can benefit, every major area of an organization
- identify the limitations of the metaphysical and empirical methods of decision making
- identify the strengths of the scientific method of decision making
- recall the three fundamental steps of the scientific method

Americans are an optimistic lot, the epitome of the "Can do!" attitude: Just give us a seemingly impossible task, and we'll land on the moon, convert perennial flood lands to agricultural gardens, and harness the energy of the atom. Indeed, we have accomplished much for which we can be proud. These feats, and countless others, were accomplished through the efforts of people working together on programs or projects in America's organizations—government agencies, public firms, private businesses.

Americans, however, are cynical too, and sometimes toward the sources of our pride. We believe government agencies, public firms, and private businesses are wasteful, inept, and sometimes unnecessary. Newspaper accounts of failures fuel our cynicism. The United States Air Force paid $999.20 to the Pratt and Whitney Company for a pair of pliers (reduced to $669.00 after a U.S. senator's letter reached the Pentagon).[1] While U.S. automakers tout the quality of their cars, one of every five autos sold in America is a Japanese export.[2] Consumer electronics follows suit. Already familiar with names such as Honda and Toyota, Americans are learning to pronounce names such as Sanyo, Toshiba, Yamaha, Nakamichi, Hitachi, Onkyo, and Casio. Reviews and evaluations in magazines such as *Consumer Reports* and *Stereo Review* document that quality originates beyond our borders. "Why," Americans ask, "can't our automobile and electronics companies manufacture products to counter these intrusions?"

On a sad note, the aftermath of the ten million gallons of oil spilled from the Exxon ship *Valdez* continues to devastate Alaskan shorelines and wildlife, despite the largest financial settlement on record.[3]

And on a sad day, an O-ring failed and television visuals etched deep into our collective memory the tragic loss of the *Challenger* space shuttle and her seven-member crew. Struggling for composure, Americans asked, "Where were the needed safety programs?"[4]

The projected $120 billion cost of covering the losses amassed during the Savings and Loan crisis contributes to a $290 billion national deficit and a $4.2 trillion national debt—a stack of thousand-dollar bills 267 miles high.[5] The fact that members of Congress bounced 4,325 checks within a six-month period only added salt to the wound.[6]

NASA launched the $1.5 billion Hubble space telescope with an ever-so-slightly misshapen mirror, but that distortion was enough to blur the returning images. Dashing the hopes of scientists, officials delayed some experiments and scrubbed others until repairs to the mirrors were undertaken. It was ironic that the engineers had accomplished the more difficult task of creating a perfectly smooth mirror surface but had erred in the easy procedure of cutting the proper curvature. NASA had access to the mirror for ten years before the launch, but quality control systems had not discovered the defect.[7]

Despite victory in the Persian Gulf, the executive branch of the government canceled billion-dollar contracts for the Navy's A-12 Stealth attack bomber because of delays and cost overruns.[8] And the B-2 Stealth bomber, designed to fly undetected, failed tests of its ability to elude enemy radar.[9]

The litany of program failures is extensive and because the failures were too dramatic to escape media attention, the list is also all too familiar. Collectively, these failures underscore the importance of effective program assessment, as each failure is traceable to a breakdown at some critical point of the organizational program. These fiascoes were well publicized, but most employees have witnessed in their workplace unpublicized, and sometimes hushed-up, program failures—orientation programs that fail to inform, training programs that fail to instruct, reward systems that fail to motivate, quality circles that fail to improve quality. Thus, the notorious examples are not exceptions: Program failures—large and small, publicized and concealed—abound. Voices from several sectors are rising, pressuring managers to assess the effectiveness of their programs. Today, the cost of failure is too great to accommodate program ineffectiveness.

Sources of Pressure to Assess Programs

Managers are encountering from a variety of sources mounting pressures to assess organizational programs.[10] Two of these sources, the tightening U.S. economy and increasing foreign competition, are interrelated. American companies are scrambling to secure diminishing resources and to maintain an increasingly costly labor force. Five of seven start-up companies fail within the first five years, and established companies contend with mounting financial pressures. Faced with a general slowdown in economic growth, organizations are "under the gun" to perform, so effective programs are essential.

Second, the expanding service sector of the economy provides impetus to assess the effectiveness of organizational programs. Government service programs such as Welfare and Medicare address important social exigencies, but their success is difficult to measure. Lacking an observable, tangible product, many service agencies are challenged to justify their existence.

Third, congressional regulation creates a need for program assessment. Government program spending continues to escalate at a time when many voters detest tax increases. Congress is insisting that government programs provide an accounting of their activities.

Fourth, consumer sophistication creates pressure for assessment of program effectiveness. Consumers have tasted imported quality and want it from American companies. The public has also "tasted" water, air, and noise pollution and rejects them. Within the organization, workers demand more than good pay, workers seek comfortable working conditions and interesting and challenging jobs. Organizations are implementing programs such as job enrichment, job enlargement, and flexible schedules to improve employees' quality of life at their workplace.

Finally, pressure to conduct program assessment results from managers' increased sophistication in the methods of evaluation. Increasingly, managers learn research and statistical methods in college and training workshops. Consultants experienced in assessment methods are also available.

The span and depth of these pressures leave few hiding places for managers who want to avoid program assessment. Now we will look at the three main components of program assessment: the program, assessment, and decision making.

The Nature of Program Assessment

Program assessment is the process of determining the effectiveness of organizational programs. The central function of program assessment is to serve organizational decision making: Should a program be continued, modified, or ended?

Types of Programs

A program is any definable set of coordinated activities aimed at producing goods or services, or at maintaining or enhancing organizational functioning. Programs can be *explicit* or *implicit,* depending on their degree of visibility. An explicit program usually has a name, specific goals, and a clear beginning. Safety awareness campaigns, communication training programs, and quality control circles are examples of explicit programs. An implicit program is an unnamed, coordinated activity that is still definable and is aimed at maintaining or enhancing organizational functioning. Procurement procedures, reward systems, and managerial style are examples of implicit programs. Each is definable, and their effects are relevant to many managers. We will use the term *program* in a general way, encompassing both explicit and implicit programs whose effectiveness is of interest.

Assessment

A fundamental characteristic of program assessment is comparison. Usually the comparison is to a similar organizational unit—one that is not experiencing the program. For example, a manager may compare the productivity of workers who received training to workers who did not. Alternatively, a comparison can be made to an established norm or quota. For example, a manager may compare employee productivity to the productivity of a large, national sample of employees in the same industry. A comparison can be made to a baseline of previous performance. For example, a manager may compare workers' monthly performance after training to their monthly performance before training.

Program assessment, then, involves comparing outcomes of explicit or implicit programs to a comparable organizational unit, to an established norm or quota, or to a baseline of previous performance. The type of comparison a manager chooses to undertake depends on the particular circumstances of the assessment, but a comparison is required for a program assessment. Without a comparison, there is no basis for interpretation.

Decision Making

It is difficult to envision an organization that does not aspire to be effective, although "effective" may vary among organizations. It is also difficult to find managers who are willing to entrust organizational success to fate or luck. Most managers believe that organizational success turns on the quality of the decisions they make and, further, that quality decision making requires accurate and relevant information. The primary benefit of program assessment is that it can provide such information and thus increases the likelihood that managers will make sound decisions about the effectiveness and the fate of organizational programs.

This is an important point. The purpose of program assessment is astonishly practical: to serve organizational decision making. The reasoning is clear as well: Program assessment can provide accurate and relevant information essential to sound decision making, and sound decision making is more likely to produce organizational success.

Scope of Program Assessment

Almost every segment of an organization is amendable to, and can benefit from, program assessment. Implemented to establish, maintain, and improve organizational functioning, programs permeate organizations, and, in the interest of sound decision making, each program is a candidate for program assessment. We will see that explicit or implicit programs exist in all four elements central to organizations. Program assessment can serve decision making in each element.

Structure. All organizations develop and operate within a structure. Organization charts identify position and hierarchy. Program assessment can support decisions about the structure of an organization. Decisions must be made about division of labor, reporting relationships, span of control, and space allocation.

Management. Program assessment can influence decisions about managing employees and their activities. Decisions need to be made about motivating, guiding, and rewarding employee behavior, as reflected in incentive programs, training programs, quality control circles, and reward structures.

Tasks. Program assessment can impact decisions about work. Decisions must be made about what should be done, how it should be done, and in what sequence it should be done.

Technology. Program assessment can inform decisions about the tools used in the workplace. Organizations are adopting a variety of innovations for the planning, operating, and monitoring stages of work that increase both efficiency and quality. Impressive advances have been made in communication—in storage, retrieval, and manipulation of information, in energy use, and in automation.

Every important element of an organization—its structure, processes, tasks, and technology—contains programs to maintain or enhance organizational functioning. In the interest of sound decision making, each program is a candidate for program assessment. With relevant and accurate program information in hand, decision making will be more sound and organizational success more likely.

Next we will examine the decision-making process in more detail. We will consider two ways managers typically make program decisions—the metaphysical method and the empirical method—and then we will examine the Scientific Method. We will discover that of these three methods of decision making, the Scientific Method is the one most likely to produce sound program decisions.[11]

Methods of Decision Making

Making decisions is an important managerial responsibility. One important decision managers face is whether to continue, modify, or end an organizational program. Because this type of decision influences organizational success, it is important to determine what decision-making method produces the most effective decisions.

There are three qualities mandatory to sound decision making. First, inquiry should focus on the merits of the program, on the program's effects. This may seem obvious because a program's effectiveness is related to its impact on the organization. Yet managers often make decisions that shift the focus away from the merits of the program.

Second, decision making should encourage inquiry. Because inquiry is basic to discovery, this quality also may seem obvious. To judge a program, you must be free to inquire about it. To attain useful and accurate information, inquiry cannot be censored or curtailed. Informed decisions are more likely to be valid than are uninformed ones, so it is important that a method of decision making emphasize the search for and use of accurate information. We will see, however, that managers make decisions in ways that do not encourage inquiry.

Third, decision making should *recognize errors* that managers can make during inquiry and in drawing conclusions from inquiry. As most managers know (and many have learned the hard way) even carefully made observations can be inaccurate. And carefully drawn conclusions can still be wrong. Organizational programs are usually complex, and the means of observation are often inexact, so errors during inquiry are almost unavoidable. A good method of decision making should acknowledge that errors during inquiry are to be expected and steps should be taken to identify their type and severity. So as we examine the three ways managers make decisions, we desire that method that focuses on the merits of the program, encourages inquiry, and acknowledges and estimates the types of error associated with inquiry.

The Metaphysical Method of Decision Making

One method of decision making that managers use is the *metaphysical* method. Using this method, people make decisions through deliberation or contemplation. It acknowledges that knowledge can be independent of and separate from direct observation. According to this method, some things just "stand to reason."

Many things stand to reason within organizations or so we often act. Some things appear obvious, and we base our decisions on that. This is a common method of decision making. Keep in mind the three traits of viable decision making: encourages inquiry, focuses on the merits of the program, and acknowledges and estimates error. There are four kinds of metaphysical decision: 1) tradition, 2) unquestioned authority, 3) consensus, and 4) intuition.

Tradition. A decision that is made by tradition values and relies on what the organization has done in the past and adapts it to the present. Decisions based on tradition maintain organizational habits. For example, the fact that an employee orientation program is in place is sufficient reason to keep it in place. Or a manager may decide to modify a program this year because the program has undergone a revision every year to date. You can identify a tradition-based decision by asking *why* something happened. If the answer is "Because we have always done it that way," you know it is tradition and not based on the merits of the program. Such a decision creates an organizational "habit," and as with our personal habits, organizational habits may go unquestioned, unexamined, and unbroken. Decisions by tradition have the potential to simply repeat previous, ineffective operations. Traditional effectiveness is productive; traditional ineffectiveness is not.

Unquestioned Authority. Managers sometimes—without question—follow the recommendations of any person in authority. For example, that one's boss says an organizational program should be continued . You can recognize this type of decision making by asking the person to justify the decision. The standard reply is "Because the boss said so, that's why." Although the boss may be right, the boss's position of authority is enough for the recommendation to go unquestioned. Questioning authority at work can buy trouble. But unfortunately, as many employees know, status alone provides no assurance of correctness. The boss may have little or no direct experience with or knowledge of the program and still issue a recommendation. Or a boss may hear one bad thing about a program and recommend its termination. Sound decision making, however, requires more than status. This method of decision making does not encourage inquiry.

Little is decided until the boss speaks, and no further inquiry is made once the boss has spoken. This method of decision making does not focus on the merits of the program. Instead, focus is shifted to the presumed expertise of the boss, bolstered by his or her authority.

Consensus. One of the more seductive modes of decision making occurs when people reach agreement. Consensus is comforting. Confidence soars and a sense of validation is felt when one's decisions are readily accepted by others. A manager may continue a program because everyone agrees it is effective. Behind the allure of this method of decision making, however, lies the risk that everyone could be wrong. Questioning shared agreement may elicit disapproval, sometimes strong, from others. When you question the consensus, others may question your loyalty.

Intuition. Decisions based on intuition are founded on faith, on beliefs. The person "just knows" what is true. An often cited example of a decision by intuition is the choice to believe in God. Some have faith, for example, that God exists. I recall as a youngster being asked to mow the lawn on "Spruce Up the Church Day." When the requester returned, he asked why I hand't cut the grass yet. I said that the grass seemed short enough to me. He replied with a zinger; "Why don't you take it to the Lord in prayer?" Returning to find the lawn still uncut, he asked if I had done what he suggested. I replied I had, and God said the lawn was okay just as it was. He became irritated with me. Questioning truths causes trouble.

Reliance on intuition is common in the workplace. Many managers value their own intuition to the point of according it priority over other kinds of evidence. Despite information to the contrary, if a manager "feels in his guts" that a program is effective, that is enough to extend the program. Intuition, however, can be wrong—as anyone who has lost at the racetrack can attest. Basing decisions on belief ends further inquiry, since one's belief is considered the truth. Information contrary to the belief is ignored. Since truth is known, contradictory information is actually "impossible" and should be ignored. Closing inquiry and ignoring contradictory information do not foster open inquiry, a quality important to a viable method of decision making.

Common sense is an interesting subset of decision making by intuition. Common sense is social wisdom so ingrained that it becomes second nature. So when we hear common sense we respond, "Oh yeah, that's true." For example, "seeing is believing" and "beauty

Tim learns that questioning truth lands trouble.

is only skin deep." But you already knew that I imagine common sense abounds. Because it is familiar and ingrained, common sense "rings true." To question common sense elicits trouble. It is risky to question what everyone *knows* is true.

You have probably ridiculed the results of funded research because the findings are just common sense. For example, if researchers report that people who share certain characteristics tend to fall in love with each other, a reader might moan over the money wasted to "discover" what common sense has known for years. "After all," the reader might offer confidently, "Birds of a feather flock together." If the researchers had concluded, however, that dissimilar people fall in love, the public still would be unimpressed: "After all," the reader would state emphatically, "Opposites attract."

Common sense sounds true in isolation. Did you notice, however, that in its infinite wisdom, common sense is a two-way street? According to common sense, both similar and dissimilar people tend to fall in love. There are no other possibilities, so common sense prevails no matter what the researchers find. Common sense often insulates itself from error by accounting for all possible outcomes. If it was determined that two people in a relationship grew *apart* when one moved far away, common sense would explain, "Out of sight, out of mind." On the other hand, if the same couple grew *closer* after one moved, the explanation would be "Absence makes the heart grow fonder." Individually, each statement rings true. Positioned side-by-side, however, we see that common sense has overextended itself, accounting for both outcomes. No matter which outcome researchers find, common sense would mock the effort and expense of the inquiry. Take a few moments to discover whether you have internalized contradictory common sense by following the instructions in Learning Module 1.1 Exploring Common Sense. Learning Modules are an integral part of the chapter content, both clarifying and extending ideas. The reader is encouraged to complete each Learning Module.

LEARNING MODULE 1.1: Exploring Common Sense

Instructions

The statements below contain common sense, except a portion of each statement is missing. Please complete as many of the statements as you can in the space provided.

1. Nothing ventured, ______________________.
2. Better safe ______________________.
3. There's no place ______________________.
4. The grass is always greener on ______________________.
5. Don't rock ______________________.
6. The squeaky wheel gets ______________________.
7. A penny saved is ______________________.
8. You have to spend money to ______________________.
9. What you see is ______________________.
10. Don't judge a book by ______________________.
11. Two heads are better ______________________.
12. If you want it done right, ______________________.
13. Many hands make ______________________.
14. Too many cooks ______________________.
15. Busy hands are ______________________.
16. Take time to smell ______________________.
17. If you got it, ______________________.
18. Pride goeth before ______________________.
19. Look before ______________________.
20. ______________________ or get off the pot.

Analysis

1. The correct responses are presented at the end of the chapter. How many statements did you complete correctly? Most people score higher than 50 percent.
2. What can you conclude about the degree to which you have internalized social values, here in the form of common sense statements?
3. How many statements, considered individually, sound true to you? Do you agree that commonsense statements usually sound true?
4. Do you agree that each pair of statements (e.g., statements 1 and 2, statements 3 and 4, etc.) represents opposite or contradictory conclusions? Take a moment to review each pair.

5. In light of this Learning Module, how useful is common sense for program assessment if it is never wrong, even when it contradicts itself?

END OF LEARNING MODULE 1.1

Common sense lacks the qualities we seek in a method of decision making for program assessment because it doesn't encourage inquiry. Questioning common sense—as does questioning truth—usually elicits correction or reprimand.

Metaphysical decision making involves tradition, unquestioned authority, consensus, intuition, and intuition's subset, common sense. We seek a method that focuses on the merits of the program, encourages inquiry, and notes the errors associated with inquiry, so metaphysical decision making does not satisfy our criteria.

Rather than examining the merits of the program, metaphysical decision making focuses on organizational habits, organizational status, shared agreement, and belief/faith. Whether the truth comes from the past, the boss, shared agreement, or faith, inquiry is closed prematurely, contradictory information is ignored, and nonbelievers (those who question) are censured. Metaphysical methods give little attention to the types of errors associated with inquiry and drawing conclusions. With truth in hand, error is not a concern. Next we turn to a second method of decision making managers typically use, again looking for an optimum method for program assessment.

The Empirical Method of Decision Making

The word empirical means "of the senses." Empirical decision making relies on what we observe through the five human senses—smell, taste, touch, hearing, and sight. Managers primarily use the last two senses, what they hear and see, to assess programs empirically. Managers listen and watch for positive program outcomes. In a quality circles program, managers listen for customers' comments about product quality. In a sales training program, managers watch for an increase in new orders. Managerial decisions to keep, modify, or end programs are based on observations of program outcomes.

The empirical method is common in organizations. We count orders, accidents, tardiness, errors, bed occupancy, and so on. Managers distribute surveys to assess customer satisfaction, employee knowledge, employee morale, company image, and so on. Managers devote considerable activity to observing the outcomes of explicit and implicit programs within organizations, and they usually employ these three steps:

1. Formulate an expectation.
2. Observe a program outcome.
3. Make a comparison.

An expectation is a statement that specifies the relationship between an organizational program and an outcome. The components of an expectation are the program, the program outcome, and the effect the program has on the program outcome. A manager may, for example, expect that a safety training program will decrease employee accidents on the job. The program (training) and an outcome (number of employee accidents) are specified, as is the effect one has on the other (training will *decrease* accidents). A manager may expect that a participative managerial style will increase employee morale. This expectation involves an implicit program: participative managerial style. The outcome is employee morale. The effect is that the program (participative managerial style) will *increase* the outcome (employee morale). An expectation is an informed guess of the effect of a program on a program outcome. The informed guess is usually based on the manager's prior knowledge and experience.

The manager then observes the program outcome. Sometimes observation is direct, as when a manager counts the number of employee accidents following a safety training program. Observation can be indirect as well, as when subordinates of a participative style manager complete a morale questionnaire. The questionnaire responses are indirect in that they are assumed be a reflection of the morale of the employees.

Finally, the manager makes a comparison. A manager may compare the observed program outcome to that of a comparable group, to a baseline of previous performance, or to established norms or quotas. For example, a manager could compare the accident rates of employees who participated in the safety training program to the accident rates of a comparable group of employees who did not. The manager could compare the number of accidents from before and after the safety training program. Finally, a manager could compare the accident rates of trained employees to the national average in the industry or to the accident rate targeted by management as the allowable quota.

The empirical method has two desirable qualities: it focuses on the merits of the program and it encourages inquiry. It is lacking, however, in the desired quality of being sensitive to errors made during inquiry. A manager using this method first formulates an expectation of the effect of the program on the program outcome and then observes the outcome. In performing these steps, two questions arise: What is the expected relationship between the program and the observed program outcome? The questions focus on the merits of the program—its outcomes—and, as questions, they emphasize inquiry. The qualities we seek from the empirical method, then, lie in its anticipation of program outcomes in the first place and in its observation of those outcomes in the second place. Both anticipation and observation are necessary to program assessment. Both require inquiry—inquiry into what we can expect and into what actually occurred. The empirical method of decision making fails to emphasize the types and magnitudes of errors that can accompany inquiry. Let's examine why this is so. The empirical method emphasizes observation through the human senses, mostly what we see and hear, but should we *always* believe what we see and hear? Are the senses always trustworthy? Most of us can think of occasions when our senses fooled us. We will see that errors can accompany each of the three steps of the empirical method; forming expectations, observation, and comparison.

Errors in Expectations. The first step in the empirical method is making an educated guess about the effect of the program on the program outcome. When we consider a specific program and a specific outcome, however—say, safety training (program) and subsequent accidents (outcome)—room for conceptual error arises. Conceptual error can occur in our use of terms. The meanings of *safety training* and *subsequent accidents* are open to interpretation. To most people, safety training is a group of employees assembled to listen to a presentation on safe work practices. But training can assume many forms in organizations: personal instruction, video instruction, computer-assisted instruction, participation in a simulation, hands-on practice, or self learning. Similarly, what constitutes an accident is open to interpretation. The definitions of training and accidents may differ among units within the same organization, or even among employees in the same unit. Most terms that managers use during program assessment, however, are more susceptible to unclarity than these. Terms need clarity, specificity, and delineation from other terms. Without clear use of terms, an expectation involving those terms will likely be unclear as well. The empirical method does not emphasize or provide a set of guidelines for clarity of terms. The common approach is to assume that everyone agrees on the meanings of terms.

Conceptual error can also occur when managers form expectations from their previous knowledge and experience in organizations. Based on previous experience, a manager may expect safety training to decrease accidents. Behind this expectation lies the manager's *explanation* of how organizations establish and maintain safety. The manager's explanation is derived from knowledge of organizational structures, processes, tasks, and technology and may go like this:

> Some kinds of behavior lead to too many accidents. Some kinds of behavior lead to fewer accidents. Training can teach new ideas and skills. Learning new ideas and skills can help employees change their behavior. The changed behavior should lead to fewer accidents.

The crux of the explanation is that employees can *learn* desired behavior. Once the explanation is articulated, it is easy to see that the expectation is drawn from it. Training decreases accidents (the expectation) because employees learn new behavior (the explanation). This is only one explanation among several possibilities. The potential for conceptual error arises because such explanations are seldom articulated in the empirical method. Managers do not lay out their thinking systematically, either to themselves or to others, and without articulation, the explanation remains unexamined.

The empirical method does not emphasize or offer guidelines for the explanations that underlie expectations. Consequently, erroneous explanations may go undetected.

Scientists have developed several criteria to judge the usefulness of explanations. An explanation should not contain internal inconsistencies or inconsistencies with other accepted explanations. An explanation should not omit important terms or the links among them, and an explanation should not be unnecessarily complex. When managers do not examine their explanations, program assessment can be based on inconsistent, incomplete, or complicated explanations.

Errors in Observation. The empirical method of decision making stresses the importance of observation. Managers verify their expectations through observation. But are the senses trustworthy? We will see that the senses can mislead us in several ways.

Inaccuracy in observation arises from the uniqueness of each person's sensory mechanisms. Although most people's eyes and ears function the same way, there are physical differences between your eyes and ears and those of others. A person who is color blind obviously sees colors differently than others. Less dramatic, but just as real, differences in the perception of color exist among most people. One person's sense of red differs slightly from another person's sense of red. Differences in observation can be expected because of the slight differences in the physical makeup of eyes. This applies to the other senses as well. What is loud for another person may be just right for you. We all have encountered people who complain the room is too hot (or cold) when we are perfectly comfortable. When slight differences in observation accumulate to a substantial inaccuracy, or when slight changes in program outcomes interest us, this source of observational error becomes very important. The empirical method of decision making, however, places little emphasis on physical differences in sensory mechanisms, and program assessment proceeds ignorant of any observational differences.

Psychologists discovered years ago that humans engage in selective perception. Of the multitude of stimuli encountered daily, much goes unnoticed or is soon forgotten. Furthermore, people miss and forget differently.[12] Psychologists have concluded that what we notice and forget is selective, based on our expectations, needs, and values.[13] Look at Figure 1.1.[14] What do you see? What people see in Figure 1.1 is influenced by their prior exposure to information, which "sets up" an expectation. This is illustrated in Figure 1.2. People who have just seen drawings of people are more likely to report that Figure 1.1 is a drawing of an old man. Those who just viewed animal drawings say it is a drawing of a rat.

Figure 1.3 shows how needs can influence perception. Driving home from work, a hungry person may longingly notice every restaurant en route, and little else. A person short on cash will miss the eateries, but scan diligently for automated teller machines. The same drive home yielded two very different observations, both influenced by need.

Figure 1.4 illustrates that values can influence perception. Some people see a fuel-efficient, economy car, while others see a low status symbol. The former group value economy over status, and that affects their impression.

Selective perception occurs within the organization as well. Managers' expectations, needs, and values influence what they observe.

Figure 1.1
Expectations Influence Perception

A manager may *expect* high employee morale because that is the program's stated goal; a manager may *need* high employee morale to justify the continued existence of the new program; and a manager may *value* high employee morale, believing it is an integral part of a successful organization. There is nothing wrong with expecting, needing, or valuing high employee morale. The problem occurs when expectations,

Figure 1.2
Prior Exposure Sets Up Expectations

Figure 1.3
Needs Influence Perception

needs, or values lead managers to observe higher employee morale than actually exists. The empirical method of decision making places little emphasis on reducing either the role of unique sensory mechanisms, as discussed earlier, or differences due to selective perception.

Errors in Comparison. To be meaningful, observations should be compared to observations from a similar group, to a standard or quota, or to previous performance. If we use our example of comparing accident rates before and after safety training, we can see the potential for error. When the program group displays fewer accidents after training than does the comparison group, the training appears to be effective. But what if the comparison group had more accidents than the program group *before* training began? The comparison is invalid because the program group was superior before training. Any program can look effective compared to a comparison group that isn't comparable initially. Differences between the program group and the comparison group are important sources of comparison error. Managers often are unaware of these discrepancies and proceed as if the groups were comparable.

Figure 1.4
Values Influence Perception

Errors in comparison can also be the result of nonprogram factors. What if new equipment was installed prior to safety training? We cannot be sure whether the decrease in accidents was due to the training or the better equipment. The empirical method gives little attention to such nonprogram influences.

Finally, comparison errors can result when only a sample of the whole is observed. It is costly and time consuming to study everyone. Sampling is useful unless the smaller group is not representative of the whole group. When not representative, observations from a sample will differ from what would be observed of the whole.

Each step of the empirical method is susceptible to error. Empiricism focuses on the merits of the program and encourages inquiry (two qualities we seek in a method of decision making), but it does not offer guidelines for detecting and dealing with errors in expectations, observation, and comparison. Lacking this, the empirical method is inadequate for program assessment.

Finally, we will consider a third method of decision making, called the scientific method. We will find that this method overcomes the limitations of the metaphysical and the empirical methods of decision making, and thus provides a viable option for program assessment.

The Scientific Method of Decision Making

A viable method of decision making for program assessment should focus on the merits of the program, encourage inquiry, and address errors made during inquiry. We have seen that the metaphysical method fared poorly on all three qualities, and the empirical method, while strong on the first two, stumbled on the third quality. The scientific method of decision making recognizes the strengths of empiricism. It embraces empiricism's emphasis on observation through the senses and adopts the three steps of empiricism: forming an expectation of the effect of the program on the program outcome, observing the program outcome, and comparing those observations to a comparable group, to established norms or quotas, or to previous performance. Like empiricism, the scientific method focuses on the merits of the program and encourages inquiry. The scientific method also addresses the important problem of errors that accompany inquiry, detecting errors made during each step and determining their magnitude. This distinguishes the scientific method from metaphysics and empiricism.

To address errors of inquiry, the scientific method uses a set of rules to guide expectations, observations, and comparisons. The rules of inquiry have been generated by scientists working on a myriad of problems over decades. These "rules" are really an array of prescriptions, principles, practices, conventions, and standards. Because much of the remainder of this book is devoted to identifying, illustrating, and practicing these rules, we will only highlight their purposes here. As you might have anticipated, the scientific method advances a set of rules for each step of the empirical method: forming expectations, observing program outcomes, and making comparisons.

Rules for Expectations. Some of these rules attempt to minimize errors that accompany the formation of an expectation. One source of error emanates from the multiple meanings of the terms used in an expectation. Because they are used differently within organizations, terms must be clear, specific, and distinct from other similar terms. The rules are particularly helpful in program assessment, where many terms such as *participative managerial style* and *employee motivation* are challenging to delineate.

Errors also arise when managers base their expectations on unexamined explanations. For example, we hope that safety training will decrease accidents because employees *learn* new behaviors. Learning and how learning functions in the organization are the key elements in this explanation, but the explanation is erroneous if learning and how it functions is misunderstood, or if something other than learning is the actual explanation. The scientific method uses rules to guide the development and critique of explanations and emphasizes that explanations should be articulated to others. Such inspection and critique reduces conceptual error. Explanations that are examined in this way become known as theories. In the scientific method, expectations are drawn from theory, from voiced and critiqued explanations. Rules attempt to ensure that theories contain all relevant terms and the pertinent links among them. Additional rules see that theories are internally consistent, consistent with other accepted explanations, and not unduly complex. The overall aim is to achieve conceptual clarity.

Rules for Observation. Observations of program outcomes are subject to both the physical limitations of human sensory mechanisms and the influences of human selective perception. What is seen and heard depends on the eyes and ears involved. What is perceived and forgotten is a result of expectations, needs, and values. Error, slight or massive, accompanies observation. The scientific method uses rules to add accuracy and consistency to observation. Rules guide what to observe, how much to observe, when and where to observe, how to observe, whom to observe, how many to observe, and who should observe. Observation is a central tenet of the scientific method, and appropriately, a comprehensive set of rules guides it.

Rules of Comparison. Comparison is a minimum requirement of program assessment, whether to a comparable group, to previous performance, or to a standard or quota. Errors in comparison occur when initial differences exist between the program group and the comparison group. The groups must be similar in all characteristics that affect the program outcome. The scientific method uses rules to ensure that the program group and the comparable group are initially comparable.

Errors in comparison can also occur if nonprogram factors influence the program outcome. New equipment, for example, may decrease accidents instead of, or in addition to, safety training. It is difficult to distinguish the benefits of the new equipment from the benefits of the training. A set of rules minimize such nonprogram influences.

There can be errors in comparison when observations are drawn from a sample of the whole. If the characteristics of the members of the sample do not reflect those of the whole, the outcomes may misrepresent how the program would affect the whole. The scientific method has rules to safeguard against this problem. Rules offer important guidance for forming expectations, making observations, and making comparisons. They seek to minimize error at each stage of inquiry.

Even with its focused and vigilant emphasis on minimizing error, and despite all its rules, the scientific method recognizes that error can elude the most diligent effort. Error can be minimized but not eliminated. Fortunately, the scientific method rules possess an important additional feature: Not only do they minimize error, but they identify the error and estimate its magnitude. Decision making can then proceed with the error minimized and with full knowledge of the type and magnitude of the error as well.

Ironically, the scientific method shuns the idea of eliminating error, for without error, we have only truth and no need for further inquiry. We would confidently ignore any contrary information and rebuff those who question. So, not only is the persistence of error, however slight, acknowledged in the scientific method, it is actually cherished, since it mandates room for additional inquiry, for challenge, for unexpected information.

In scientific research you will frequently see the expression $p < .05$. The p refers to probability, and the $<$ is the math symbol for "is less than." The .05 represents the level of risk of making an error. The expression indicates the probability that the study's decision is incorrect. The expression means that if we repeated the study many times, we would decide incorrectly less than five times in each 100 replications. This translates into 95 percent confidence that the decision is correct. Imagine for a moment that you had the opportunity to wager on a horse, with 95% confidence it would be first across the finish line. Or imagine that you could buy a lottery ticket with 95% confidence of winning millions. Unless morally opposed to these activities, would you buy tickets where success is so assured, almost a sure thing? This is how confident scientists have agreed to be before believing the results of a study. Scientists report the expression $p < .05$, however, as a reminder that room for error still exists, and room for contradictory information and further inquiry exists as well. We will see this expression later in the book when we examine the rules that guide comparison, the third step of the scientific method of decision making. Here, it reminds us that the scientific method looks for and estimates the size of error and yet stops short of reaching "truth," lest certainty close inquiry.

The scientific community values persistent inquiry, even into topics obvious to common sense. It embraces contrary information, making the scientific method self-corrective. Program assessment should welcome a method that focuses on the merits of the program, encourages inquiry, and identifies and estimates errors in inquiry, producing decisions with known risk of being incorrect. Rule-guided procedures should make sound decision making, and in turn, organizational success—more likely.

Table 1.1 shows the strengths and weakness of the three methods of decision making we have examined. As the only method that focuses on the merits of the program, encourages inquiry, and addresses the types of error that accompanies inquiry, the scientific method emerges as the method of choice to serve decision making to determine the fate of organizational programs.

The notorious failures we examined at the beginning of this chapter foretell the myriad of lesser-known program failures in organizations nationwide. Together with mounting pressures from a variety of sources for program accountability, these failures underscore the importance of assessing the effectiveness of organizational programs. The scientific method of decision making provides the means to reach sound program decisions. Much of this book identifies and illustrates the rules of the scientific method. To this end, two general instruc-

Table 1.1
Strengths and Weaknesses of the Three Methods of Decision Making

	Focuses on the Merits of the Program	Encourages Inquiry	Addresses Errors That Accompany Inquiry
Metaphysical Method	–	–	–
Empirical Method	+	+	–
Scientific Method	+	+	+

tional goals are pursued throughout the book. The first goal is to help readers attain the knowledge and skills needed to become educated consumers of program assessment reports. Of special importance is the ability to ask questions to discover if the study successfully followed the rules of science that guide expectation, observation, and comparison. The second goal is to prepare readers to contribute to the planning and conduct of program assessments within organizations. Again, emphasis is on the ability to ask questions to discover if the planned study follows the rules of science. Upon approaching each topic in the book, consider how the concepts or skills will help in the critical review of program assessment reports and help in the planning and conduct of program assessment projects.

Main Points of Chapter 1

- Program failures, both notorious and commonplace, signal the need for program assessment.
- Managers face pressures to undertake program assessments.
- Explicit programs are usually named, have stated objectives, and have clear beginnings. Implicit programs are organizational activity not officially recognized as programs but whose effectiveness is still of interest.
- Assessment requires a comparison to a comparable group, an established norm or quota, or to previous performance.
- The metaphysical method of decision making focuses on information apart from the merits of the program and tends to prematurely close inquiry, ignore contradictory information, and punish those who question.
- The three steps of the empirical method of decision making—forming expectations, observing program outcomes, and making comparisons—focus on the merits of the program and encourage inquiry, but they do not address errors made during inquiry.
- Adopting the three steps of the empirical method, the scientific method of decision making also focuses on the merits of the program and encourage inquiry. It adds a set of rules to guide conceptualization, observation, and comparison, which generate decisions with confidence of being correct.
- The scientific method of decision making emerges as the optimum method for program assessment.

ANSWERS TO LEARNING MODULE 1.1

1. Nothing ventured, nothing gained.
2. Better safe than sorry.
3. There's no place like home.
4. The grass is always greener on the other side of the fence.
5. Don't rock the boat.
6. The squeaky wheel gets the grease.
7. A penny saved is a penny earned.
8. You have to spend money to make money.
9. What you see is what you get.
10. Don't judge a book by its cover.
11. Two heads are better than one.
12. If you want it done right, do it yourself.
13. Many hands make light work.
14. Too many cooks spoil the stew.
15. Busy hands are happy hands.
16. Take time to smell the roses.
17. If you got it, flaunt it.
18. Pride goeth before the fall.
19. Look before you leap.
20. (I better not put it in print) or get off the pot.

Chapter Notes

1. Refund on $999 pliers. The *Washington Post*, Vol. 113, No. 225, July 18, 1990, p. A21.
2. *World Motor Vehicle Data*, 1990 Edition, The Public Affairs Division of the Motor Vehicle Manufacturers Association of the United States, Inc., 1990, p. 29.
3. Exxon to pay $1 billion to settle oil spill claims. The *Sun* [Baltimore], Vol. 308, No. 101, March 14, 1991, pp. 1A,

10A; Valdez oil cleanup complete, but its effects linger. The *Sun* [Baltimore], Vol. 309, No. 58, July 23, 1991, 13A; Malcolm W. Browne, In once-pristine sound, wildlife reels under oil's impact. The *New York Times*, Vol. CXXXVIII, No. 47830, April 4, 1989, pp. C1, C5.

4. Phillip M. Boffey, NASA studies role of headquarters. The *New York Times*, Vol. CXXXV, No. 46809, June 18, 1986, A20.
5. Lower bailout costs seen. The *New York Times*. Vol. CXVII, No. 49225, January 28, 1993, D2; Neal R. Peirce, Clinton calls on governors for help. The *Sun* [Baltimore], Vol. 312, No. 72, February 8, 1993, 9A; Scott Pendleton, National debt: Good or bad? Pick your perspective. *Christian Science Monitor*, Vol. 85, No. 75, March 16, 1993, p. 11.
6. Bounce the house bank. The *Washington Post*, Vol. 114, No. 292, September 23, 1991, A10.
7. Luther Young, Starry-eyed scientists struggle with loss. The *Sun* [Baltimore], Vol. 307, No. 64, July 30, 1990, 1A; Warren E. Leary, NASA is assailed on quality control. The *New York Times*, Vol. CXXXIX, No. 48282, p. 10A.
8. A-12's demise sends defense industry firm message. The *Sun* [Baltimore], Vol. 306, No. 46, January 9, 1991, pp. 1F, 9F.
9. Air Force admits stealth failed recent radar test. The *Sun* [Baltimore], Vol. 309, No. 102, 4A.
10. The following discussion draws heavily from Emil J. Posavac and Raymond G. Carey, *Program evaluation: Methods and case studies*. 2nd ed., Englewood Cliffs, NJ: Prentice Hall, 1985, 19–22.
11. The discussion is drawn from Earl Babbie, *The practice of social research*. 6th ed., Belmont, CA: Wadsworth, 1992, pp. 17–27; Louise H. Kidder and Charles M. Judd, *Research methods in social relations*. 5th ed., NY: Holt, Rinehart and Winston, 1986, 8-19; Morris R. Cohen and Ernest Nagel, *An introduction to logic and scientific method.* NY: Harcourt, Brace, and Co. 1934, 193–195; Eugene Stone, *Research methods in organizational behavior*. Santa Monica, CA: Goodyear, 1978, pp. 5–12.

12. R. Buckhout, Eyewitness testimony. *Scientific American,* 1974, *231,* pp. 23–31.
13. Werner J. Severin and James W. Tankard, Jr., *Communication theories: Origins, methods, uses.* 2nd ed., NY: Longman, 1988, pp. 120–129.
14. Arno F. Wittig and Gurney Williams III, *Psychology: An Introduction.* NY: McGraw-Hill, 1984, p. 326; B. R. Bugelski and D. A. Alampay, The role of frequency in developing perceptual sets. *Canadian Journal of Psychology,* 1961, *15,* pp. 205–211.

2

An Overview of Program Assessment

Chapter Preview

This chapter provides an overview of program assessment. We will discover that an evaluator typically progresses through a series of eight steps, each step specifying an activity to be performed. While completing these steps, however, the evaluator must be mindful of error that can accompany inquiry. Therefore, this chapter also advances a scientific model of program assessment. The model applies the principles of the scientific method of decision making to program assessment. Evaluators should use the program assessment steps and the scientific model in tandem: one to direct activity, the other to minimize error accompanying the activity.

Learning Objectives

After reading Chapter 2, you should be able to:

- describe the activity of each step of program assessment
- explain the purpose of the scientific model of program assessment
- describe the components of the scientific model of program assessment
- identify the steps of program assessment that are susceptible to the error that accompanies inquiry
- describe how the error of inquiry can be minimized
- explain why evaluators should use the steps of program assessment and the scientific model of program assessment in tandem
- describe the logic of the scientific model of program assessment

While organizational effectiveness has interested and sometimes eluded bosses and managers for many years, it is only recently that program evaluators adopted the methods of science. Increasingly, managers appreciate that program assessment requires inquiry—as does science—and that scientists' alertness to the errors that accompany inquiry would benefit program assessment as well. As do scientists, program evaluators collect information and draw inferences from it. That information will likely be sound, as will be subsequent inferences, when evaluators identify and attempt to minimize any error that accompanies inquiry. Drawing from years of experience, scientists have sharpened their awareness of potential error that accompanies inquiry. In response, they have developed strategies and procedures that minimize the role of error while data are gathered and analyzed.

This chapter examines eight major steps of program assessment, and explores how to integrate into these steps an awareness that error accompanies inquiry.

The Steps of Program Assessment

A program assessment progresses through a set of activities that can be consolidated into eight major steps. (See Table 2.1.)

The first four steps are completed before collecting data. The remaining steps help ensure that decision makers obtain, understand, and act on evaluation information. We will discuss each step in turn to give an overview of the Program Assessment process.

Table 2.1
The Steps of Program Assessment

Step 1	Involve stakeholders throughout the assessment.
Step 2	Specify the expected program outcome.
Step 3	Establish a measure of the program outcome.
Step 4	Plan a method for gathering the data.
Step 5	Collect the data.
Step 6	Analyze the data.
Step 7	Communicate the results.
Step 8	Make program decisions.

Involve Stakeholders Throughout the Assessment

As the first step in program assessment, the evaluator should involve stakeholders—those who have a vested interest in the program. Stakeholders include the key decision makers, employees, and clients affected by the decisions made from the assessment, including those who administer or participate in the program. For example, the stakeholders for a management training program include the decision makers who oversee the program, the program trainers, and the program trainees.

Involving the stakeholders early and throughout a program assessment is important. Stakeholders know the program best—its history, purpose, design, strengths, limitations, and vulnerabilities. They also will be affected by any program changes after the assessment—changes in purpose, design, size, and possibly even its existence.

Stakeholders are more likely to support decisions in which they participate, even if the decision counters their input. When excluded from the decision process, stakeholders may feel that decisions are "handed down," and they may resist change. It is a practical step, then, to enlist stakeholder involvement from start to finish of a program assessment.

Stakeholders can assist in different steps. Representatives should be selected when stakeholders are numerous or unavailable. To encourage candor and independent thinking, stakeholders should submit their ideas in writing before discussion. This way stakeholders provide valuable information and buy into the assessment process and its outcome.

Specify the Expected Program Outcome

Effective programs produce desired outcomes. To gauge a program's effectiveness, we must know its intended outcome. The second step of program assessment identifies what we expect of the program and why. For example, the goal of an employee orientation program may be for new employees to learn basic organizational information. Stakeholders can be especially helpful in establishing goals or clarifying those that are vague.

Especially when they represent varying constituencies, stakeholders sometimes disagree over expected program outcomes. If this happens, it is a good idea to work with stakeholders to reach consensus and, if that fails, observe multiple outcomes linked to multiple goals. New stakeholders can evaluate a variety of "mock" results of the program assessment, to identify the type of information they find meaningful for making decisions. If they cannot identify at least one scenario that accurately reflects the program's goal, they will be forced to realize that they must be clearer about expected outcomes. This preliminary exercise can help insure that stakeholders will have faith in and can interpret the results of the program assessment.

Stakeholders, however, are seldom content to merely indicate *what* they expect from a program; they usually want to know *why* it produces the desired outcome. Without such understanding, there is no way to know how to improve a program that doesn't work. Consider an employee orientation program, for example. A manager may expect new employees to become familiar with the organization during the employee orientation. Why? Because the employees *learn* the information, the manager reasons. *Learning* is the explanation for the program's success. If employees don't become familiar with the organization, learning did not take place. Therefore, strategies to improve an ineffective orientation program would focus on factors that facilitate learning. Program explanations are usually drawn from published theory and research on the topic and from the decision makers' personal knowledge and experience.

Establish a Measure of the Program Outcome

To gauge a program's effectiveness, we must measure its expected outcome. Often, a measure of the outcome already exists, developed by others during their previous research. You can find existing measures in published evaluation reports and, more quickly, in compilations of measures like those cited in Appendix 6 of this book. If an outcome measure is unavailable, the evaluator must develop one. Stakeholders can be valuable resources for selecting or developing a measure. They know what questions to ask and what kind of vocabulary to use.

To assess an employee orientation program, for example, the evaluator would need a measure of the employees' knowledge of basic organizational information. Since the information is specific to the organization, there will be no preexisting measure and one will have to be developed. In this case, the measure could be a set of questions, much like a quiz, to see how much information the new employees can recall from the orientation.

On the other hand, it is likely that a measure already exists for a diversity training program that develops gender and racial or cultural sensitivity. The topic of employee diversity has gained wide attention today, and someone has no doubt already worked on such a program. Questionnaires that measure attitudes in the workplace are common and are usually in the Likert-type format. This format presents a set of statements with which respondents are asked to agree or disagree. The statements are often worded in both positive and negative forms, so that the respondent must agree with some and disagree with others to show a positive attitude. For example, the Women as Managers Scale (WAMS) contains twenty-one Likert-type statements to assess employee attitudes about the ability of women to be effective managers.[1] Table 2.2 presents four items from the questionnaire.

To score this questionnaire, the responses are numbered one through seven, beginning with *strongly disagree*. Because items 1 and 3 are worded negatively, their scores are reversed (i.e., the responses are numbered seven through one). Then the scores for all items are summed, so that a high total score indicates a gender-based stereotype.

Questionnaires should contain instructions to help the respondent understand how to complete the questionnaire. There is usually a cover letter that explains the purpose of the questionnaire, who will have access to the results, if the results will be shared with the respondents, and if the responses will remain anonymous. When feasible, an evaluator should administer the questionnaire to a few stakeholders to verify that it is easy to understand and complete.

Plan a Method of Gathering Data

During the first three steps, stakeholders helped specify what they expect of the program and why, and they have helped select an existing measure or design a new one. The fourth step of program assessment is to make a plan for gathering the data. Stakeholders can also make valuable contributions in this activity.

Program assessment contains a comparison, whether to a comparable group, to previous performance, or to a national norm or quota. If comparison is to a comparable group, the group needs to be identified. If needed, permission to distribute a questionnaire must be secured. Which and how many people will be asked to complete the questionnaire must be identified. If a sample of employees will be asked to complete the questionnaire, how that sample will be selected must be planned. All logistics about distributing the questionnaire should be planned, including when, where, and how it will be distributed. How the questionnaires will be returned is also planned, including setting a return deadline. Finally, how the questionnaire will be scored and analyzed must be planned.

Plans should be confirmed as much as possible, and contingency plans for addressing unexpected difficulties should be developed. The

Table 2.2
Items from the Women as Managers Scale

1. It is less desirable for women than for men to have a job that requires responsibility.
   - ☐ strongly disagree
   - ☐ disagree
   - ☐ slightly disagree
   - ☐ neither disagree nor agree
   - ☐ slightly agree
   - ☐ agree
   - ☐ strongly agree

2. Women have the objectivity required to evaluate business situations properly.
   - ☐ strongly disagree
   - ☐ disagree
   - ☐ slightly disagree
   - ☐ neither disagree nor agree
   - ☐ slightly agree
   - ☐ agree
   - ☐ strongly agree

3. Challenging work is more important to men than it is to women.
   - ☐ strongly disagree
   - ☐ disagree
   - ☐ slightly disagree
   - ☐ neither disagree nor agree
   - ☐ slightly agree
   - ☐ agree
   - ☐ strongly agree

4. Men and women should be given equal opportunity for participation in management training programs.
   - ☐ strongly disagree
   - ☐ disagree
   - ☐ slightly disagree
   - ☐ neither disagree nor agree
   - ☐ slightly agree
   - ☐ agree
   - ☐ strongly agree

evaluator should complete all planning before collecting data. Advance planning ensures that, when it is time to collect the data, everything will be ready and will proceed smoothly. Planning completes the preparatory work that is undertaken before data collection.

Collect the Data

The fifth step of program assessment is data collection. The evaluator should distribute and then collect the questionnaires as planned, careful to preserve anonymity if it was promised. The evaluator should use the contingency plans as unexpected events dictate. Stakeholders who helped plan the assessment would not receive questionnaires because they already know the expected outcome.

The easiest way to gather data is to give questionnaires to an assembled group. You can give uniform instructions and secure a high return rate. When employees are dispersed, they need to know when, where, and how to return the questionnaires. Including a preaddressed envelope often encourages respondents to return the questionnaires. Most employees want their responses to be anonymous, and some appreciate receiving a summary of the results. If time allows, the evaluator can send a reminder or a second questionnaire to those who are slow to respond. Questionnaires from the comparable group are so labeled to prevent them from being confused with those from the program group. Finally, the evaluator can thank the respondents for completing the questionnaires and for their help in the assessment process.

Analyze the Data

After the data are collected, it is time to discover if the program is effective. The sixth step of program assessment is to analyze the data. First, score the questionnaires. If the questionnaire is in a quiz format, a correct response usually counts as a 1 point, and an incorrect response 0. This format might be appropriate, for example, when measuring new employees' retention of information presented in an orientation program.

To score a Likert-type questionnaire, the researcher assigns successive numbers to each possible response, careful to reverse responses for negatively-worded items before summing the scores.

Next, the researcher analyzes the questionnaire scores. The analysis can examine the questionnaire's reliability and validity, reveal the existence of a program impact, and determine if the results can be generalized to other employees.

Communicate the Results

The data analysis reveals the success of the program. The seventh step of program assessment is to communicate the results to relevant decision makers and stakeholders, so they clearly understand the purpose, nature, and results of the program assessment and are able to use the information to decide the fate of the program. The presenter should tailor the information to the listeners' needs, interests, and knowledge of research, and package the information in a style that will increase interest and credibility.

The presentation can be oral, which allows for clarification and discussion. Oral communication can be personal conferences with key decision makers, small-group meetings with decision makers and representative stakeholders, or large-group meetings for all who are interested. A written report can be a lengthy, documented account, a short executive summary, or a memo, bulletin, and newsletter. Sometimes the evaluator will give a draft of the formal written report to key decision makers for review and incorporate their suggestions into the final version. If promised to them, the evaluator provides a summary of the results to those who completed the questionnaires. Effective communication is essential if decision makers and other stakeholders are to use the program assessment results in subsequent decisions about the program.

Make Program Decisions

The eighth and final step of program assessment is to decide the fate of the program. Will it continue without change, undergo modifications, or end? It is often useful to involve key decision makers and stakeholders in this decision. Programs with successful outcomes are usually continued and, if warranted, expanded to service a wider clientele. Strategies to modify less successful programs can be drawn from the theory on which they were based. For example, if the effectiveness of an employee orientation program is due to new employees absorbing the information presented, unsuccessful programs should concentrate on enhancing the factors that facilitate learning.

Extensive program modifications often engender fear and resistance. People hate change, fearing it carries judgement that they are inadequate. Involving stakeholders in the decision process helps alleviate this fear. Decisions reached through consensus are most readily accepted, but stakeholders may still embrace decisions even without consensus if they believe their input was seriously considered.

We have considered the steps of program assessment in some detail to provide an overview of the process and the involvement of stakeholders throughout as feasible. The steps of program assessment, however, should include concern for the errors that can accompany inquiry. As we saw in the scientific method of decision making, inquiry is vulnerable to errors in expectations, observations, and comparisons. The scientific method contains rules to address each type of error, and they should be incorporated into the eight steps.

The Scientific Model of Program Assessment

Because they gather information and draw inferences, program assessments are susceptible to the inevitable errors that accompany inquiry. By themselves, the steps of program assessment do not emphasize these errors, as does the scientific method of decision making. The scientific method stresses that evaluators should attempt to identify and minimize the errors that accompany inquiry so the principles of the scientific method should be added to the eight steps. This is accomplished with the Scientific Model of Program Assessment, shown in Fig. 2.1.

Figure 2.1
The Scientific Model of Program Assessment

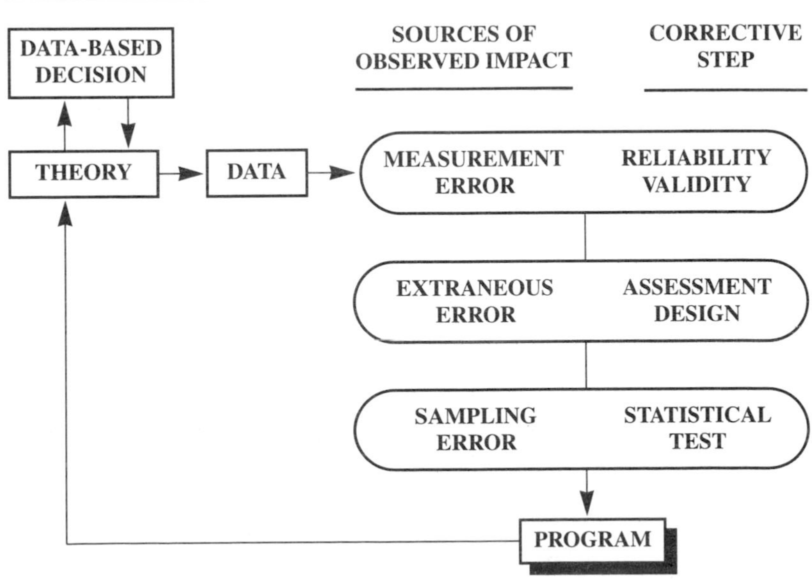

The model draws heavily on the principles of the scientific method of decision making discussed in Chapter 1. Later we will see that the steps and the scientific model complement one another and are used in tandem. The steps are sequential activities that must be completed, and the model concentrates on the errors that accompany those activities. Used together, they produce sound information on which managers can base decisions about the fates of programs.

The Components of the Scientific Model

The scientific model of program assessment contains components that call attention to the errors that arise during inquiry. The components add the logic of the scientific method to program assessment. Refer to Fig. 2.1 as we examine each component.

Data-Based Decision Making. Program assessment begins with the need to decide the fate of a program. In Fig. 2.1, Data-Based Decision reflects the value that the scientific method places on obtaining and using sound information. In program assessment, this reminds us to draw program decisions from information that focuses on the merits of the program, not from tradition, unquestioned authority, consensus, or intuition. Managers should base program decisions on sound information. Data-based decision corresponds to Step 8 of Program Assessment (Make Program Decisions), except it adds the admonition that those decisions be data-based.

Theory. The Theory component is analogous to Step 2 of program assessment, in which one specifies what one expects of the program and why. The scientific method's penchant for minimizing error surfaces dramatically here, as the theory component of the model requires more than specifying a program's expectation and an explanation for it. The theory component also requires attention to the error that managers may make as they formulate expectations and explanations.

Expectations and explanations can contain conceptual error. Expectations, for example, sometimes contain unclear or poorly defined terms that can have multiple meanings in different organizations, in different units within the same organization, and even among members of the same unit. An expectation is only as clear as the terms used to define it. For example, the meanings of the terms *employee orientation program* and *knowledge about the organization* must be clear if we are to have a clear expectation that one produces the other. If people have differing interpretations for the terms, they will have different expectations, as well. Defining important terms ensures concurrence among people, and reduces conceptual error.

Explanations can also contain conceptual error, especially when explanations are not spelled out or shared with others for critique. Explanations sometimes contain internal inconsistencies or are inconsistent with other related explanations; they sometimes omit important terms or important links among terms; they sometimes include unnecessary terms or are needlessly complex. The scientific method instructs that we spell out and share our program explanation with others, and that our explanation should be consistent, complete, and not needlessly complex. Chapter 3 discusses the tenets for constructing theory.

Data. In Fig. 2.1, to the right of Theory, is Data. Data collecting is the fifth step of program assessment, often achieved by distributing a questionnaire to the people who use the program. The scientific method adds the importance of treating people similarly during data collection. The only difference among respondents should be whether they did or did not experience the program. If, for example, a company is assessing a morale-boosting program and the employees are from different settings, it cannot be known with certainty that their high morale is due to the morale-booster program or is instead a factor of the setting.

Ideally, respondents should be in a similar setting and receive the same instructions, explanations, assurances, and time frames to complete the questionnaire. Similarity is especially important when some respondents are within a comparison group and when respondents are dispersed. The scientific model reminds us to keep this principle in mind while collecting data.

Sources of Observed Impact. Analysis of the data may reveal an observed impact, suggesting program effectiveness. For example, the results may show that managers who attended diversity training workshops displayed more sensitivity toward coworkers than those who did not. At first glance the diversity training program appears to be effective, but the scientific method reminds us that error can accompany inquiry. Three types of error appear under Sources of Observed Impact on the model. This is important. The scientific method stipulates that while an observed impact may be caused by the effectiveness of the program, it can also be caused by error accompanying inquiry. An observed impact can contain three major types of error, and each occupies its own line in the model.

Corrective Step. We can address each type of error through a Corrective Step. The Corrective Step controls or reduces the error that may accompany an observed program impact.

Measurement Error. Measurement error occurs if we measure the program outcome inconsistently or inaccurately. Following diversity training, for example, we may attempt to measure "sensitivity toward fellow employees" with a questionnaire that unwittingly measures employee morale. Any conclusion we draw from this measurement more accurately reflects morale. As a result, we would unknowingly mistake high morale ratings for sensitivity toward fellow employees. In Fig. 2.2, Measurement Error and its corresponding Corrective Step are highlighted for easy reference.

Because measures of the program outcome can be inconsistent or inaccurate, the scientific method recommends a corrective step. The

Figure 2.2
Measurement Error

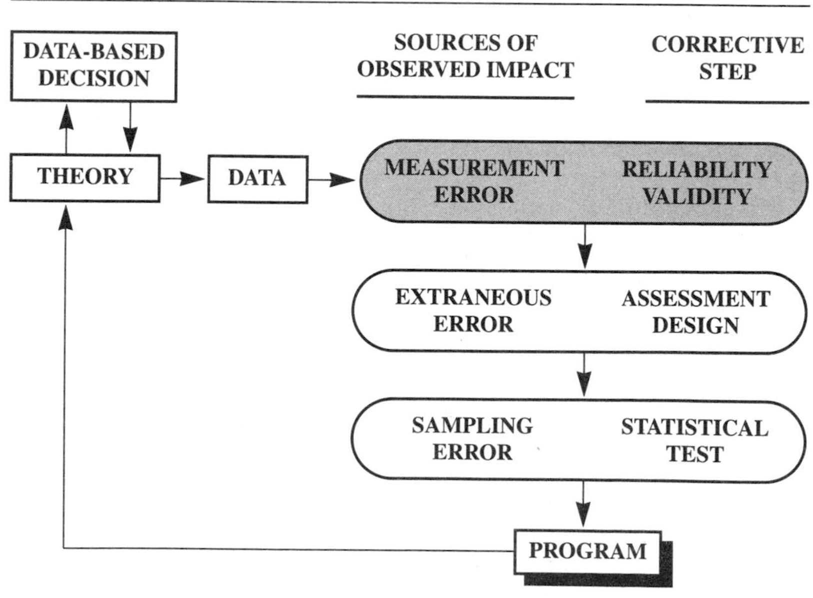

corrective step analyzes the data to assess measurement consistency, commonly referred to as *reliability,* and measurement accuracy, commonly referred to as *validity.* If measures are inconsistent or inaccurate, you risk mistaking the influence of measurement error for the impact of the program. In Chapter 4 we discuss measurement error and explain how to establish measurement reliability and validity.

Extraneous Error. A second type of error arises while making a comparison to a comparable group, to previous performance, or to a norm or quota. This type of error is called an error in comparison, or extraneous error. The term *extraneous error* occupies the second row of the scientific model. Fig. 2.3 shows this important term with its corresponding corrective step highlighted for easy reference.

Extraneous error occurs when the observed impact actually results from an influence other than the program. For example, new employees may be familiar with company benefits after completing an orientation program because they had access to relevant company booklets. We would be incorrect to praise the orientation program if

Figure 2.3
Extraneous Error

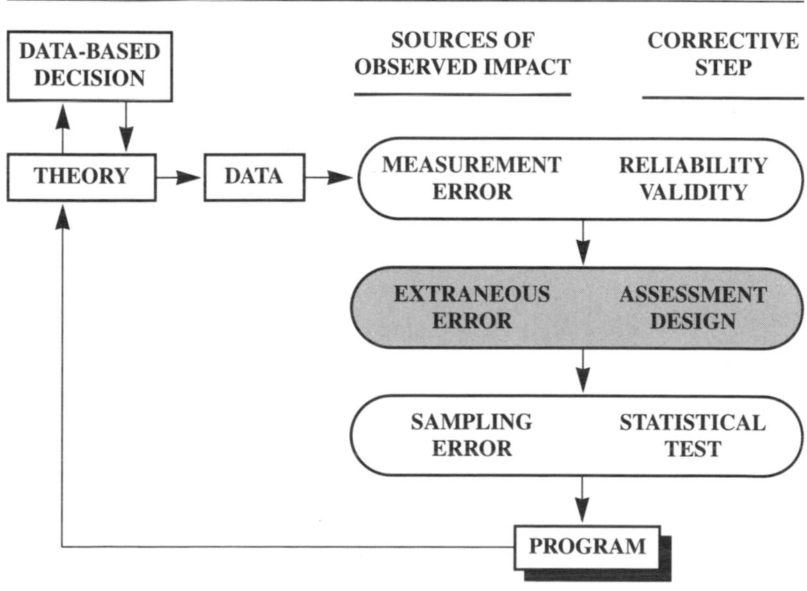

employees arrived already informed. We call this *extraneous* because interest centers on determining the impact of the program, not the impact of irrelevant, extraneous factors. Trouble occurs when the impact of an extraneous influence is mistaken for success of the program.

To minimize extraneous error, the scientific method recommends a corrective step, called Assessment Design. An assessment design summarizes how and on whom observations were made. Observations can be made before or after the program, on one or more groups, and on one occasion or many. It takes into account if the employees are a random sample of the whole. Some combinations of these design components are more susceptible to the influence of extraneous error than others. When we use an assessment design that is susceptible to extraneous error, we risk mistaking the influence of extraneous error for a program impact. The common types of extraneous influence are identified, and the types of assessment design that minimize their influence are discussed in Chapter 5.

Sampling Error. The third type of error occurs when the results from a sample differ from the results from the whole, yet are unwittingly generalized to the whole. We call this type of error an error in generalization, or sampling error. Sampling error also occurs if employees assigned to Program and Control Groups initially differ. When a random process governs the selection or assignment, the error produced is random sampling error. The Scientific Model of Program Assessment is presented in Fig. 2.4 with this important term and its corresponding Corrective Step highlighted for easy reference.

Because observing the program's impact on a large number of people is often difficult and expensive, program assessments commonly observe only a sample. Sample results usually differ from what would be observed of everyone. The corrective step is to perform a Statistical Test on the data. The statistical test determines whether the observed impact exceeds the influence expected from sampling error, and if so, attributes the observed impact to the effectiveness of the program. Chapter 6 explains how to secure samples that will produce results similar to the whole, and Chapter 7 explains how to conduct statistical tests of the data. Once we observe a program impact, the scientific method reminds us that the impact could be caused by three types of error as well as by the program itself.

The Logic of the Scientific Model

The logic of the scientific model centers on the Sources of Observed Impact. An observed impact can be caused by any of four influences:

Figure 2.4
Sampling Error

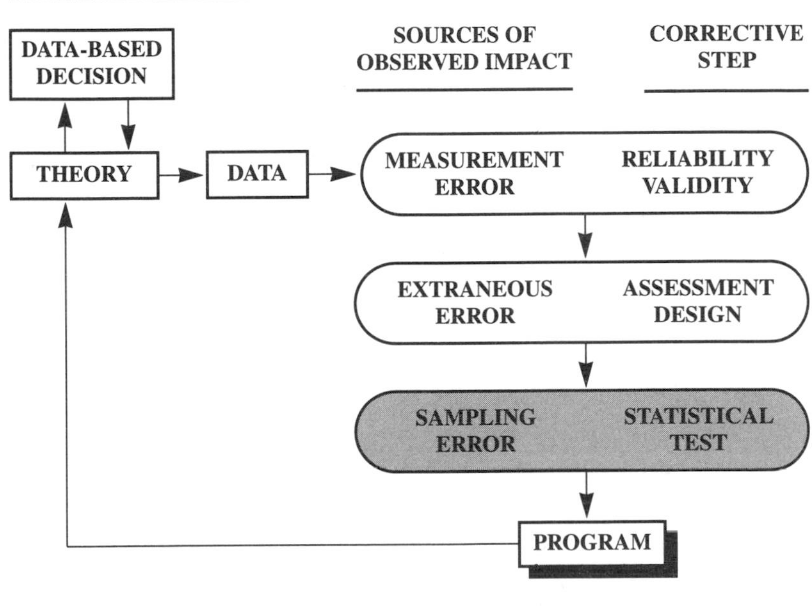

measurement error, extraneous error, sampling error, and the effectiveness of the program itself. Appreciate that initially, all four influences are intertwined and indistinguishable from each other. Consequently, measurement error, extraneous error, and sampling error can masquerade as, and thus be mistaken for, a program impact.

The rule of program assessment contained in the model is: *Only after the first three influences have been addressed in succession can we attribute an observed impact to the effectiveness of the program.* If you are unable to minimize one of the three types of error, stop there; do not continue to move down in the model, and draw no firm conclusion about the effectiveness of the program. The program may be effective, but the observed impact may be error, too. You can't say either way. Within the logic of the scientific method, when error is minimized, conclusions can be drawn with confidence. But with substantial error, no firm conclusions are justified.

The first step of the scientific model is to start at the first line in the model, measurement error, and apply the corrective step to establish

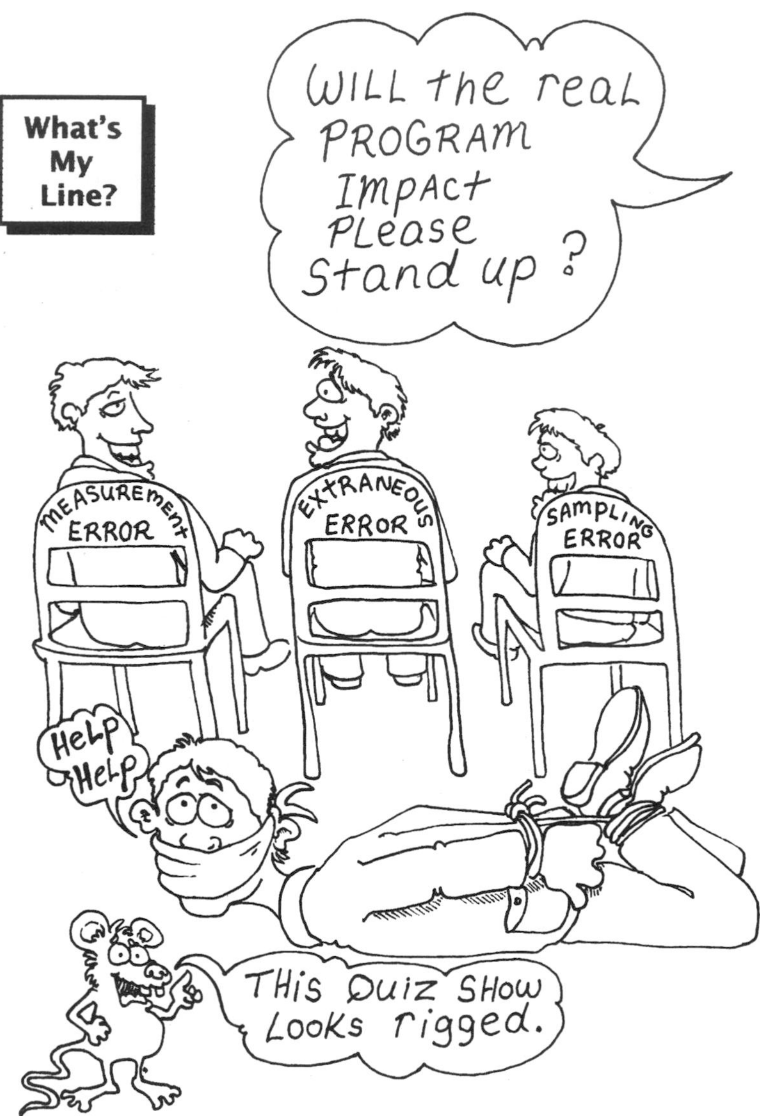
What's My Line?
WILL the real PROGRAM Impact Please Stand up?
MEASUREMENT ERROR
EXTRANEOUS ERROR
SAMPLING ERROR
Help Help
THis Quiz SHow Looks rigged.

measurement reliability and validity. This assures that the program outcome was measured consistently and accurately.

With measurement error minimized, move down one line in the model to extraneous error and its corrective step. Here you determine if the assessment design is vulnerable to extraneous error. This you do by examining whether observations were made before or after the program, on one group or more, on few occasions or many, and on random or nonrandom groups.

If the assessment design is appropriate, move down another line in the model to sampling error. The corrective step determines if the observed impact exceeds the influence expected from sampling error. If it does, you rule out sampling error as the cause of the observed impact.

This done, move down one line in the model. The program remains as the only logical cause of the observed impact. Because you have minimized each type of error, you can conclude that the observed impact is due to the effectiveness of the program.

Finally, note the arrow that returns from the program to the theory. When you can conclude that the observed impact is due to the program, the theory from which this expectation was drawn is empirically supported. Consistently supported theories gain stature.

Combining the Model and the Steps

The steps of program assessment specify a set of sequential activities common to all program assessments. The scientific model of program assessment extends these activities to minimize error during the process. Evaluators should use the two in tandem, one directing activity, the other minimizing error. The steps secure information on which to decide the fate of a program; the scientific model clarifies concepts and validates measurement, comparison, and generalization. Based on the assumption that sound information engenders sound decisions, the scientific model brings the rigors of science to the assessment process.

Figure 2.5 presents the links between the components of the model and the steps of program assessment. Adding the steps to the model emphasizes that program assessment entails more than completing a set of steps, although that is important. It also needs to address the types of error that can be made while completing the steps.

Involving stakeholders throughout the assessment as much as feasible helps to ensure relevant results. Stakeholders can be especially helpful in specifying program theory, selecting measurement

Figure 2.5
The Scientific Model and the Steps of Program Assessment

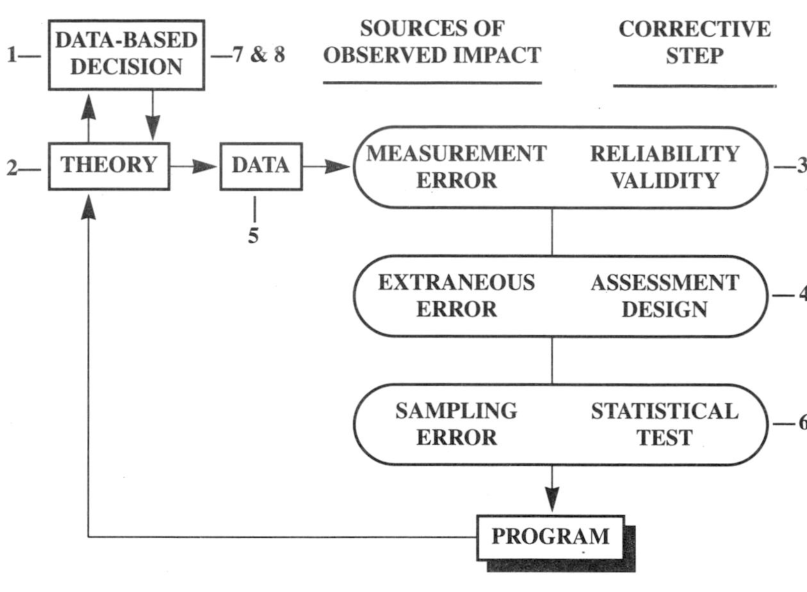

tools, and making program decisions. Their input can provide the conceptual clarity important to formulating program expectations and explanations, and their input can provide important insights and deepen their "buy-in" during the decision process.

When completing Step 2, specifying the program's expected outcome, take measures to avoid the conceptual error that can accompany those expectations. This step entails forming both an expectation and an explanation, both what to expect from the program and why. The expectation should contain clear terms, lest stakeholders have dissimilar meanings for important terms. The explanation should be consistent, complete, and not unduly complex.

In completing Step 3, establishing a measure of the program outcome, be mindful of measurement error, line one in the model. The Corrective Step establishes that measures of the program outcome are reliable and valid.

When completing Step 4, planning the logistics of who, when, where, and how the data will be gathered, be mindful of extraneous error, line 2 in the model. By adequately planning the Assessment's Design, you minimize the influence of factors other than the program. In your planning, you need to decide whether to make observations before or after the program, on one or more groups, on one or more occasions, and on random or nonrandom samples. Choose among these options to guard against extraneous error.

Step 5, collecting the data, is analogous to the Data component of the model, except to Step 5 the model adds the recommendation that we treat respondents as similarly as possible during data collection. Similar treatment ensures that the only influence at play is whether or not people experienced the program.

When completing Step 6, analyzing of the data, attend to sampling error, line 3 in the model. When you use a sample of the whole or assign employees to groups randomly, analysis of the data will indicate if the observed impact exceeds the influence expected from sampling error. If it does, you can generalize the results to the whole.

When communicating results of the program assessment, Step 7, again be mindful of the error that can accompany how we think about the effectiveness of programs, what we expect from them and why. The expectation should be clear, the explanation consistent, complete, and not unduly complex. Results are communicated to key decision makers and stakeholders to use in decision making. The scientific method also values reporting the results in a public forum (e.g., professional conference, academic journal, trade magazine, world wide web) when feasible. In this way, interested parties in other organizations or academic institutions can use and critique the study. Knowing which theories correctly anticipate program outcomes advances our collective understanding of how organizations attain effectiveness.

Step 8, making program decisions, pertains to the Data-Based Decision component of the model. It adds, however, that evaluators should focus on the merits of the program, not tradition, unquestioned authority, consensus, or intuition. The assumption is that decisions are more likely to be sound if based on sound information.

In the remainder of this book we will examine more closely the important topics of conceptual error, measurement error, extraneous error, and sampling error; and we will present methods that evaluators can use to minimize each one. Each chapter begins with a list of the Steps and a diagram of the model with the topics covered in the chapter highlighted. By referring to the diagram, you will always know where you are in the assessment process.

Main Points of Chapter 2

- Program assessment progresses through a series of eight steps.
- Stakeholders should be involved as much as practical throughout the assessment process.
- Before collecting data, you should specify what is expected of the program and why, secure a measure of the program outcome, and plan the logistics of who, when, where, and how the data will be gathered.
- After collecting and analyzing the data, the results should be communicated to key decision makers and stakeholders and used in deciding the fate of the program.
- The steps of program assessment, however, are susceptible to the error that inevitably accompanies inquiry.
- The scientific model of program assessment identifies the types of error that accompany program assessment and provides corrective steps to minimize each type of error.
- The steps of program assessment and the scientific model of program assessment are used in tandem; one directs activity, and the other minimizes the error accompanying the activity.
- Conceptual error can cause the program expectation to be misunderstood or its explanation to be wrong. The scientific model insists that program expectations contain clear terms and that explanations be consistent, complete, and not unduly complex.
- Measurement error, extraneous error, and sampling error can be mistaken for program effectiveness. The scientific model calls for these errors to be addressed while planning the logistics of an assessment and while analyzing the data.
- The logic of the scientific model of program assessment stipulates that only after you have minimized in succession each type of error can you attribute the observed impact to the effectiveness of the program.

Chapter Note

1. James R. Terborg, Women as managers scale (WAMS). *The 1978 annual handbook for group facilitators.* University Associates, pp. 79–83.

3

Constructing Program Theories

Chapter Preview

This chapter explores managers' expectations about program outcomes and the importance of explicit explanations for achieving expectations. We will see that program assessment is guided by theory, and we will learn how to construct theories to use within program assessments.

Learning Objectives

After reading Chapter 3, you should be able to:

- appreciate that managers expect organizational programs to produce desired outcomes for specific reasons, that they attempt to anticipate and understand program impacts
- define the term *theory*
- explain why a theory should be spelled out, shared, and tested
- identify the main functions of a theory
- define the components of a theory
- prepare a diagram of a theory
- identify the qualities of useful theory

The Focus of Chapter 3

The program assessment steps discussed in this chapter, along with their corresponding components in the Scientific Model, are highlighted below.

The Steps of Program Assessment

1. **Involve stakeholders throughout the assessment.**
2. **Specify the expected program outcome.**
3. Establish a measure of the program outcome.
4. Plan a method of gathering data.
5. Collect the data.
6. Analyze the data.
7. Communicate the results.
8. Make program decisions.

The Scientific Model of Program Assessment

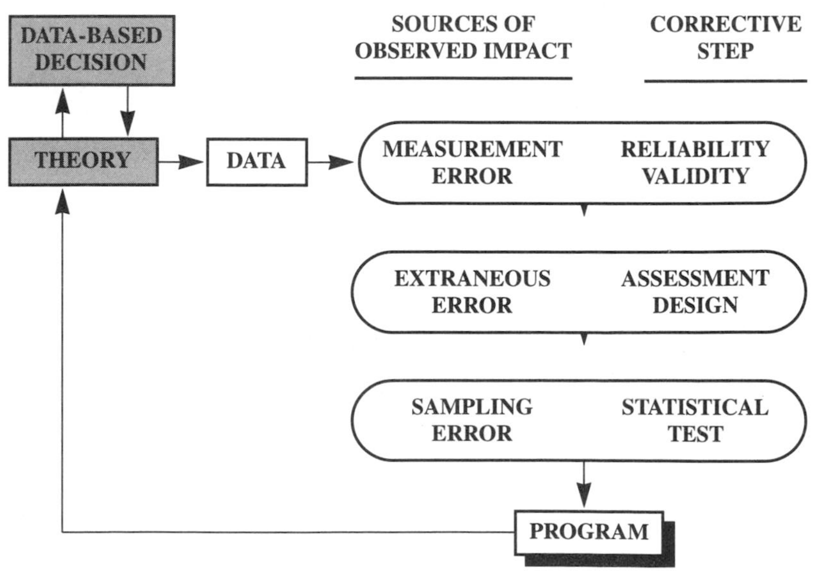

Expectations are commonplace. All of us expect things—that setting the alarm clock will awaken us, that brushing our teeth will prevent cavities, that donning shorts and our favorite T-shirt will bring frowns at work, that eating breakfast will sustain us through the morning, that leaving at a certain time will get us to work on time, that turning the ignition key will start the car, and so on. An expectation links an activity to an outcome, and to properly plan our lives, we need to know what to expect. Expectations help us decide to set the alarm for a particular time, to add toothpaste and breakfast food to our shopping list, and to put our car keys where we can find them.

Sometimes we don't know why an activity leads to an outcome, but we may be content not to know, even if others do. We may not know how that key starts our car, and we don't really care as long as the car starts. Automakers and mechanics know how, and that's good enough for us.

Often, however, we do have an understanding of why an activity leads to an outcome. We know that the fluoride in toothpaste helps fight tooth decay, that nutrients in cereal can give us energy, and that our workplace has a dress code. We often know both what to expect and why to expect it; beyond expectations, we have explanations, an understanding of why things occur.

Explanations allow us to "fix" the unexpected. If we get a poor report from our dental checkup, we can request a fluoride treatment; if we typically grow weary before lunch, we can plan more nutritious breakfasts; and if we encounter displeased looks at work, we can wear more appropriate clothing. To make things work, expectations may suffice. To design things and fix things, explanations are critical.

Expectations are also common in the workplace. All decision makers have expectations about the activities that will produce effectiveness. They also have expectations about the effects of organizational programs. For example, a manager may expect an incentive program to increase employee productivity. Managers draw their expectations from a combination of sources, including their formal education and job experience.

Decision makers are seldom content to just expect program effectiveness; they also want to understand why the program produces its outcome—why, for example, incentives increase productivity. Without knowing why, it is difficult to design incentives effectively or to modify a defective incentive program. Explanations are as useful at work as they are in daily life.

Program Theories

Although decision makers may not realize it, their explanations are theories. A theory specifies the expected relationship between an organizational activity and an organizational outcome, and states why that relationship is expected. In program assessment, a theory specifies what we expect of a program and why. The main functions of a theory are to predict and explain organizational functioning, to anticipate what will happen and to understand why it happened.

That all decision makers have and frequently use theories will surprise those whose notion of a theory is something produced by a scientist in some laboratory, peppered with words they don't know, and unrelated to life in organizations as they know it. To the contrary, each expectation you have about how and why things work in your organization is a theory.

The theories held by decision makers and the more formal theories found in textbooks both aim to predict and explain organizational functioning. In either case, the distinguishing feature among theories is the degree to which they are spelled out, shared with others, and tested. One useful way to delineate a theory is to describe it on paper, using words and drawings. As we delineate our theory, we can clarify unclear terms, add relevant terms, delete irrelevant terms, and resolve inconsistent reasoning.

When we share our theory with others, they may recognize limitations and possibilities we missed: They can point out vague terms, missing and unnecessary terms, and faulty reasoning. A theory shared also allows others to further their understanding of how organizations work; others may find your theory interesting and use it in their own decision making or research.

To test a theory, we examine it under conditions where its predictions can fail. A program assessment is just such an opportunity, because the expected program outcome may fail to materialize, providing no support for the theory on which it was based. Conversely, if the program produces its expected outcome, the theory is supported. The theory is not proved—no theory is, for there always exists the possibility that it may fail a future test. Rather, theories garner support by weathering occasions to be incorrect. Scientists value theories that withstand many trials.

Components of a Theory

Theories assume different forms. We will adopt one approach to constructing a theory that is well suited to program assessment. In this approach, a theory is composed of four components: the program, the program outcome, an expectation, and an explanation. Two additional components, moderators and boundaries, are optional but often useful in constructing a theory.

The Program

A program is a definable set of organizational activities designed to maintain or enhance organizational functioning. For example, some companies use incentive programs to increase employee productivity. Programs occur in all segments of an organization, its structure, processes, tasks, and technology.

Programs may be explicit or implicit. Explicit programs are usually named, have stated goals, and include recognizable beginnings. Implicit programs are any informal set of organizational activities we can define and whose effectiveness interests us. Often, implicit programs are unnamed, lack stated goals, and are not called programs; but they exist and they attempt to maintain or enhance organizational functioning. Table 3.1 gives examples of explicit and implicit programs within the main segments of an organization.

Table 3.1
Examples of Explicit and Implicit Programs

	Explicit Programs	**Implicit Programs**
Structure	Decentralization Matrix organization Autonomous work groups	Communication networks Downsizing
Processes	Quality assurance program Performance appraisal system Information management system	Decision making/leadership Resource allocation Managerial style
Tasks	Training program Safety awareness programs Job enlargement/enrichment Job rotation	Task description Task load Work flow
Technology	Modernization Innovation	Worker-machine relationship

The Program Outcome

A program outcome is the change effected by the program. For example, increased employee performance is the outcome of an incentive program. The program outcome is a concept, a component of a theory, and not the actual observed outcome.

Identifying an appropriate outcome is not always easy, because it turns on the definition of organizational success, which can mean different things to different people. The nature of the organization and the vantage of the person making the judgement also affects the interpretation of results. Table 3.2 presents examples of program outcomes used by decision makers, theorists, and researchers.

Table 3.2
Examples of Program Outcomes

1. **Overall Effectiveness**: A general evaluation that takes in as much criteria as possible and results in a single judgment about the effectiveness of the organization.
2. **Productivity**: The quantity or volume of the major product or service that the organization provides, which can be measured at three levels: individual, group, and total organization.
3. **Efficiency**: A ratio that reflects a comparison of some aspect of unit performance to the costs incurred for that performance.
4. **Profit**: The revenue from sales remaining after all costs and obligations are met. Percent return on investment and percent return on total sales are sometimes used as alternative definitions.
5. **Quality**: The quality of the primary service or product provided by the organization.
6. **Accidents**: The frequency of on-the-job accidents resulting in lost time.
7. **Growth**: An increase in such variables as total manpower, plant capacity, assets, sales, profits, market share, and number of innovations.
8. **Absenteeism**: The relative frequency with which people are absent from work. The usual definition stipulates unexcused absences, but even within this constraint there are a number of alternative definitions.
9. **Turnover**: This is usually some measure of the frequency and amount of voluntary terminations and refers to a change in actual personnel within the organization however the change occurs.

10. **Satisfaction**: Satisfaction has been defined many ways, but perhaps the modal view references satisfaction to the achievement or possession of certain outcomes provided by the organization and defines it as an individual's perception of the degree to which he or she has received an equitable amount of the outcome.
11. **Motivation**: The strength of the predisposition of an individual to engage in goal-directed action or activity on the job.
12. **Morale**: A predisposition in organizational members to put forth extra effort in achieving organizational goals and objectives. It includes feelings of commitment and is a group phenomena involving extra effort, goal communality, and feelings of belonging.
13. **Control**: The degree of and distribution of management control that exists within an organization for influencing and directing the behavior of organization members.
14. **Conflict/Cohesion**: A bipolar dimension defined at the cohesion end by an organization in which the members like one another, work well together, communicate fully and openly, and coordinate their work efforts. At the other end lies the organization with verbal and physical clashes, poor coordination, and ineffective communication.
15. **Flexibility/Adaptation**: The ability of an organization to change its standard operating procedures in response to environmental changes.
16. **Planning and Goal Setting**: The degree to which the organization systematically plans its future steps and engages in explicitly goal setting behavior.
17. **Goal Consensus**: The degree to which all individuals perceive the same goals for the organization, which is distinct from actual commitment to those goals.
18. **Role and Norm Congruence**: The degree to which the members of an organization are in agreement on such things as what kinds of supervisory attitudes are best, performance expectations, morale, and role requirements.
19. **Managerial Interpersonal Skills**: The level of skill and efficiency with which the management deals with superiors, subordinates, and peers and includes the extent to which managers give support, facilitate constructive interaction, and generate enthusiasm for meeting goals and achieving excellent performance.
20. **Managerial Task Skills**: The overall level of skills the organization's managers, commanding officers, or group leaders possess for performing tasks centered on work to be done.

Table 3.2 *(continued)*

21. **Information Management and Communication**: The collection, analysis, and distribution of information critical to organizational effectiveness.
22. **Readiness**: An overall judgment concerning the probability that the organization could successfully perform some specified task if asked to do so.
23. **Utilization of Environment**: The extent to which the organization successfully interacts with its environment and acquires scarce, valued resources necessary to its effective operation.

Program outcomes vary in several ways: Some are global indices of effectiveness, others are specific; some are abstract, others concrete; some pertain to producing goods, others to providing services. Next we discuss the link between the program and its outcome, the expectation.

The Expectation

An expectation postulates that a program will change the program outcome and specifies the direction of the change. For example, the expectation may be that an incentive program will improve employee performance. The expectation contains two components: that incentives will alter employee performance and the change will be for the better. Several types of relationships that may exist between a program and its outcome are shown in Fig. 3.1.

Figure 3.1(a) is the most common expectation: that the program causes the outcome to increase, as in the case of an incentive program increasing employee productivity. Fig. 3.1(b) is also a common outcome, a decrease. For example, a safety awareness program should reduce on-the-job accidents. The effect of a program may rise and then plateau, or level off, as illustrated in Fig. 3.1(c). For example, repetition of information enhances recall to a point and then levels off. Eventually repetition is no longer effective. Employees may have absorbed all they can or become bored and tuned out. Finally, the outcome may increase to a point and then decrease, as illustrated in Fig. 3.1(d). For example, reprimand may initially improve employee behavior but then engender resentment and resistance.

Figure 3.1
Some Possible Expectations of a Program

a. Program causes outcome to increase.

b. Program causes outcome to decrease.

c. Program causes outcome to increase and then plateau.

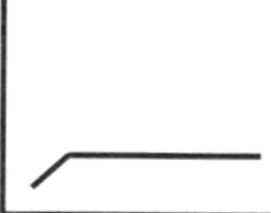

d. Program causes outcome to increase and then decrease.

The Explanation

The explanation is why the program changed the program outcome. A *force* in the environment may have produced the results, or a change may have occured through the steps of some *process*. Theorists have advanced many forces and processes to explain human behavior. If we posit that incentive programs motivate employees, the explanation—motivation—resides within the employees, and that is the force that prompts productivity. Motivation, an internal force, is the causal link for program and outcome: Incentives motivate workers, and motivation prompts productivity.

Alternatively, explanations can point to forces or processes external to the person—social, organizational, or cultural forces. Task ambiguity, for example, can be a normal part of the employee's environment, but it can cause stress.

Researchers have expended considerable time and energy developing and testing explanations for organizational functioning. Table 3.3 presents a brief description of selected explanations applic-

Table 3.3
Explanations

Explanation	Premise
Needs	Behavior is initiated to satisfy unfulfilled needs. For example a thirsty person will drink, and a hungry person will eat.
Learning	Behavior that is reinforced is learned.
Dissonance	People find it uncomfortable to hold conflicting opinions and attempt to find resolutions.
Social Comparison	People form their own opinions, including opinions about their self-worth, by comparing them to the others' opinions.
Social Exchange	People govern their relationships according to business rules, exchanging goods, services, and sentiments with others instead of cash. People seek fairness in their exchanges with others.
Organizational Fit	An organization's structure should match its environment. Tall structures are suitable for steady environments; flat structures are required for unsteady environments.
Uncertainty Reduction	Organizational activities function to reduce the equivocality of information received from the environment

able to a variety of organizational programs. Each explanation may account for the effects of a variety of organizational activity. These and other explanations are described in books on organizational behavior.[1]

Explanations are sometimes referred to as theories, but we will continue to call them explanations and reserve the term *theory* to encompass all four components: the program, outcome, expectation, and explanation. Two additional components of a theory are optional but often prove useful. These are moderators, that under some conditions a program will not produce its expected outcome, and boundaries, that a theory may not apply to all employees in all situations.

Moderators

The effect of the program can depend on a variety of mitigating influences called moderators. A feature of the program, the individual, or the environment, a moderator intervenes and prevents or reverses the program outcome. For example, incentives increase productivity, unless employees lack the requisite knowledge to perform the task. Employee knowledge is a moderator; it prevented the outcome from materializing. Similarly, the impact of incentives may depend on the employees' level of skill, another moderator. Despite knowing how to perform the task, employees' lack of skill may hinder productivity.

Knowledge and skill are employee traits, but moderators can also be characteristics of the environment, as when incentives are ineffectual during times of high economic prosperity. Here the economy is a moderator, preventing the expected impact of an incentive program on employee productivity. Aspects of the program—its length, content, mode of instruction—can also be moderators. For example, if the incentives are too small, an incentive program will not increase productivity, So size of incentive is the moderator.

When a theory has several moderators, they are usually grouped into categories for convenience. Moderators that describe conditions of or within the individual are called internal (or psychological or individual). Those that describe processes or structures outside or external to the individual are called external (or social or environmental). Moderators that are part of the program are called aspects of the program. Table 3.4 gives examples of each category.

Moderators intervene between a program and its outcome and prevent or reverse the outcome. Researchers include in their theories moderators that likely affect the outcome or that hold theoretical interest. They omit rare and theoretically uninteresting moderators.

Table 3.4
Moderators

Internal	External	Aspects of the Program
Demographics (age, gender)	Task demands	Program length
Intelligence, knowledge	Group pressure	Program content
Skills	Resources	Program facilitators
Goals	Working conditions	Program cost
Personality types	Organizational climate	Program location
Attitudes	Economy	Program frequency

The final component of a theory, also optional, identifies the topics that a theory does and does not address.

Boundaries

A boundary identifies the domain of a theory, what topics the theory does and does not address. Much as a fence encloses and defines an area, a boundary circumscribes the topic area of a theory. For example, just as the theory of gravity applies to objects but not ideas—ideas don't fall with the regularity that rocks do—a theory of motivation applies to employees but not, say, customers. We can't expect a theory to predict the effects of a program for all possible employees in all possible situations. Instead, we may limit a theory to labor force workers in manufacturing companies. It is up to the theorist to specify the boundary of a theory, the range of people and situations the theory finds interesting and attempts to explain.

A boundary can delimit the range of three aspects of a theory. First, it can specify the range of people to which a theory applies. A theory can apply to all employees or only to hourly employees, clerical employees, or male employees. Second, a boundary can specify the range of situations to which a theory applies: organizations in general or limited to for-profit organizations, or sales departments. Third, a boundary can specify a span of time. It can include all time periods or limit itself to employees with five years or more at the firm, or to new employees only.

The boundary of a theory usually remains unstated unless there is concern about misunderstandings. Such concern prompted

Cody explains that the theory pertains to dogs only.

Newcomb to identify two boundaries to his theory of interpersonal influence: that two people like each other and each has strong feelings about an issue. Newcomb makes clear that his theory does not apply to adversaries or unimportant topics. Further, his theory does not apply to falling objects, but he needn't mention it because no one would have thought so anyway. Thus, boundaries circumscribe what a theory does and does not pertain to, but needn't be mentioned unless confusion is likely.

Theorists sometimes convert a moderator of little theoretical interest to a boundary. Instead of including knowledge and skill as moderators, for example, you could stipulate that your theory deals only with employees who have the requisite knowledge and skill to be productive. This automatically eliminates all other possibilities.

Defining Theoretical Concepts

The first step in building theory is to define clearly each important term in the theory. We refer to theoretical terms as concepts; at the theoretical level, we think with concepts. If we are exploring whether incentives motivate employees to higher productivity, incentives, motivation, and productivity are all concepts. To reflect the sometimes subtle and complex elements and processes within organizations, theories necessarily use concepts with multiple meanings.

Theories with unclear concepts are unclear themselves. Consider again whether incentives motivate employees to higher productivity. Without definition, our notions of an incentive program likely differ, and our meanings for concepts such as motivation and productivity likely differ. As a result, our interpretations of the theory based on those concepts will differ. Unless we discover we are using the same concepts differently, we will not know our interpretations of the theory differ. Unclear theories are difficult to understand, critique, and test.

The objective, then, is to eliminate all interpretations except the one we want to use. We want meanings that help us single out elements of the organization that interest us. We can often draw useful definitions from previous theory and research on the topic. There is no reason to reinvent definitions if others have defined concepts like incentives, motivation, and productivity in theoretically useful ways. We should, however, identify the sources of the definitions we adopt. If we can't find precise definitions, we can adapt them to our theoretical

How good is a theory if it contains terms with multiple meanings?

purpose, changing the language as needed. Finally, we can assign a new meaning to a concept, along with a rationale for its introduction.

Commonly, theorists clarify concepts with verbal definitions, a set of words used in place of another word to explain a person's mind.[2] Table 3.5 presents three useful strategies for defining theoretical concepts.

Let's define a simple word first. To define *car,* we would consider categories of objects that include cars: moving objects, modes of transportation, vehicles, and motor vehicles. We will use the least general category that still includes cars, but "motor vehicles," also includes trucks, buses, motorcycles, and tractors. So, we next identify the attributes of a car that distinguish it from other motorized vehicles. For example, a car generally moves on four wheels and can carry two to six passengers and a small amount of cargo. A verbal definition assumes the following form:

$$\text{word} = \text{category} + \text{differentiating attributes}$$

Thus we can define a car this way: A car is a motorized vehicle that moves on four wheels and can carry two to six passengers and small amounts of cargo. You can think of motorized vehicles other than cars that fit this description, but this definition excludes most of them. If not, you can add an element to the definition that would eliminate other examples.

For a more complex topic, we can again consider whether incentives motivate employees to higher productivity. How can we define *incentives*? First, we would think of the least general category that includes incentives among its elements, then identify attributes of incentives that differentiate them from other elements in the category.

Table 3.5
Strategies for Defining Theoretical Concepts

1. Identify a category that includes the concept as an element, then specify traits that distinguish that concept from others in the category.
2. Specify how the concept is similar to and different from related theoretical concepts.
3. Specify how the concept differs from its usage in common language or in previous theory and research.

Relevant categories we could use include: things, stimuli, things of value, and things of value to employees. Taking the least general category for our theory—things of value to employees—we then add attributes of incentives that distinguish them from other things of value to employees. For example, we could follow Klein and Ritti and define incentives as things of value that employees strive for.[3]

In researching previous theory on this topic, I discovered a category that seemed theoretically more appealing. I was drawn to the idea that an incentive is a promise, a promise that employees will receive something. This category shifts interest from tangible things, such as money bonuses, to a verbal statement, to a promise. I recognized that a promise is a communication message, and this intrigued me; it is a category I find theoretically useful. Although there are certainly other meanings for incentive, we want the one we consider theoretically useful to our purposes. A meaning that is theoretically useful in one theory may serve another theory less well.

Now we need to identify attributes of incentives that distinguish them from other types of promises. Consider the following: An incentive is a promise to employees of something extra, considered valuable, if they perform in specified ways.[4] This description differentiates incentives from most other promises. I included the word *extra* to distinguish incentives from usual pay. I included the word *considered* to emphasize that managers may not realize what employees value; managers offer what *they* consider valuable. If the incentive was phrased "something extra that is of value to employees," but employees did not find it valuable, it is not an incentive. Consequently, we cannot identify an incentive until we observe employee reaction to it. Some find this provision useful, but I do not, because I want to think of an incentive as a communication message, whether or not employees value what managers promise.

Now let's illustrate the second strategy for defining a concept. We can specify how a concept is similar to or different from related theoretical concepts, for example, how incentives are similar to or different from rewards. Campbell, *et al.,* note that sometimes people fail to distinguish between incentives and rewards.[5] They offer a temporal distinction: Incentives, once received, become rewards, but not before. So a bonus can be both an incentive and a reward, depending on whether it is sought or obtained.

The third strategy for defining concepts is to specify how the concept differs from usage in common language or in previous theory and research. In common usage an incentive means "something, as the fear of punishment or the expectation of reward, that incites to action or effort."[6] Most definitions of incentives found in organizational theory, however, emphasize things employees value rather than things that instill fear of punishment.

Now we can refine our definition of incentives as a promise. We can stipulate that once obtained, things of value are rewarding, but not before, and we can stipulate that incentives do not include threats of punishment. Considering that managers sometimes misjudge what employees value and threaten punishment to incite change, our definitions stipulate that this theory does not entertain these ideas. We are not saying we are correct, only that we find these definitions theoretically useful. Finally, appreciate the importance of defining incentives, since our usage differs from that in common language and from that in some previous theories.

Let's define *motivation*. After reviewing previous theory and research, I chose the following: Motivation is a predisposition to reduce the discrepancy between an actual and a desired state of being.[7] By *predisposition,* I mean an existing inclination or readiness to do something. The definition implies that motivation is goal oriented; people seek ways to reduce discrepancies between their actual and desired states. Incentives, however, do not cause or increase motivation. Rather, motivation already exists as a discrepancy between an actual and a desired state. If employees believe incentives will reduce the discrepancies between their actual and desired states, they will engage in behavior in an effort to obtain the incentives.

Finally, by *productivity* I mean the quantity of the major product or service an organization, department, or individual creates from organizational resources.[8]

I hope you can now appreciate how defining terms clarifies concepts. What might have been open to multiple interpretations is narrowed to one usage that is theoretically useful. We should not be surprised if defining our concepts makes them clearer even to us. We shall discover soon that clear theoretical concepts aid theory building. Clear theoretical concepts also help others understand, critique, and test the theory we build. With clear concepts in hand, we are ready to use them to construct theory.

Constructing a Program Theory

In constructing a theory, its components must be identified and the relationships among them made clear. You can do this by casting your theory as a diagram that has the program on the left, the program outcome on the right, and an arrow connecting the two, as shown in Fig. 3.2.

Figure 3.2
Incentive Program and Employee Productivity

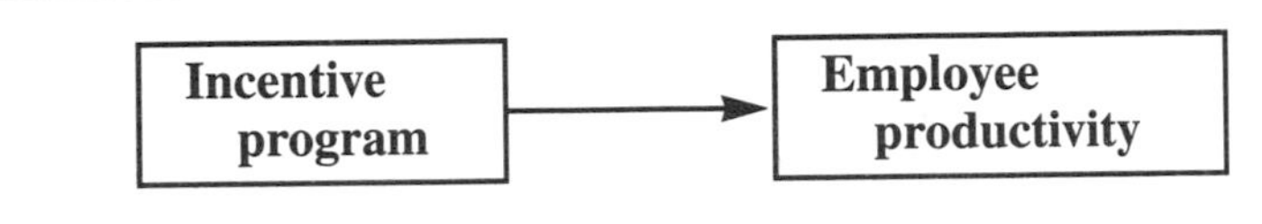

The arrow represents the expectation that the program will change the outcome. Unless stated otherwise, the arrow indicates that you expect the program to increase the program outcome. Fig. 3.2 posits that incentives will increase employee productivity. The next step in constructing a theory is to identify *why* the program is expected to produce this outcome. Thus we need to specify why we expect incentives to increase productivity. One likely explanation is that incentives motivate workers to work harder. Motivation explains why this program increases productivity, and it would be incorporated into the diagram as shown in Fig. 3.3.

Because it is a logical interim step in producing the outcome, the explanation is placed between the program and the outcome. Here, incentives motivate employees, which in turn stimulates employee productivity. Fig. 3.3 contains the four components essential to a theory: the program, the program outcome, an expectation (the arrow), and an explanation.

Certain aspects of the employees, the environment, or the program however, can prevent a program from having its expected effect. We should consider if any moderators exist for our theory. Low employee knowledge and skill, for example, could neutralize the effect of incentives. Productivity will not increase when employees lack the requisite knowledge or skills to perform their tasks. Fig. 3.4 incorporates several moderators into this theory, grouped as internal (upper box) and external (lower box).

Figure 3.3
Incentive Program/Motivation/Employee Productivity

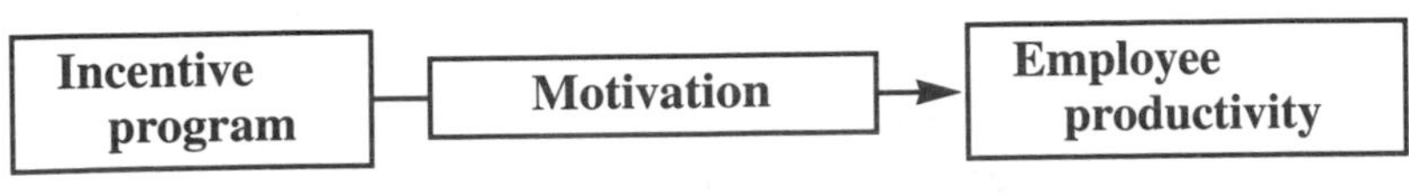

Figure 3.4
Full Model of Incentive Program

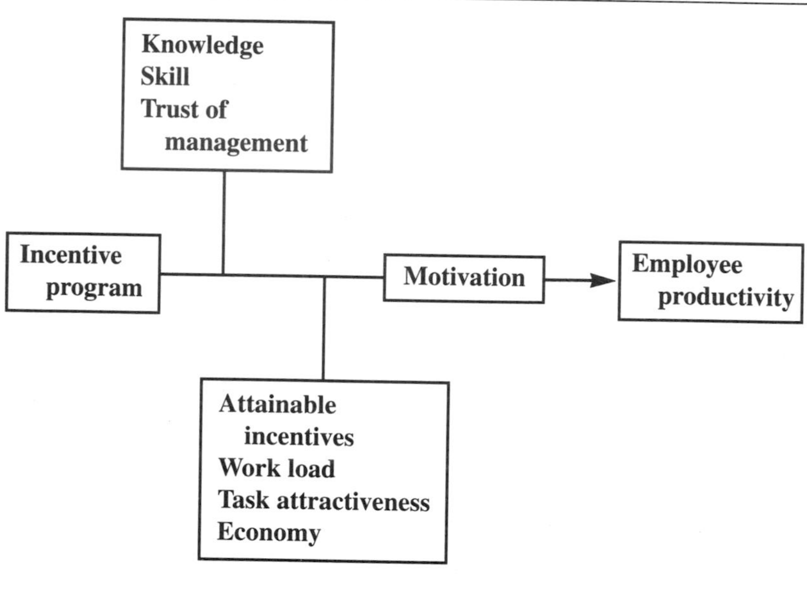

We posit three internal moderators. When employees lack knowledge, skill, or trust in management, productivity may not increase, despite incentives. There are four external moderators. If incentives are unattainable, the work load is high, the task is unattractive, or the national economy is strong, productivity may not increase, incentives or not. The addition of these moderators allows the theory to more accurately reflect the complexity of organizational functioning.

A boundary to a theory is presented in the narrative accompanying a diagram. Since no boundaries were mentioned, the theory is not limited to any one type of worker, organization, or time period.

In summary, follow five general steps when constructing a diagram of a theory:

1. Place the program on the left, the program outcome on the right.
2. Connect the program and the program outcome with an arrow. If other than positive, specify the anticipated relationship in the accompanying narrative.

3. Position an explanation between the program and the outcome.
4. Group moderators as internal or external, and place them between the program and the explanation, extending above or below the arrow line; place moderators that are aspects of the program in a box under the program.
5. Specify any boundaries to the theory in the accompanying narrative.

A theory offers a reasoned expectation for the effectiveness of a program. The main functions of a theory are to predict and explain program success, to anticipate and understand organizational functioning. Theories help in the design, assessment, and improvement of organizational programs. Learning Module 3.1 Constructing Program Theories provides an opportunity for you to become more familiar with the components of a theory, how they interrelate, and how they can be diagramed. Please complete the Learning Module. Feel free to return to and review the text as you proceed.

LEARNING MODULE 3.1: Constructing Program Theories

This Learning Module lists the components of two different theories. The components are in no particular order. Please construct a diagram for each theory using all components in the list. When you are done, compare your diagrams to those presented at the end of the chapter in Figs. 3.5 and 3.6.

Theory 1	**Theory 2**
Study Skills	Accident Frequency
Learning	Age of Equipment
Family Demands	Survival Instinct
Amount of Study	Skills
Desire	Complexity of Task
Job Demands	Safety Awareness Program
Course Grade	Attitude
Intelligence	Time Constraints
Course Difficulty	Habits

END OF LEARNING MODULE 3.1

The learning module provides practice in building theories. Quite possibly, the ones you built may have differed from those presented as answers. Now we need criteria to judge the quality of the theories we build or encounter and to choose between competing theories.

Qualities of Useful Theories

Theory-guided program assessment helps decision makers anticipate and understand program effectiveness. However, accurate prediction and rich explanation require good theorizing. Wrong theories predict poorly, explain erroneously. We now turn to the issue of judging the quality of theories. Theories benefit when they are spelled out and shared with others, steps that expose shortcomings and encourage revision. Above this, however, good theories have qualities poor theories do not, or they have more of these qualities than do poor theories. We will discover that useful theories have power and integrity. We seek these qualities in theories we encounter, in those we build, or in those that compete with each other.

Power

Power refers to a theory's usefulness. Useful theories explain how and why organizations function as they do. Useful theories also predict accurately the effects of organizational activity, allowing managers to anticipate program effectiveness. Finally, useful theories inspire new thinking and research, stimulating others to test, refine, and expand their application. That is, useful theories have explanatory power, predictive power, and heuristic power.

Explanatory Power. Good theories provide compelling explanations of important organizational events. They untangle and illuminate the causal links between organizational activity and organizational outcomes. They do this in part by identifying relevant components of the organization and delineating the causal relationships among them. But more, good theories bring to the fore the causal forces, processes, or structures that underlie organizational functioning. That is, they explain why organizational activities produce the outcomes they do. Good theories enrich our understanding of life in, and the life of, organizations.

Predictive Power. Good theories anticipate accurately the effects of organizational activity. They predict organizational outcomes. A theory's predictive accuracy is tested through empirical observation. Researchers await or initiate specific organizational activity, then observe what follows. Good theories predict what actually occurs. In allowing managers to anticipate accurately the effects of organizational activity, good theories provide managers a valuable element of control. Drawing from theory, that is, managers can initiate organizational activity in anticipation of the organizational outcomes that should follow. Managerial decisions become theory guided.

More generally, good theories withstand repeated testing, gaining support with each successful trial. We say testing supports rather than proves a theory because theory testing is never complete; in the future, the theory could encounter a new opportunity to fail, and do so.

Heuristic Power. Theories that capture the imagination of theorists and researchers—enticing them to test, refine, expand, and apply them—serve a heuristic function. Good theories stimulate theorizing and research. Anxious to increase their knowledge, scientists embrace theories that render organizational functioning more understandable and more predictable; they apply them in new ways, generate new questions, gain new insights. Thus, good theories impact beyond their original design.

Together, a theory's explanatory, predictive, and heuristic power marks its usefulness. Good theories are useful. They explain organizational functioning, they predict organizational outcomes, they inspire new thinking and research. Few things are of more practical value to managers than understanding how and why organizations function as they do and anticipating accurately the effects of organizational activity.

In turn, the power of a theory depends on the conceptual soundness of both its components and the relationships among them. When we judge the quality of the theories we encounter or build, or when we choose between competing theories, we should look for integrity.

Integrity

Integrity refers to a theory's conceptual soundness. Conceptually sound theories are clearly and logically specified so that they are refutable, clear, coherent, and parsimonious. Good theories have these qualities, or at least more of these qualities than do poor theories.

Refutability. Good theories are refutable. That is, we can specify a set of circumstances in which the predictions of the theory could fail. We can indicate what stipulates failure. Short of this, we could not disprove theories; we would not detect and replace incorrect theory. For example, theories that interpret opposite outcomes as support may not be refutable. Freud's theory that people repress the memory of traumatic events into the unconscious falls into this category.[9] Whether or not someone is helped by therapy reflects opposite outcomes. Yet repression theory accepts both as support, claiming success in the first case, because repressed memories moved into consciousness, and claiming no surprise in the second case that the memory remains repressed. In this regard, no one can disprove repression theory because either improvement or nonimprovement supports the theory. Good theories avail themselves to the possibility of failing. They need not fail; they just have to be able to fail.

Clarity. In good theories, the meanings of theoretically important terms are clear. This suggests that terms used to denote the program, the program outcome, and the explanation do not have multiple uses to different audiences. To achieve clarity, theorists define their terms and delineate them from other, related terms. Good theories generate similar, shared meanings for important terms.

Coherence. A good theory is coherent, both within itself and in relation to accepted external theory and knowledge. When coherent within itself, a theory has no logical inconsistencies among its own elements; one part of the theory does not contradict another part. Additionally, good theories are specified correctly, having neither missing nor extra terms, and having neither mis-sequenced nor misgrouped terms. That is, all important terms are present—including relevant moderators and theoretical boundaries—but trivial, unrelated, or repetitious terms are absent. As well, elements of the theory are sequenced in the order and timing of their influence, and moderators with similarities are grouped together.

When coherent in relation to accepted external theory and knowledge, a theory has no logical inconsistencies with the related body of knowledge accumulated through previous theorizing and research. Good theories build on previous knowledge. They do, that is, unless the theory purposely rejects the accepted view, offering in its place a "jump in thought," a unique, innovative view. In this case, good theories may depart from, or recast, existing knowledge. Commonly, however, good theories accommodate previous thought and observation.

Parsimony. Good theories are no more complex than required to establish explanatory, predictive, and heuristic power. Needless complexity distracts. Simplicity—as when a few principles explain a complex process—is valued. For example, between two theories that explain and predict equally well, we prefer the simpler of the two. Theories that are only as complex as required display parsimony.

In sum, good theories have both power and integrity. Appreciate that power and integrity are ideals, more or less attainable. Few theories enjoy exceptionally high levels of all qualities of good theory. Rather, most theories have higher levels of some qualities than others. Often, a theory's possession of one quality compensates for low levels of other qualities. Regression theory is one such theory. As previously mentioned, in accepting as support opposite outcomes, regression theory is not refutable. However, regression theory has explanatory and heuristic power. It offers a compelling explanation for memory loss, and it has spurred additional thinking, new insights, and new applications. So we judge theory by its relative power and integrity.

Inveritably, managers have theories about Program effectiveness, even if those theories are not spelled out, shared with others, or tested. But since our expectations guide program assessment, we should make those theories explicit and as sound as we can.

Main Points of Chapter 3

- All decision makers have expectations about the kinds of organizational activities that lead to effectiveness
- A theory specifies the expected relationship between an organizational activity and an organizational outcome, and states why that relationship is expected.
- The main functions of a theory are to predict and explain organizational functioning, to anticipate what will happen and why.
- Theories should be spelled out and shared so that unclear terms can be clarified, relevant terms can be added and irrelevant terms deleted, and inconsistencies in reasoning can be resolved. Theories whose predictions undergo and withstand testing are valued.
- Theories contain four components: the program, the program outcome, an expectation, and an explanation. Theories can also contain moderators and boundaries.

- To diagram a theory, place the program on the left, the program outcome on the right, and connect them with an arrow. Insert an explanation between the program and the outcome. Insert any moderators between the program and the explanation and above or below the arrow line. Finally, specify the type of expectation, if other than positive, and any boundaries to the theory in the narrative accompanying the diagram.
- Useful theories have power and integrity. Powerful theories explain, predict, and inspire new thought and research. Theories with integrity are refutable, clear, coherent, and parsimonious.

ANSWERS TO LEARNING MODULE 3.1

1. ***Theory 1***

Figure 3.5
Amount of Study

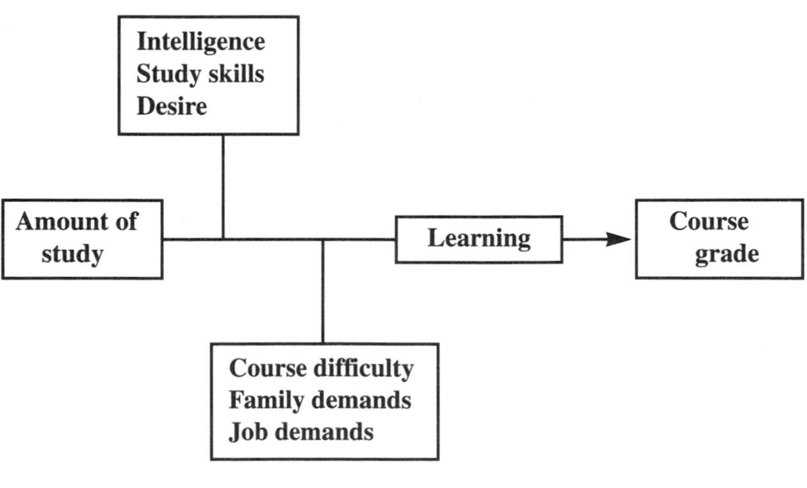

Theory 2

Figure 3.6
Safety Awareness Program

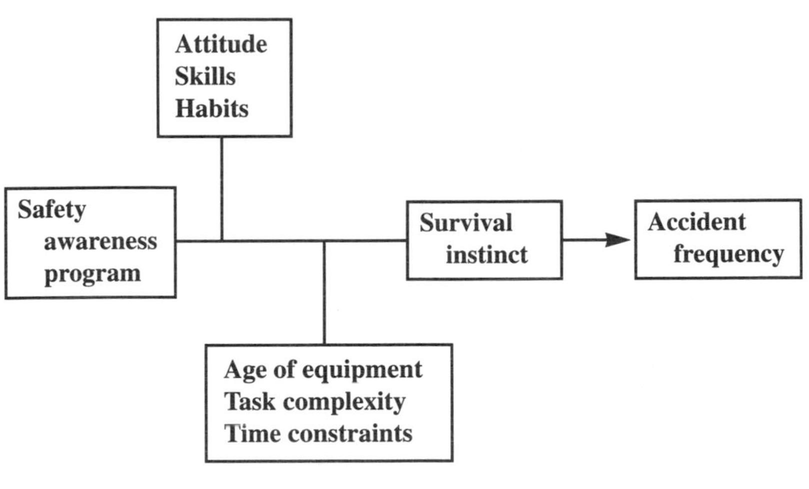

Chapter Notes

1. James L. Gibson, John M. Ivancevich, and James H. Donnelly, Jr. *Organizations: Behavior, Structure, Processes.* 7th ed., Homewood, IL: Irwin, 1991; Gregory Moorhead and Ricky W. Griffin, *Organizational Behavior.* 2nd ed., Boston: Houghton Mifflin, 1989. Also see Marvin E. Shaw and Philip R. Costanzo, *Theories of Social Psychology.* New York: McGraw-Hill, 1970.
2. I. A. Richards, quoted in Em Griffin, *A First Look at Communication Theory.* 3rd ed., New York: McGraw-Hill, 1977, p. 63.
3. Stuart M. Klein and R. Richard Ritti, *Understanding Organizational Behavior.* Boston: Kent, 1984, p. 213.
4. This definition was adapted from Klein and Ritti, p. 213.

5. John P. Campbell, Marvin D. Dunnette, Edward E. Lawler, III, and Karl E. Weick, Jr., *Managerial Behavior, Performance, and Effectiveness.* New York: McGraw-Hill, 1970, p. 345.
6. *The American Heritage Dictionary: Second College Edition.* Boston: Houghton Mifflin Company, 1976, p. 650.
7. This definition was adapted from Don Hellriegle and John W. Slocum, Jr., *Organizational Behavior.* 2nd ed., St. Paul, MN: West, 1979, p. 390.
8. This definition was adapted from Gregory Moorhead and Ricky W. Griffin, *Organizational Behavior.* 2nd ed., Dallas: Houghton Mifflin, 1989, p. 154.
9. Shaw and Costanzo, p. 13.

4

Controlling Measurement Error

Chapter Preview

This chapter examines how evaluators measure program outcomes. When a program assessment shows that the program was effective, there is always the risk of faulty measurement. Poor or inadequate measures can produce an *apparent* program impact, one that can masquerade as a real program impact. In this chapter we explore the important topic of measurement error, its nature, its sources, its effects, and its remedies.

Learning Objectives

After reading Chapter 4, you should be able to:

- define the term *measurement error*
- define the two general forms of measurement error
- identify the main sources of measurement error
- define the term *apparent program impact*
- explain the effects of each form of measurement error on the apparent program outcome
- explain the term *correlation*
- identify the two major factors that increase or decrease correlation
- define the terms *measurement reliability* and *measurement validity*
- describe the methods to establish measurement reliability and identify which method is most useful
- identify the three approaches to establish measurement validity and describe the methods to establish each

The Focus of Chapter 4

The program assessment step discussed in this chapter, along with its corresponding components in the Scientific Model, is highlighted below.

The Steps of Program Assessment

1. Involve stakeholders throughout the assessment.
2. Specify the expected program outcome.
3. **Establish a measure of the program outcome.**
4. Plan a method of gathering data.
5. Collect the data.
6. Analyze the data.
7. Communicate the results.
8. Make program decisions.

The Scientific Model of Program Assessment

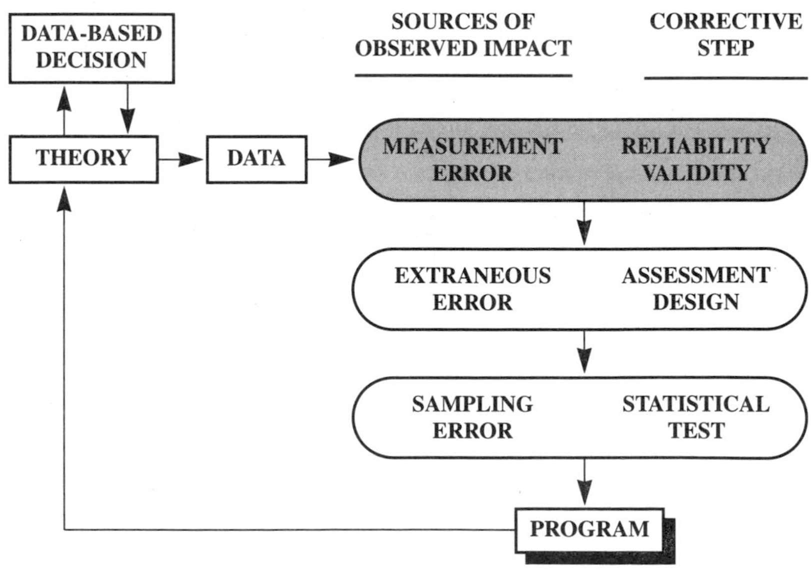

In the course of assessing the effectiveness of a program, the evaluator observes empirically the program's impact and compares past and present performances, people who have not experienced the program and those who have, or norms or quotas. Any difference signals an *apparent program impact*. We use the word *apparent* because the observed difference can stem from nonprogram influences. One of these crucial influences, called measurement error, arises whenever we measure a program outcome. This chapter illustrates that measurement error can masquerade as a program impact and presents tools to gauge whether measurement error is small enough that we can attribute an observed difference to the effectiveness of the program.

Measurement error accompanies all measures. Even in the physical sciences, where highly accurate measurement is routine, scientists know that measurement error is to be expected. Error is inevitable because scientific concepts are neither measured nor measurable. Concepts such as time, weight, and distance are just that—concepts—invented to explain what we observe, that objects age, have mass, and move. As inventions, they are not directly measurable. Instead we observe indicators presumed to possess parallel characteristics or to behave as the concept would behave. For example, sand falling through an hourglass, while not time in itself, can be used as an indicator of time.

Because few perfect indicators exist, expect a gap, however small, between an indicator and the concept it measures. Attempts to minimize measurement error have been surprisingly elaborate, even in the physical sciences, and even with such seemingly rudimentary concepts as time, weight, and distance. Despite extensive effort to refine the second as a unit of time, it remains inexact. Since 1964, the U.S. Naval Observatory in Washington, DC, the official timekeeper of the United States, has defined the second by the oscillations of the cesium-133 atom in an atomic clock.[1] This clock not only outperforms anything you could wear on your wrist, it surpasses the accuracy of the clocks that time Olympic events. Despite its precision, the atomic time of the official clock needs adjusting. Periodically, one second is added to keep the official clock in sync with the rotation of Earth, which spins slower ever-so-slightly each year. For instance, a second was added at 7:59 p.m. eastern daylight time, June 30, 1992. Between 1972 and 1992, sixteen one-second additions were made to correct the official U.S. clock. The spectacle of two people arguing over the accuracy of their wristwatches is all the more amusing now that we know it is unlikely that either party made allowances for the slowing rotation of Earth.

Weight is another seemingly easy attribute to measure. To measure their weight, most people consult the common bathroom scale, although some stare in disbelief. Some discount the scales at the doctor's office as well. The world's official unit of weight, a one-kilogram platinum-iridium cylinder, is safely housed in a vault in Paris. However, scientist Paul T. Olsen at the National Institute of Standards and Technology outside Washington, DC, suspects that the official kilogram is slightly off.[2] He is building an ultrasensitive scale to measure the accuracy of the official kilogram. Capable of measuring weight as precisely as one part in ten million, the scale is two stories tall and generates a magnetic field about 2000 times stronger than Earth's. Olsen's work reflects growing concern among scientists that the official one-kilogram cylinder emits or absorbs gases, causing slight fluctuations in its weight. Although such slight inaccuracies in a bathroom scale alarms no one, precision is critical to scientists who theorize about and conduct research on the weight of subatomic particles. When Olsen's work is completed, scientists may know more about how much error accompanies their measures of the minute but significant particles that comprise matter.

Not that measurement error is always minute, for considerable error accompanies measures of some concepts in the physical sciences. For years, scientists have vigorously sought to determine the age of the universe.[3] Following the Big Bang, they theorize, galaxies have been speeding through space, distancing themselves from each other. Because galaxies scatter from a common origin, we should be able to fix the age of the universe from its rate of expansion. Scientists measure the rate of expansion using the ratio between the velocity with which galaxies move and the distance from Earth they have traveled. Whereas scientists readily can measure velocity from the wavelengths of light coming from a galaxy, they find distance difficult to measure owing to the enormous expanses. The Andromeda galaxy and the M81 Group, for example, lie 2.5 million light-years, and 10 million light-years from Earth, respectively (a light year is the distance traveled by light in one year, or about 5.88 trillion miles). Because measuring distance is so problematic, the rate of expansion of the universe remains a controversy today among scientists, with some fixing it at 50 and others at 100 kilometers per second per megaparsec (a megaparsec is the distance light travels in 3.26 million years). In turn, they reason, this rate of expansion fixes the age of the universe between 10 billion and 20 billion years old. The span between 10 billion and 20 billion years represents measurement error.

Ralph gives Erma a lesson in measurement error

That's 20 − 10 = 10 billion years of measurement error. Using the most sensitive technology available, including readings from the Hubble space telescope currently orbiting Earth, scientists have narrowed the age of the universe to a 10-billion-year window. Considerable error accompanies measures of vast distances.

Similar problems plague behavioral scientists and, invariably, those who assess programs by measuring the individual and collective behaviors of human beings. Behavioral scientists confront the additional challenge that human beings think and feel. As a result, measures of such concrete program outcomes as absenteeism likely contain some measurement error. As in the physical sciences, program outcomes are concepts and as such, are not measurable directly. Instead, we define and measure empirical indicators of the concept. We may measure absenteeism, for example, by examining personnel records. Personnel records, however, can be incomplete or incorrect. Occasionally, one employee "covers" for another employee's absence; a supervisor may forget to record an absence; one supervisor may mark an employee who misses half a day absent while another supervisor may not; more often, supervisors "forgive" absences accompanied by good excuses, or poor excuses well-presented expect small discrepancies between actual and recorded performance.

Considerable error accompanies measures of more abstract Program Outcomes like motivation. Motivation is an invented description of a presumed internal state of an employee. Finding observable and accurate indicators of employees' internal states is difficult. We could watch for indicators of motivation, such as working overtime, initiating work, or volunteering for work, but there is no guarantee that observable traits represent personal feelings.

Forms of Measurement Error

Despite efforts to minimize it, error is indigenous to all measures, and it assumes two forms: measures can be inaccurate and inconsistent. We may measure the wrong thing, or we may measure the right thing but measure it inconsistently. We can also measure the wrong thing inconsistently.

The three targets in Fig. 4.1 demonstrate each type of error. Target 1 portrays an ideal measure of a program outcome: The target's center has been hit and hit consistently. This is what we want when measuring a program outcome like motivation—to measure motivation and measure it consistently. Target 2 shows measures that,

Figure 4.1
Inaccurate and Inconsistent Measures

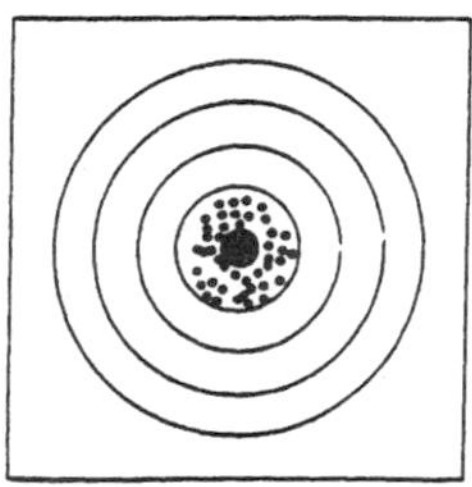 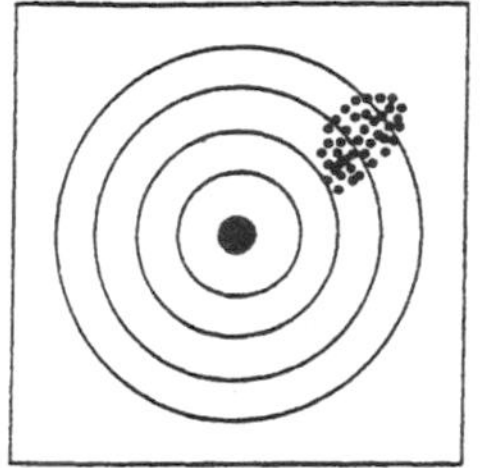 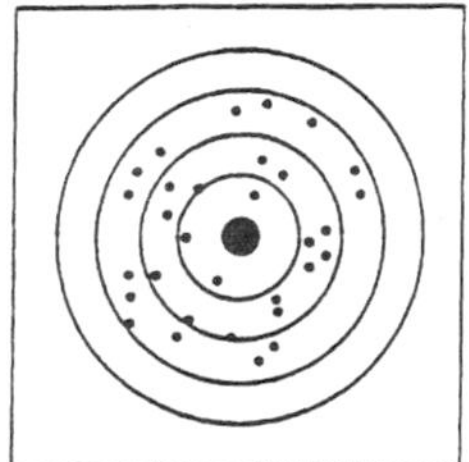

while consistent, are inaccurate, favoring a spot off-target. That we hit the spot off-target consistently affords no consolation. Although we measured something consistently, that something, whatever it was, wasn't motivation (not the bull's-eye). Target 3, where the hits are scattered all over, portrays the worst-case scenario: Measures are neither accurate nor consistent. Not only have we not measured motivation, we haven't measured anything meaningful. To be useful, measures should conform to the pattern displayed in Target 1.

Sources of Measurement Error

Measurement inaccuracy and inconsistency stem from a variety of sources that are readily understood within the context of a program assessment. Here's an example: To determine the effectiveness of the company's new sales training program, a manager randomly assigned to it sixteen salespeople. Sixteen other salespeople performed their duties as usual, receiving no training. At the completion of the training, all thirty-two salespeople completed a questionnaire designed to measure employee motivation. The manager found this difference in the average motivation level between trained and untrained salespeople.

	Motivation Level
Trained Salespeople	4.2
Untrained Salespeople	3.2

Motivation level differed between trained and untrained salespeople, signaling an apparent program impact. Before attributing the impact to the effectiveness of the sales training program, however, the manager should be mindful that the apparent program impact could represent measurement error instead.

The manager's measures of motivation could be inaccurate, inconsistent, or both. The measures would be inaccurate if the questionnaire systematically measured the wrong thing—something less than, other than, or in addition to motivation. Measuring less than motivation occurs when the questions underrepresent the meaning of *motivation*, or when the questions do not ask about important components of motivation. For example, the questionnaire may contain no items about initiating work without being asked, a potentially important ingredient of motivation.

Measuring something other than motivation occurs when the questionnaire items measure a concept other than motivation. For example, if it mostly contains items about feelings toward coworkers and the workplace, the questionnaire may measure morale instead of motivation.

Measuring more than motivation occurs when the questionnaire contains items that measure a concept in addition to motivation. For example, the questionnaire may contain items about opinions of the workplace, reflecting morale, in addition to items reflecting motivation. The measures reflect morale and motivation.

Beyond being inaccurate, measures can be inconsistent. The measures of motivation would be inconsistent if random influences altered how people would *normally* answer. These nonsystematic influences cause the observed score to depart from the person's *true score.*

Random influences can emanate from (1) the questionnaire, (2) the respondent, or (3) the immediate environment. Characteristics of the questionnaire can influence respondents' answers and yet be irrelevant to their motivation. For example, ambiguous instructions can cause some respondents to proceed differently than normal; instructions that become clearer while completing the questionnaire can alter how a respondent proceeds; and typographical errors in the questionnaire can alter how someone answers.

Influences within the respondents can also alter their performance. Respondents can become fatigued, impatient, or nervous. Some may make careless errors when recording answers. Some may guess at answers, inadvertently skip questions, or take longer than others. Some may be distracted by personal problems.

Influences within the immediate environment can alter how respondents perform, too. Changes in lighting, temperature, or sound can be distracting. Whether from the questionnaire, the respondent, or the environment, these random influences are unrelated to motivation and can alter how respondents answer the questionnaire. To the degree any of these influences intrude, measures will be inconsistent.

Effects of Measurement Error

Measurement error misrepresents the actual impact of the program in either of two ways. When measures are inaccurate, the apparent program impact represents an impact in the wrong thing—something less than, other than, or more than the program outcome. When measures are inconsistent, the relationship between the program and its impact will underestimate the relationship between the program and its true impact. That is, the results will underestimate the relationship we would have observed if there had been no measurement inconsistencies.

Remember the manager who observed an apparent program impact: Motivation level was higher among employees who received sales training (4.2) than among employees who did not (3.2). This is merely an apparent program impact because the measure of motivation may contain measurement error. Measurement inaccuracy alters the results we would have obtained had we accurately measured the program outcome. When measures are inaccurate, the apparent program impact represents an impact in the wrong thing. In this case, the observed difference between the trained and untrained salespeople would represent a difference in something less than, other than, or in addition to motivation. To attribute this apparent program impact to the effectiveness of the program would be misleading because the program influenced the wrong, and unspecified, program outcome.

Measurement inconsistency underestimates the actual relationship between the program and the program outcome. When we determine the relationship between sales training and employee motivation, we will underestimate their true relationship.

An apparent program impact contains both measurement error and whatever impact the program has. Moreover, the two—measurement error and the impact of the program—are initially intertwined, indistinguishable from one another. Thus, the amount of measurement inaccuracy needs to be gauged, lest it masquerade as a program impact. The amount of measurement inconsistency must be gauged to avoid underestimating the relation between the program and its impact.

Although impossible to eliminate, we can reduce measurement error and gauge its remaining level. Correlation procedures provide the principal means of assessing the magnitude of measurement error.

Correlation

When measurement error is negligible, we can attribute an apparent program impact to the effectiveness of the program. To gauge measurement error, we use correlation procedures. Correlation is easier to understand if we use a set of data. Table 4.1 shows the weights of seven people obtained both from their home scales and from the scale at the doctor's office. In this instance, the two scales produced identical measures. Exact agreement between measures however, is rare.

Table 4.2 presents a second, more typical, set of measures for seven other people. This time the two types of scales produced similar but not identical measures. We can summarize the similarity of the measures in alternate ways. For example, the home scale weights were all within five pounds of the doctor's scale weights. Alternatively we could say that the measures were identical for person 12, the doctor's scale weight was less than the home scale weight for person 8, and it exceeded the home scale weight for all the rest.

Finally, we could say that everyone who weighed above average on the home scales also weighed above average on the doctor's scale, and everyone who weighed below average on the home scales also weighed below average on the doctor's scale.

Table 4.1
Weights of Seven People

Person	Home Scale	Doctor's Scale
1	130	130
2	175	175
3	123	123
4	160	160
5	122	122
6	185	185
7	141	141
Average	148	148

Table 4.2
Weights of Seven Others

Person	Home Scale	Doctor's Scale
8	176	173
9	136	138
10	123	124
11	160	161
12	122	122
13	185	186
14	141	146
Average	149	150

These descriptions, however, are unwieldy if not confusing. Fortunately, mathematicians have derived a formula that produces a concise summary of the similarity between successive measures. The procedure was developed by Karl Pearson and is formally called the Pearson product-moment correlation coefficient. The procedure examines the relative position or location of each person's score within two sets of scores and produces a single, numerical index, designated as r, of the relationship between the two sets of scores. Correlation examines the position of each person's score within each set of scores in terms of its distance from the average. For example, the average weight on the home scales is 149 pounds, and person 8's weight is a distance of $176 - 149 = 27$ above average on the home scale. The average weight on the doctor's scale is 150 pounds, and person 8's weight is $173 - 150 = 23$ above average on the doctor's scale. Therefore, person 8 is *located* above average on both scales, as depicted in Fig. 4.2.

The correlation will be high when those who score above average on one measure score above average on the other, and when those who score below average on one measure score below average on the other. The correlation will be low when there is little correspondence between successive measures, as when half of those who initially score above average subsequently score above average but

FIGURE 4.2
Location of Person 8

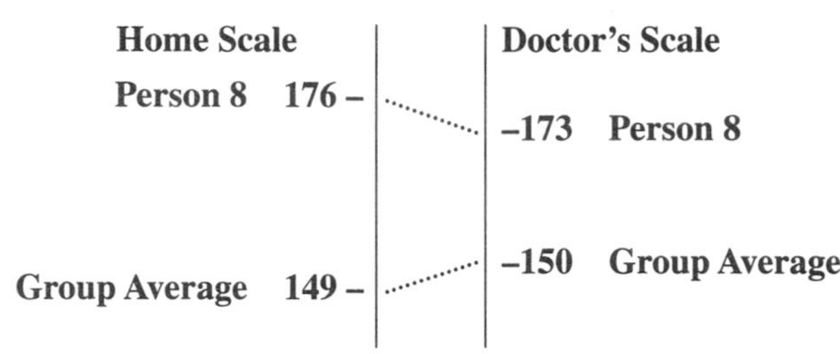

the rest score below average. Total dissimilarity between successive measures produces a correlation of zero, and perfect similarity, as exhibited in Table 4.1, produces a correlation of +1.00, the largest value *r* can assume.

The weights of the people in Table 4.2 are repeated in Table 4.3, in which the middle columns show whether each score is located above the average of its group, signified by a plus sign, or below average, signified by a minus sign. For example, since person 8's weight (176) exceeds the home scale average weight (149), it lies above average and receives a plus sign. Because person 9's weight (136) is less than 149, it lies below average and receives a minus sign. Note that everyone who scored above average (+) on one measure scored above average (+) on the other, and, everyone who scored below average (−) on one measure scored below average (−) again. Peoples' weights hold similar positions (either above or below average) on both measures.

Finally, the numerical differences between each score and the average of its group are presented in Table 4.4, with the home scale differences in the left column (designated *x*) and the doctor's scale differences in the middle column (designated *y*). The pattern of plus and minus signs preceding each difference remains the same as in Table 4.3, while the actual numerical values obtained by subtracting each score from the average of its group have been added.

The *xy* column contains the products of values *x* and *y*, and these values are totaled at the bottom. In this instance, all *xy* values are positive. Multiplying positive numbers results in a positive number, as does multiplying two negative numbers. Thus, *x* and *y* values

Table 4.3
Each Weight's Location from Average

Person	Home Scale			Doctor's Scale
8	176	+	+	173
9	136	–	–	138
10	123	–	–	124
11	160	+	+	161
12	122	–	–	122
13	185	+	+	186
14	141	–	–	146
Average	149			150

Table 4.4
Multiplying Differences and Summing Their Products

Home Scale x	Doctor's Scale y	xy
+ 27	+ 23	+ 621
– 13	– 12	+ 156
– 26	– 26	+ 676
+ 11	+ 11	+ 121
– 27	– 28	+ 756
+ 36	+ 36	+ 1,296
– 8	– 4	+ 32
	Total	3,658

with similar signs increase the correlation. Conversely, x and y values with dissimilar signs (there are none in Table 4.4) produce a negative product (a positive number times a negative number produces a negative number), and when added to the other numbers, decrease the correlation. This is the key feature of the formula for the correlation: Scores that occupy similar locations in both measures (i.e., above average in both or below average in both) increase r, and scores that occupy dissimilar locations (one above average one below average) decrease r.

The resulting value—3,658 in this case—has two shortcomings as a useful index of relationship. First, as a total it increases as a function of the number of people and thus can overrepresent the relationship. Second, the total can increase without limit, making it difficult to compare one correlation to another.

To restrict the size that the total can assume, it is divided by a second value, symbolized as $(Ns_X s_Y)$. This last step will not be elaborated on here, except to emphasize that dividing by N, the number of people, "averages" the summed values so that the result is insensitive to the number of people measured. Dividing by $s_X s_Y$ "standardizes" the correlation so that it will never exceed +1.00.[4] In this form, $r = 0$ indicates no similarity between two sets of measures; $r = +1.00$ indicates total similarity; and values of r between 0 and +1.00 indicate varying degrees of similarity.[5]

Using the computer to divide 3,658 by the value of $(Ns_X s_Y)$ provided a correlation coefficient of $r = .95$. Because .95 is so close to +1.00, it shows that high similarity exists between the measures of the home scales and the doctor's scale.

Although s_X and s_Y will not be discussed in detail until Chapter 7, the formula for the correlation coefficient is presented here for reference:

$$r = \frac{\Sigma xy}{Ns_X s_Y}$$

where x and y are the differences between each score and the average of its group, xy are the products of these differences, and Σxy is the sum of these products. Σ is the Greek letter sigma and means "sum the values." In this case, x and y are the numbers in the two left columns of Table 4.4, xy are the products in the right column, and Σxy is the total at the bottom of the table.

Although this explanation of correlation is complex, the formula for the correlation coefficient can be performed easily on a computer. Two principles should be kept in mind. The numerator (top portion) of the formula ensures that values of x and y with similar signs increase the correlation, while values of x and y with dissimilar signs decrease the correlation. Thus, the correlation coefficient reflects the degree to which scores have the same relative positions (either above average on both measures or below average on both measures). Second, the denominator (bottom portion) of the formula ensures that the correlation never exceeds $+1.00$.

The correlation coefficient, then, describes the similarity between two sets of measures, with $r = 0$ indicating no correspondence and $r = +1.00$ indicating perfect correspondence. High correlations signal the presence of similarity between successive measures of the program outcome. This last feature allows us to gauge the error that accompanies measures of the program outcome. When the correlation among successive measures of the program outcome is high, measurement error is low, and we can attribute the apparent program impact to the effectiveness of the program. The people in both Tables 4.1 and 4.2 could go on a diet and use their home scales to monitor progress. With $r = 1.00$ and $r = .95$, respectively, the measures from the home scale would either be identical to, or very close to, the doctor's scale.

Correlation is a viable means to gauge the degree to which measures are inaccurate or inconsistent. *Measurement validity* is the degree to which measures are accurate, and *measurement reliability* is the degree to which measures are consistent. When measurement error is high, measurement validity and/or reliability is low; when measurement error is low, measurement validity and/or reliability is high. Attributing an apparent program impact to the effectiveness of a program requires both measurement validity and measurement reliability.

Over the years, scientists have evolved conventions for how large the correlation coefficient should be before concluding that measurement error is small enough to attribute the apparent program impact to the effectiveness of the program. Now we will see how we can use correlation procedures to establish measurement validity and reliability using the conventions for the size of the correlation coefficient. Since to be interpreted, measures must at least be consistent, we will look at measurement reliability first.

Measurement Reliability

Measurement reliability is the degree to which measures of a program outcome are consistent, free of random influences emanating from the questionnaire, the respondents, or the immediate environment. Two general approaches have evolved to establish measurement reliability. The first, stability, establishes the similarity of measures of the program outcome on successive occasions. The second, internal consistency, establishes the similarity within the set of measures itself on a single occasion. In each case, a high correlation coefficient indicates that measures display similarity and thus contain low measurement error. Ideally, you should check if a questionnaire is reliable before using it for your program assessment. You can do this in two ways: First, consult previous research to see if other researchers have reported information that shows the questionnaire is reliable. Second, assess the questionnaire's reliability for a subset of your program target audience, a subset that will not be involved in the subsequent program assessment. When using a questionnaire in program assessment, you should again assess its measurement reliability to ensure that the measures are reliable in that specific instance.

Stability

Measurement stability refers to the degree to which measures of the program outcome are similar on successive occasions. To establish measurement stability, researchers gather measures from the same group of people on two separate occasions, separated by time. Two methods have evolved to assess if measures are stable—the test-retest method and the equivalent forms method.

The Test-Retest Method. In the test-retest method, the evaluator administers the same questionnaire to the same people on two separate occasions. A high correlation between the two sets of measures shows that people responded similarly on both occasions, that the measures are stable over time, and are thus reliable. This method reasons that reliable questionnaires produce very nearly the same results on successive occasions.

How large the correlation coefficient must be to indicate good measurement reliability depends on the concreteness of the outcome measure. For concrete outcomes, such as timing a runner with a stopwatch, expect very stable measures, say as reflected by $r = .95$. But for abstract outcomes, such as measuring employee motivation with a questionnaire, expect less stability between successive measures. For abstract outcomes, behavioral scientists agree that the correlation coefficient should be .80 or above to indicate good measurement reliability, and no lower than .70 to indicate minimal measurement reliability. Correlations below .70 are usually unacceptable except for preliminary or exploratory research. Researchers report the correlation coefficient so readers can evaluate the adequacy of the measures for themselves.

Although seeking similarity between successive measures seems a sensible way to establish measurement reliability, the test-retest method suffers from three limitations. First, assembling people twice to complete a questionnaire is often inconvenient and sometimes impossible. Second, this method assumes no change occurs in the program outcome between administrations of the questionnaire, an assumption that is not always tenable. When the program outcome does change, the correlation coefficient underestimates measurement reliability. What looks like unreliability instead reflects a change in the program outcome. As a remedy, you can shorten the interval, reducing the possibility that the program outcome changes. Finally, the correlation coefficient can overestimate measurement reliability if on the second occasion respondents remember their initial answers. What looks like reliability may reflect the respondents' memories. As a remedy, you can lengthen the interval, reducing the possibility that respondents recall earlier responses. Unfortunately, lengthening the interval to minimize recall increases the likelihood that the program outcome will change in the interim. One is left with the difficult task of selecting an interval short enough that the program outcome doesn't change but long enough that respondents don't recall initial answers.

The Equivalent Forms Method. To alleviate the difficulty of selecting an optimum interval between administrations, the equivalent forms method administers two distinct, yet comparable, forms of the questionnaire to the same people—one questionnaire on one occasion, the comparable version on another. This method parallels the test-retest method, except the evaluator administers two *equivalent* forms of the questionnaire instead of the same questionnaire. As an initial step, the evaluator develops equivalent forms of the questionnaire so that each measures the program outcome but with different questions. This method reasons that respondent memory is immaterial if each questionnaire contains unique questions. Consequently, the researcher can shorten the interval, reducing the possibility that the program outcome will change.

A high correlation between scores on the equivalent forms indicates that the measures are stable over time. As with the test-retest method, a correlation of .80, one as low as .70, and one below .70 indicate good, at least minimal, or unacceptable measurement reliability, respectively.

While allowing for a short interval, this method unfortunately retains the necessity to assemble the same group of people on two occasions, and moreover, adds the necessity to develop equivalent forms of a questionnaire, usually a difficult and time-consuming task.

Internal Consistency

Designed in part to overcome the pitfalls of the two methods to establish measurement stability, internal consistency methods gauge the similarity with which various parts of a questionnaire measure the program outcome. To their credit, these methods assess measurement reliability on a single occasion. Two methods to establish internal consistency exist, but the latter we discuss is superior.

The Split-Half Method. In the split-half method, the questionnaire is administered on a single occasion, and the scores from one-half of the questionnaire, selected arbitrarily, are correlated with the scores on the other half of the questionnaire. If separate portions of the questionnaire can produce similar measures, it is consistent within itself, and considered reliable. Typically, peoples' answers to the odd-numbered questionnaire items are correlated with their answers to the even-numbered items. For a questionnaire consisting of ten questions, for example, the procedure correlates peoples' answers to items 1, 3, 5, 7, and 9 with their answers to items 2, 4, 6, 8, and 10. The resulting correlation coefficient indicates the measurement reliability of the questionnaire when separated into halves, so it underestimates the measurement reliability of the questionnaire as a whole. The Spearman-Brown prophecy formula, named after the two statisticians who developed it, adjusts the r obtained on the questionnaire halves to arrive at the measurement reliability of the questionnaire as a whole. The formula is

$$r' = \frac{2r}{1 + r}$$

where r is the measurement reliability for the questionnaire when separated into halves and r' (pronounced *r prime*) is the measurement reliability of the questionnaire as a whole. For example, for an r of

.75 obtained on questionnaire halves, r' for the questionnaire as a whole is

$$r' = \frac{2(.75)}{1 + .75} = \frac{1.5}{1.75} = .86$$

Because r' usually exceeds r, you should always perform this conversion. Similar to other indices of measurement reliability, an r' of .80 or above indicates good measurement reliability; one as low as .70 indicates minimal measurement reliability; and one below .70 indicates unacceptable measurement reliability.

A problem arises: You can subdivide a questionnaire into halves in alternate ways (e.g., even and odd items, top and bottom halves, randomly formed halves), and various halves typically produce different values of r'. Consequently, dividing the questionnaire one way can produce an r' that exceeds .70, and dividing it another way may not. As you can see, depending on how you divide the questionnaire, it may or may not meet the established conventions for measurement reliability.

Cronbach's Alpha. Named after its developer, and denoted by α, the Greek letter alpha, Cronbach's alpha is based on the average of the set of correlations produced by correlating every questionnaire item with every other questionnaire item. For a 10-item questionnaire, the procedure correlates item 1 successively with items 2 through 10, item 2 with item 1 and successively with items 3 through 10, item 3 with items 1 and 2 and successively with items 4 through 10, and so on. This produces a set of inter-item correlations. Finally, the procedure averages this set of inter-item correlations by adding them and dividing by the number of correlations in the set. The average of the inter-item correlations is designated as $\bar{r}$ (pronounced *r bar*). The formula for Cronbach's alpha adjusts $\bar{r}$ by the number of people on whom the measures were drawn, as follows:

$$\alpha = \frac{n\,\bar{r}}{1 + \bar{r}\,(n - 1)}$$

where $\bar{r}$ is the average of the set of inter-item correlations and n is the size of the sample. The value for α is interpreted as other indices of measurement reliability. An α of .80 or above indicates good measurement reliability; one as low as .70 indicates minimal measurement reliability; and one below .70 indicates inadequate measurement reliability.

Derived from a single administration of a questionnaire, Cronbach's alpha averts the shortcomings of the test-retest and the equivalent forms methods of establishing measurement reliability. It also yields a single index, unlike the split-half method. Cronbach's alpha emerges as the method of choice to establish measurement reliability.

The researcher using the test-retest method should be prepared to address the concerns surrounding the length of the interval between tests: To what degree is the correlation coefficient inflated due to the respondents' memory of their initial answers, and to what degree is the correlation coefficient deflated due to changes in the outcome that occurred during the interval? Researchers using the split-half method should be prepared to address the concern that the value of r' depends on the method of dividing the questionnaire into two halves. In turn, these same questions should be raised by consumers of research reports who encounter these methods. The best recourse is the habitual use of Cronbach's alpha to establish measurement reliability.

Increasing Measurement Reliability

Evaluators can increase measurement reliability in two ways. They can lengthen the questionnaire, adding items at least as good as those already in the questionnaire. Other things equal, lengthening a questionnaire increases its measurement reliability, although there is a point of diminishing return.[6] Evaluators can also remove items that correlate minimally with other items. Removing poor items from a questionnaire increases its measurement reliability, although a sufficient set of items must remain to fully measure the program outcome.

To be useful, measures must be consistent, reliable. Once measurement reliability is established, focus turns to whether what is measured consistently is measured accurately.

Measurement Validity

Measurement validity is the degree to which measures accurately represent the program outcome and only the program outcome, as it is defined conceptually. We can use three approaches to establish the measurement validity of a questionnaire. The first approach, content validation, explores the degree to which the items on the questionnaire fully represent the program outcome. Not amenable to correlation procedures, an evaluator addresses content validation while selecting or preparing a questionnaire. The second approach, called construct validation, explores the degree to which measures of the program outcome relate as expected with conceptually related outcomes: high relationship with equivalent outcomes, moderate relationship with similar outcomes, and low relationship with unrelated outcomes. Assessed through correlation procedures, an evaluator addresses construct validation before undertaking a program assessment. The third approach, called predictive validation, explores the degree to which measures of the program outcome relate to a desired criterion behavior, such as job performance. Predictive validation also uses correlation procedures.

Content Validation

Content validation assures that measures fully reflect the program outcome, that measures thoroughly cover its content. Conversely, imagine measuring a student's mastery of a college course with one true-false question. Fortunate are the students who know or guess the answer to the question. Others will likely complain that the examination wasn't fair, that it didn't give them a chance to show what they knew, that one question can't begin to represent the breadth and depth of information covered in a college course. (This would all be said rapidly and in one breath.) A one-item exam necessarily overlooks large portions of the course content, and thereby lacks content validity. Similarly, imagine measuring employee motivation by the number of times they come to work early. Motivation, however, entails more than early arrivals. There is also willingness to work, initiating new work without being told, working late, and so on. Measures that omit relevant aspects of an outcome lack content validity.

You can establish content validity for a questionnaire with these three steps:

1. Specify the domain of the program outcome.
2. Generate questionnaire items.
3. Judge whether the items fully represent the domain.

Domain refers to the array of phenomena—behaviors, attitudes, needs, skills—encompassed by your definition of the program outcome. Define the program outcome before selecting or preparing a questionnaire, consulting previous theory and research on the topic as needed. For example, if attempting to define motivation, you could consult the work of Abraham Maslow. Maslow described motivation as a hierarchy of five needs, physiological, safety, love, esteem, and self-actualization, wherein the next, higher-order need motivates behavior when the preceding, more basic need is relatively satisfied.[7] These five needs are the content domain of motivation, as Maslow defines the term. A questionnaire would need enough items to fully reflect each need.

Next, you generate numerous questionnaire items to reflect each dimension of the program outcome. You can often draw ideas for questionnaire items from previous research on the topic. You may also interview employees about what motivates them or ask them to write about it. The key is to generate an array of statements that reflect all relevant ideas on the topic. Then you cast the ideas into a consistent form, such as:

1. It is less desirable for women than for men to have a job that requires responsibility.
   - ☐ strongly disagree
   - ☐ disagree
   - ☐ slightly disagree
   - ☐ neither disagree nor agree
   - ☐ slightly agree
   - ☐ agree
   - ☐ strongly agree

Finally, ask experts in this topic area to judge the items, using your definition of the program outcome, on the degree to which each item represents the content domain of the program outcome. You would delete items that the experts consider outside of or irrelevant to the content domain. The experts could also suggest motivation factors that your items fail to reflect. Together, these steps help ensure that the questionnaire items fully reflect the content domain of the Program Outcome.

Construct Validation

Construct validation establishes whether the measure of a program outcome *behaves* as researchers expect it to. Whether, for example, it finds a difference between people who are known to differ. Whether it relates highly to another measure of the same program outcome. And more generally, whether measures behave empirically as expected theoretically. The word construct typically refers to phenomena such as intelligence and motivation that reside within individuals and are not directly observable. We will use the term construct to refer to any program outcome of interest.

You should establish the construct validity of a questionnaire before using it in a program assessment with these two steps:

1. Specify how you expect the measure of the program outcome to perform.
2. Verify whether the measure of the program outcome performed as you expected.

Two methods pertinent to program assessment use the above steps to establish the construct validity of measures. These are the known-groups method and the convergent method. Researchers use either or both methods to establish the construct validity of questionnaires, although they use the convergent method more often.

The Known-Groups Method. This method assesses whether a measure can detect the difference between people who are already known to differ on the program outcome. The evaluator identifies people who already differ on the program outcome, administers the questionnaire to them, and checks if the results show that the people differ. As Step one, the evaluator expects the questionnaire will detect the difference known to exist between these people. As Step two, the evaluator checks if the questionnaire detected the difference. Questionnaires that detect known differences display construct validity. This method reasons that if people already differ on a construct, and a questionnaire detects this difference, the questionnaire must be measuring that construct. For example, if supervisors have identified motivated and unmotivated workers, we would expect the first group to score higher than the second group on a questionnaire of employee motivation. If the people's scores on the questionnaire differ, we have evidence that the questionnaire measures motivation. If the questionnaire fails to detect this known difference in motivation, we know it is invalid.

The Convergent Method. This method assesses whether the measurement of a program outcome relates as expected to another measure of this program outcome or to measures of other program outcomes. The questionnaire of interest, whose validity is unknown, is correlated with others of established validity. If the questionnaire can obtain results as expected relative to known standards, then the new questionnaire is valid.

The evaluator first specifies the relationships expected between the measures. Then the evaluator administers the set of questionnaires to employees similar to those that will participate in the program assessment. Finally, the evaluator computes the correlation between the measure of the program outcome and the other measures and checks whether the correlations conform to what was expected. A valid questionnaire correlates as expected with the other measures.

Just how many and what combination of measures researchers use varies, limited in part by the researcher's time and interest. Often, researchers at least correlate the program outcome questionnaire with another valid measure of the same topic, or if one doesn't exist, with a valid measure of the most similar topic for which a questionnaire exists. The most complete picture emerges when a measure is correlated with a combination of other valid measures. Each time a questionnaire correlates with other valid measures as expected, we gain additional evidence of its construct validity. In this sense, construct validity is not an either-or quality but a matter of degree, where more evidence is better.

Researchers form expectations about how a measure should relate to other measures based on how the topics have been defined previously and on the commonalities among those definitions. Measures of constructs with highly similar definitions should correlate highly. Conversely, measures should converge successively less toward successively less-related constructs. For example, one should expect a questionnaire that measures motivation to do the following:

1. Correlate highly, say above .80, with another, already existing questionnaire of motivation from the same theoretical perspective
2. Correlate moderately high, say about .65, with a preexisting questionnaire of motivation from a different theoretical perspective
3. Correlate only moderately, say about .45, with measures of related constructs, such as need for achievement and organizational commitment
4. Correlate minimally, say below .20, with measures of unrelated constructs like general intelligence and reading ability

Let's review each possibility using motivation as the Program Outcome. You may have selected a questionnaire or may have developed one that measures motivation as defined by Maslow and wonder if it provides a valid measure. You prefer this questionnaire because it contains a small number of clear items, and language more suitable to your organization. Your measure is valid if it can duplicate the results from a preexisting questionnaire already known to measure motivation accurately. You know it does if it correlates highly, say above .80, with the valid measure of motivation.

You would administer both questionnaires—the one you like and the valid one—to a group of employees similar to those you plan to use in a program assessment. Then you correlate the scores from the preferred questionnaire with the scores of the valid questionnaire. Finally, you would judge if the resultant correlation is above .80 as you expected. Two measures of motivation drawn from the same theoretical perspective should correlate highly. If they do, the high correlation suggests that the questionnaires measure equivalent things, that they are interchangeable.

Conversely, two measures of motivation from different theoretical perspectives should correlate moderately high, but not too high, lest they be duplicates, and thereby question the theoretical distinctions between the perspectives. A moderately high correlation, say about .65 shows that, as expected, the questionnaires measure something in common, motivation, yet, each measures something the other doesn't, something unique. That something, is attributed to the conceptual differences between the perspectives, to how each defines motivation differently.

If it is valid, a measure of motivation should correlate only moderately, say around .45, with measures of related but conceptually distinct constructs such as need for achievement and organizational commitment. These constructs share some conceptual common ground with motivation, but they reflect new territory. For example, while those who feel the need for achievement may be motivated, they also want to advance. Motivation does not necessarily entail the desire for advancement. And while those who feel committed to the organization may be motivated, they also identify with the organization. Motivation does not require identification with the organization. Because the related measures represent new territory beyond their conceptual common ground with motivation, we should expect only moderate correlations.

Finally, a measure of motivation should correlate only minimally, say below .20, with unrelated constructs like general intelligence or reading ability. Motivation has little if any conceptual common ground with either. Should a measure of motivation correlate with intelligence or reading ability, it is likely due to the difficulty level of the instructions or the difficulty of the language in the items. The complexity of the questionnaire needs to be reduced, the language simplified.

To verify any of the above expectations, you would administer the relevant questionnaires to a group of employees similar to those who will participate in the program assessment and correlate the scores. Then you would check if the correlations emerge as expected. Measures that perform empirically as expected theoretically provide evidence of convergent validity.

Predictive Validation

Predictive validation establishes whether measures relate to a criterion behavior as expected from theory. The criterion behavior is an element of organizational effectiveness. For example, the expectation may be drawn from theory that current employee motivation (a measure) is predictive of future high sales (a criterion behavior). Measures that predict what is expected theoretically display predictive validity.

To this end, a manager could correlate measures of motivation with year-end sales. A moderate correlation, say about .40, suggests that the measures predict the criterion behavior. We expect a moderate correlation because sales are influenced by a myriad of factors besides motivation, such as supply and demand and the prevailing economic climate. Managers often use this method in selecting and placing personnel. The manager hires or promotes those employees who score high on a questionnaire that measures motivation, assuming that motivation predicts high sales.

Please take time to complete Learning Module 4.1 Assessing Measurement Reliability and Validity. It is designed to increase your familiarity with these important topics.

LEARNING MODULE 4.1: Assessing Measurement Reliability and Validity

This learning module will make you more familiar with how evaluators establish measurement reliability and validity. You will see two types of questionnaires used frequently in research, and you will examine the initial efforts to assess their measurement error. After reading about each questionnaire, you will be asked to identify the method the authors used to assess measurement reliability and validity, and to gauge the degree of success. Please read the description in each example carefully and then answer the questions.

Example 1 Job Satisfaction Index

Source: Arthur H. Brayfield and Harold F. Rothe, An index of job satisfaction. *Journal of Applied Psychology*. 1951, *35*, 307–311.

Measure: The Job Satisfaction Index is a general index of job satisfaction inferred from the individual's attitude toward work. The questionnaire consists of 18 items with five-step responses ranging from *strongly agree* to *strongly disagree*. The 18 items were drawn from a larger pool of 255 questions. Criteria for item selection included the degree to which items referred to overall job satisfaction rather than specific aspects of a job.

Item Examples: My job is like a hobby to me.
My job is usually interesting enough to keep me from getting bored.
I consider my job rather unpleasant.
Most days I am enthusiastic about my work.

Reliability: The Job Satisfaction Index was administered as part of a study of 231 female office employees. One of the investigators personally administered the tests to employees in small groups. The odd-even reliability coefficient computed for this sample was .77, which was corrected by the Spearman-Brown formula to a reliability coefficient of .87.

Validity: The Job Satisfaction Index was able to discriminate between groups who were assumed to be differentially satisfied with their jobs. The mean scores of 40 students in an adult night school course in Personnel Psychology who were also employed in a personnel position were contrasted with 51 students in the same course but who were not employed in personnel positions. The authors assumed that students employed in occupations appropriate to their expressed interest should be more satisfied with their jobs than students employed in occupations unrelated to their expressed interest in personnel work. The personnel group's mean job satisfaction score was 76.9 and the non-personnel group's was 65.4. The difference between the means was significantly different at the 1 percent level.

The Job Satisfaction Index was also reported to correlate .92 with the Hoppock Blank administered to the same night school population. The Hoppock Blank is a general measure of job satisfaction developed much earlier.

Analysis Questions for Example 1

This section poses questions about the ways the authors in Example 1 assessed measurement reliability and validity. Answer each question fully, referring to the description as needed.

1. What method did the authors use to assess the measurement reliability of the Job Satisfaction Index?
2. Why was the result "corrected"?
3. How successfully did the authors establish the measurement reliability of the Job Satisfaction Index?
4. What two methods did the authors use to assess the measurement validity of the Job Satisfaction Index?
5. How successfully did the authors establish the measurement validity of the questionnaire?

When you are done, please compare your answers to those at the end of the chapter, before beginning Example 2. The idea is to learn as much as you can before proceeding.

Example 2 Dogmatism Questionnaire

Source: Milton Rokeach, *The Open and Closed Mind.* New York: Basic, 1960.

Measure: The Dogmatism questionnaire is designed to measure the openness or closedness of the individual's belief system. An open belief system reflects "the extent to which the person can receive, evaluate, and act on relevant information on its own intrinsic merits, unencumbered by irrelevant factors . . ." (p. 57). Closed-minded (dogmatic) people prefer certainty, prefer people like themselves, and respect authority figures. Respondents indicate the degree to which they agree or disagree with each item on a seven-step scale.

Item Examples: We must guard against subversion from within.
To know what's going on, rely on leaders.
Pick friends who believe as you do.
I hate some people because of what they stand for.
There is only one correct philosophy.
A person who believes in too many causes is wishy-washy.

The questionnaire has been revised several times (Forms A–E) to improve its reliability and to incorporate refinements in the theoretical formulation.

Respondents: Form A was completed by 202 MSU students. Form B was completed by 207 students in New York City colleges. Form C was given to the 207 New York City college students and to two groups of MSU students, 153 and 186. Form D was administered to 137 students at University College in London. Finally, 80 students at Birbeck College (England) and 60 English workers completed Form E.

Reliability: The following split-half reliabilities (corrected) were obtained for each form.

Form	# of Items	Group	*N*	*r*
A	57	MSU I	202	.70
B	43	NY Colleges	207	.75
C	36	NY Colleges	207	.84
		MSU II	153	.73
		MSU III	186	.71
D	66	English Colleges I	137	.91
E	40	English Colleges II	80	.81
		English Workers	60	.78

Validity: The following table presents the correlations between Dogmatism (D) and Authoritarianism (A), and between Dogmatism and Ethnocentrism (E).

		Correlations	
Group	***N***	**D/A**	**D/E**
MSU I	202	.67	.36
NY Colleges	131	.61	.49
MSU II	153	.61	.33
MSU III	186	.54	.31
English Colleges I	137	.57	.39
English Colleges II	80	.62	.32
English Workers	60	.77	.53

Finally, graduate students in psychology were asked to nominate other graduate students (outside the field of psychology) as being either high or low in Dogmatism. The highs scored significantly higher on the Dogmatism questionnaire.

Analysis Questions for Example 2

The Dogmatism Questionnaire measures the openness or closedness of a manager's belief system. Before accepting the results of such a questionnaire, we would want to know the degree to which its measures are reliable and valid. Please answer each question below, referring to the description as needed.

1. What method did the author use to assess the measurement reliability of the Dogmatism Questionnaire?
2. How successfully did the author establish the measurement reliability of the Dogmatism Questionnaire?
3. What two methods did the author use to assess the measurement validity of the Dogmatism Questionnaire?
4. What two methods did the author use to assess the measurement validity of the Dogmatism Questionnaire?
5. How successfully did the author establish the measurement validity of the questionnaire?

When you are done, please compare your answers to those at the end of the chapter.

END OF LEARNING MODULE 4.1

Content, construct, and predictive validation entail substantial effort. Delaying program assessment until attaining a complete picture of a measure's validity is usually not practical. Measurement validity, however, is a matter of degree rather than an either-or proposition, and evidence of validity is sought on an ongoing basis: During questionnaire construction, during pilot studies conducted on employees similar to those who will participate in the program assessment, and during program assessment itself.

In practice, researchers often accept evidence of measurement validity that they consider "good enough" for the immediate purpose. Depending on the purpose of the research, one or another type of measurement validity is initially more salient and emerges as a particular concern. For example, content validation is especially important when measuring employees' mastery of the knowledge and skills covered during a course of instruction or training. Questionnaire items should fully represent the content domain encompassed by the objectives of instruction. Conversely, construct validation is especially important when building or using theory to understand and predict organizational effectiveness. The evaluator needs to explain how the program outcome relates to other measures of this outcome and to measures of other relevant outcomes. Finally, predictive validation is important when managers select and place personnel based on how they answer a questionnaire. These managers assume that the questionnaire results predict how employees will perform on the job. Thus while all three types of measurement validity are desirable, researchers often favor one over the others, at least initially, depending on the purpose of the research.

Measurement validity ensures that measures accurately represent the program outcome as defined conceptually. When measurement validity is low or unknown, an apparent program impact is uninterpretable. Initially, measurement error and the apparent program impact are intertwined, indistinguishable from each other. With evidence of both measurement reliability and measurement validity, of consistent and accurate measures, researchers can consider measurement error inconsequential and attribute the apparent program impact to the effectiveness of the program.

Main Points of Chapter 4

- Measurement error, however small, accompanies all measures. Measures of program outcomes can be inconsistent, inaccurate, or both.
- Inconsistent measures reflect random influences unrelated to the program outcome and emanating from the questionnaire, the respondent, or the immediate environment. Inconsistent measures underestimate the relationship we would have observed had there been no measurement inconsistencies.
- Inaccurate measures systematically reflect the wrong thing—something less than, other than, or in addition to the program outcome as defined conceptually. Inaccurate measures question the integrity of the apparent program impact: Is it the program outcome that is being reflected?
- Initially, measurement error and the impact of the program, if any, are intertwined, indistinguishable from each other.
- The amount of measurement error can be gauged by correlation procedures. Correlation describes the relationship between two sets of scores, where $r = 0$ indicates no relationship, and $r = +1.00$ indicates perfect correspondence.
- Measurement reliability is the degree to which successive measures of the program outcome are consistent.
- Cronbach's alpha, interpreted the same as correlation, is based on the average of the intercorrelations among the

questionnaire items and is the recommended method to establish measurement reliability.

- Measurement validity is the degree to which measures accurately represent the program outcome, and only the program outcome, as defined conceptually.
- The three approaches to establish measurement validity—content validation, construct validation, and predictive validation—establish whether measures represent the full spectrum of the program outcome, whether measures of the program outcome relate to other program outcomes as expected conceptually, and whether measures relate to a criterion behavior as expected from theory, respectively.
- Measurement validity is established on an ongoing basis, where the goals of the research may make one validation method more relevant initially than the others.
- When measurement error is negligible, the apparent program impact can be attributed to the effectiveness of the program.

ANSWERS TO LEARNING MODULE 4.1

Example 1 Job Satisfaction Index

The authors used the split-half method to assess the measurement reliability of the Job Satisfaction Index. The questionnaire was divided into two halves, whereby the responses to the odd-numbered items were correlated with the responses to the even-numbered items. Because this method divides the questionnaire into halves, the correlation needs to be "corrected" (i.e., converted to r' to reflect the reliability of the questionnaire as a whole. An r' value of .80 or above indicates good measurement reliability. The authors found $r' = .87$, so the Job Satisfaction Index displayed good measurement reliability.

The authors assessed the measurement validity of the Job Satisfaction Index using both the method of known groups and the method of convergent validation. The known-groups method seeks to discover if a questionnaire can differentiate between groups already known to differ. A valid questionnaire will detect a difference when one exists. The known groups in this case were represented by (1) students in a personnel class who also held jobs in personnel, and (2) students in the same class whose jobs were outside the personnel field. The authors reasoned that students employed in their field of interest would be more satisfied in their jobs than students employed outside their area of interest. Both groups completed the Job Satisfaction Index. The results showed that, as anticipated, students employed in their field of interest were more satisfied with their jobs than students employed outside their area of interest. The questionnaire differentiated between groups already known to differ in job satisfaction, thus providing evidence of measurement validity.

The authors also used the convergent method to assess the measurement validity of the Job Satisfaction Index. The convergent method seeks to discover if one's questionnaire correlates with one or more preexisting, and presumed valid, questionnaires that measure the same or related topics. The author used a preexisting questionnaire of the same topic. A correlation of .80 or above is expected between two measures of the same topic. In addition to completing the Job Satisfaction Index, the students in the personnel class completed the Hoppock Blank. The Hoppock Blank, which also measures job satisfaction, was created much earlier and evidence of its measurement validity has already been reported. The correlation between the Job Satisfaction Index and the Hoppock Blank was .92, indicating that the questionnaires measure essentially the same thing. Since the Hoppock Blank is presumed valid, the Job Satisfaction Index should be valid, too, since its measures are so similar.

Please return now to Example 2 in the chapter before reading the next set of answers.

Example 2 Dogmatism Questionnaire

The Dogmatism Questionnaire measures the individual's degree of open- or closed-mindedness. The author used the split-half method to assess the measurement reliability of five versions (Forms A–E) of the Dogmatism Questionnaire. The revisions were undertaken to improve the measurement reliability and the theoretical integrity of the topic. Correlations of .80 or above would indicate good measurement reliability, with .70 to .80 indicating minimal reliability. The authors administered the questionnaire to U.S. and English college students and to one group of English workers, producing a total of eight split-half correlations for the five forms of the questionnaire. The correlations ranged from .70 to .91, with four of eight in the .70s. The correlations indicate that the Dogmatism Questionnaire exhibits at least a minimal level of measurement reliability. On an encouraging note, most of the higher correlations were associated with recent versions of the questionnaire

(Forms D and E). Nonetheless, we want better than minimal evidence of measurement reliability, especially with recent and U.S. samples. Even so, using this minimally reliable questionnaire is better than using a questionnaire whose measurement reliability has not been determined.

The author assessed the measurement validity of the Dogmatism Questionnaire using both the convergent method and the method of known groups. In convergent validation, one locates one or more preexisting, presumed valid questionnaires and specifies how highly they should correlate with the new questionnaire. We should expect the new questionnaire to have a high correlation, say above .80, with a preexisting questionnaire measuring the topic from the same theoretical perspective; correlate less highly, say above .65, with a preexisting questionnaire of the same topic but from a different theoretical perspective; correlate moderately, say above .45, with measures of different but related topics; and correlate minimally with measures of unrelated topics.

Here, the author used preexisting and presumed valid measures of authoritarianism and ethnocentrism. By definition, dogmatic people value authority, certainty, and people like themselves. So the Authoritarianism Questionnaire measures an important part, but not the only part, of dogmatism and thus should correlate moderately highly but not too highly with dogmatism. The correlation should be moderately high, say about .65, because valuing authority is an essential component of both questionnaires. The correlation should not be too high, however, in that dogmatism contains components other than valuing authority.

Ethnocentrism refers to a person's belief in the superiority of the groups to which he or she belongs, especially one's race, but including one's country, gender, and age. Believing in the superiority of one's own groups is related to liking people similar to oneself, a component of dogmatism. Thus, the definition of ethnocentrism overlaps a component of dogmatism, and we should expect the two questionnaires to correlate moderately, about .45.

So we expect correlations above .65 between dogmatism and authoritarianism and above .45 between dogmatism and ethnocentrism. The authors found correlations between dogmatism and authoritarianism ranging from .54 to .77, with four of eight correlations in the .60s, as expected. The correlations between dogmatism and ethnocentrism ranged from .31 to .53, with five of eight correlations in the .30s, a little lower than expected. Nonetheless, the pattern of correlations generally emerged as expected, with higher correlations consistently associated with authoritarianism, and lower correlations associated with ethnocentrism. These results support the convergent validity of the Dogmatism Questionnaire.

Finally, the author assessed the measurement validity of the Dogmatism Questionnaire using the method of known groups. In this method, one assesses whether the Dogmatism Questionnaire can detect a difference between groups already known to differ in dogmatism. Graduate students in psychology nominated fellow students outside of psychology as being high or low in dogmatism. Members of both groups completed the Dogmatism Questionnaire. As expected, scores for the group identified as high dogs (highly dogmatic) were significantly higher than the scores for the group identified as low dogs. This result further supports the measurement validity of the Dogmatism Questionnaire.

Chapter Notes

1. Paul Overberg, If you can't find the time, wait until June 30. *USA Today,* June 22, 1992, p. 1A.
2. Douglas Birch, Scientist builds toward weighty endeavor: Scale could check kilogram accuracy. The *Sun* [Baltimore], Vol. 311, No. 129, October 16, 1992, pp. 1A, 4A.
3. Wendy L. Freedman, The expansion rate and size of the universe. *Scientific American,* November 1992, pp. 54–60.
4. Dividing by $s_X s_Y$ also allows two correlations to be compared to see which is larger than the other.
5. Values of r can also be negative but typically not when gauging measuring error.
6. The generalized form of the Spearman-Brown prophecy formula can be used to determine the impact of lengthening the questionnaire. The measurement reliability of a questionnaire lengthened by a factor k is given by:

$$r'' = \frac{k\,r}{1 + (k - 1)r}$$

where k is the factor by which the questionnaire is increased, r is the initial measurement reliability of the questionnaire, and r'' is the measurement reliability of the lengthened questionnaire. For example, doubling the length of a five-item questionnaire whose initial measurement reliability was .60 increases the measurement reliability to:

$$r'' = \frac{2(.60)}{1 + (2 - 1)(.60)} = \frac{1.2}{1.60} = .75$$

Increasing the length of the questionnaire to 15 items, then to 20 items, increases the measurement reliability to .82 and .86, respectively.

7. Abraham H. Maslow, A theory of human motivation, *Psychological Review,* 1943, *50,* pp. 370–396.

5

Controlling Extraneous Error

Chapter Preview

This chapter alerts us that influences other than the program can alter the outcome and be mistaken for program impact. The degree to which the program and nonprogram influences co-occur is controlled by one's assessment design: During an assessment, what happens, to whom, and when? We will discover that some assessment designs provide more protection than others against co-occurring, nonprogram influences. Evaluators should use the best assessment design feasible in an assessment.

Learning Objectives

After reading Chapter 5, you should be able to:

- identify three prerequisites to inferring a causal relationship between a program and its outcome
- define the terms *extraneous error* and *assessment design*
- identify and describe the common sources of extraneous error
- identify three deficient assessment designs and the sources of extraneous error that accompany each
- identify two true assessment designs, and explain why each controls extraneous error
- identify three quasi-assessment designs, and explain why each controls extraneous error
- appreciate that evaluators should strive to use the best assessment design the assessment situation allows
- remember that evaluators can use quasi-assessment designs when a true assessment design is not feasible, although they should avoid deficient assessment designs

The Focus of Chapter 5

The program assessment step discussed in this chapter, along with its corresponding components in the Scientific Model, are highlighted below.

The Steps of Program Assessment

1. Involve stakeholders throughout the assessment.
2. Specify the expected program outcome.
3. Establish a measure of the program outcome.
4. Plan how to gather the data.
5. Collect the data.
6. Analyze the data.
7. Communicate the results.
8. Make program decisions.

The Scientific Model of Program Assessment

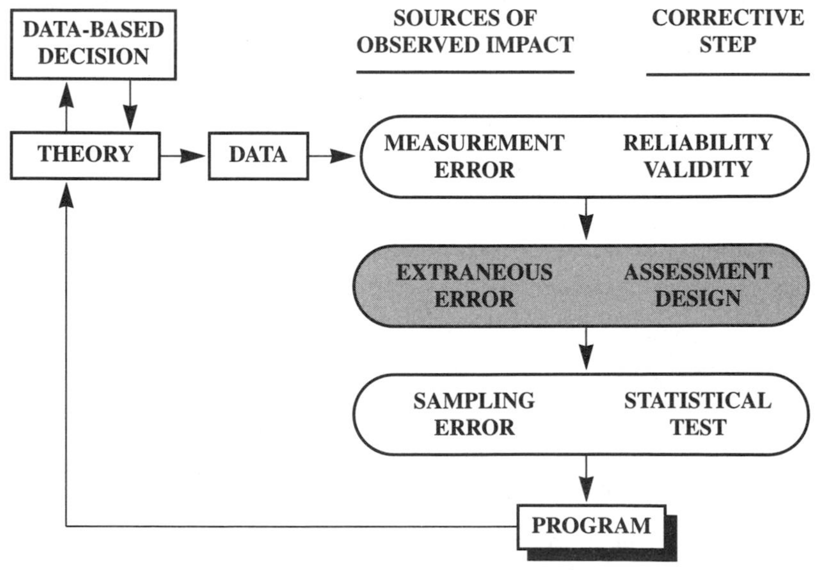

The program-outcome link is important. We expect a program to produce a desired outcome: For example, a safety awareness program should reduce accidents. The idea of cause is central to program assessment since we believe the program causes the outcome we observe. The role of cause in science is complex, but we can identify three prerequisites for infering a causal relationship between a program and its outcome. First, the program must be in place before we observe its outcome. Second, influences other than the program cannot cause the outcome. Third, the program and the outcome must covary, that is, changes in the outcome must be associated with the presence or absence of the program. Consider the issue of cause for a company that began a sales training program to improve employee motivation. A manager could conclude little about the program's effectiveness if high employee motivation was observed *before* the sales training instead of after it, or if a nonprogram influence such as a handsome pay raise, co-occurred with the sales training program. Should a pay raise occur during the sales training, its influence and the influence of the sales training would be indistinguishable from each other. If subsequent employee motivation was high, the manager wouldn't know if it was caused by the pay raise or the training. A variety of influences related to employee motivation exist in most organizations: Cellular phones may be added to company cars, flexible work schedules may be offered, or an unpopular manager may depart. Should any of these co-occur with the sales training, its influence would be intermixed with the effects of the program.

Sources of Extraneous Error

Nonprogram influences are called extraneous error because they are irrelevant, thereby extraneous, to the question of program effectiveness. Any factor that co-occurs with the program and that influences the observed outcome contributes to extraneous error. When we observe an apparent program impact—for example, employee motivation 3.2 *before* and 4.2 *after* the sales training program—it could be caused by either the program or extraneous influences. Cook and Campbell compiled the following list of the general sources of extraneous error.[1]

History

Any event that coincides with the program and influences the outcome. This could be a pay raise, a change in equipment, a change in supervisor, or a change in the economy.

Maturation

Any process that is naturally occurring within employees, which coincides with the program and influences the outcome. This source includes learning from practice, becoming stronger, and becoming more confident.

Mortality

Any loss of employees occurring during the span of the program and influencing the outcome.

Selection

Any preexisting difference between employees who receive the program and others to whom they are compared that influences the outcome. Differences could include initial higher employee motivation among those employees who experience the program, as compared to those who do not.

Testing

Any impact of a test on how employees retest. These influences include alerting employees to errors they made, to the specific topics covered by the test, or to how the test is constructed.

Instrumentation

Any change in testing procedures that influences the outcome. These changes include testing by different means, by different persons, or by the same person who adopts different criteria, such as when observation skill improves over time.

The preceding list serves as a useful reminder of the sources of extraneous error, whether we are helping to plan a program assessment or reading an assessment report that crosses our desk. We would want to be aware of the possible nonprogram factors that might influence the results of the assessment. Several illustrations of each type of extraneous error are presented in the remainder of the chapter; it may be useful to refer to this list as you proceed.

Effects of Extraneous Error

Ideally, an apparent program impact reflects the effectiveness of the program. Nonprogram influences, however, can inflate the apparent program impact, raising the danger of mistaking extraneous error for the impact of the program.

Keep in mind that the effects of the program and the effects of extraneous factors are initially intermingled. Consequently, extraneous error can mask program impact. Fig. 5.1 illustrates the important relationship between extraneous error and program impact.

Part A portrays an apparent program impact. Part B illustrates high extraneous error masking program impact (represented by the white box). In contrast, Part C illustrates that low extraneous error is unlikely to mask program impact. It is essential to control or minimize extraneous error so that it does not masquerade as program impact.

Assessment Design

Extraneous error can be controlled by what is called assessment design. An assessment design is simply a structuring of what happens, to whom, and when. For example, an assessment design might entail exposing employees to a sales training program, after which they complete a questionnaire that measures job motivation. *What happened* is the completion of training and a questionnaire, *to whom* is employees; and *when* is completing the training before completing

Figure 5.1
The Role of Extraneous Error

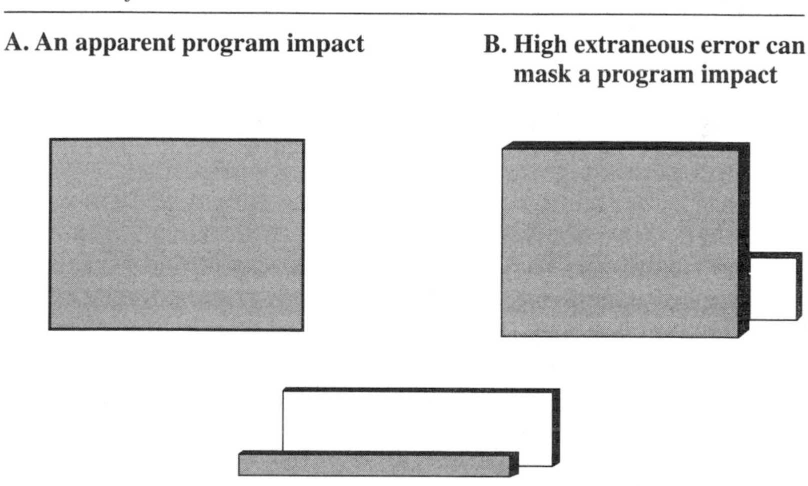

the questionnaire. The purpose of assessment design is to ensure evaluators that the program is the cause of the outcome they observe. To that end, assessment designs structure activities (who, what, and when) to guard against extraneous error.

Assessment designs include a variety of activity and sequence combinations; some of which provide more control of extraneous error than others. Three general strategies are available to guard against extraneous error:

1. Observe the outcome both before and after the program.
2. Use a control group consisting of similar employees who do not experience the program.
3. Assign employees to the program group and the control group randomly.

We will consider three categories of assessment designs that differ in how they use these three strategies.

1. Deficient assessment designs, which provide trivial protection against extraneous error
2. True assessment designs, which provide excellent protection against extraneous error
3. Quasi-assessment designs, which provide substantial protection against extraneous error.

We will discover that evaluators should avoid deficient assessment designs altogether, and should use quasi-assessment designs only when a true assessment design cannot be feasibly used in a particular setting.

To recognize assessment designs, we will adopt a notation system that depicts what happens, to whom, and when during an assessment. The system allows us to summarize a variety of assessment designs succinctly with minimal effort. At the same time, the notation system helps expose the types of extraneous error that may accompany each design. The notation system uses the following symbols:

RG = Random assignment of employees to groups
NRG = Nonrandom assignment of employees to groups
P = Program
O = Observation

We can represent all assessment designs using these symbols and the following two rules:

1. Represent each group of employees on a separate line.
2. Make the chronological order of activities proceed left to right.

For example, if one group of employees attended a training program and one group did not, but then both completed a questionnaire measuring motivation, we would denote this situation as

$$\begin{array}{lll} NRG_1 & P & O \\ NRG_2 & & O \end{array}$$

Each group gets a separate line, so first determine the number of employee groups that were used. This design needs two lines because there were two groups of employees: one that received training and one that did not. The group that did not is called a "control group" and consists of similar employees who performed their usual duties rather than participate in the program.

As a second step, determine if the evaluator assigned employees to the two groups randomly. If this is not indicated, assume they were not. Use *NRG* for this design because it was not mentioned if employees were assigned to groups randomly. You can add a subscript to each *NRG* to help differentiate the groups.

The third step is to represent the sequence of events—what happened and when. For this design, *P* should come before *O* because employees participated in a program before they completed the outcome measure. The sequence of events is represented left to right, in this case first *P* then *O*. That the control group did not participate in the program is represented by a blank in the space where the *P* would normally go had they participated in the program. We will use the notation system as we consider three categories of assessment designs.

Deficient Assessment Designs

Some designs provide inadequate protection against extraneous error, and are thus called deficient assessment designs. Unfortunately, evaluators too often use deficient assessment designs when better ones are available. You should be alerted to them, to both avoid them yourself and to recognize them when others use them. You should interpret results based on these designs with extreme caution. There are three deficient assessment designs.

One-Group Observation Design

The One-Group Observation design exposes employees to a program and then observes the outcome. For example, employees may receive sales training and then complete a questionnaire measuring their motivation. Using our notation system, this design is depicted as

NRG P O

This design uses one group of employees, so the diagram has one line. Because it was not specifically mentioned, you can assume that the employees were not assigned to the training randomly, represented by *NRG*. Next, the diagram chronicles the sequence of events, moving left to right. Employees first completed training (program), then completed the questionnaire (observation).

The question is, "Is the training the cause of the observed high motivation?" To attribute cause, the outcome must follow the program (it does) and cannot be caused by nonprogram influences. The One-Group Observation design meets the first condition, but succumbs to the second concern. Many nonprogram influences could cause high motivation instead of, or in addition to, the influence of the program. These nonprogram influences contribute to extraneous error and are therefore intermingled with and inseparable from the impact of the program. The genuine danger exists that nonprogram influences will be mistaken for program influence.

The One-Group Observation design is vulnerable to the influences of many types of extraneous error, as described below for the effects of a sales training program on employee motivation.

History

Instead of, or in addition to, being caused by the training program, high employee motivation may be caused by a pay raise, new equipment, a new supervisor, or any other event that co-occurs with the program and that influences employee motivation.

Maturation

In addition to the influence of the training, employee motivation may be caused by an increase in employee knowledge or skill, or any other internal process that naturally occurs with the passage of time and that influences motivation.

Mortality

Irrespective of the influence of the program, motivation may be high because unmotivated employees dropped out during the training, leaving those motivated employees who stuck it out.

Selection

Because employees were not randomly assigned to the training, they may be highly motivated to begin with, as when training is optional and those who volunteer tend to be highly motivated.

Selection is a concern whenever an assessment design lacks random assignment of employees to groups. History, maturation, and mortality are concerns in the absence of a control group of employees who did not experience the program. Most concerns about testing and instrumentation arise when there is an observation before as well as after the program. This design has a troublesome list of possible extraneous influences, influences that would be combined with the impact of the training program, if any. Differentiating extraneous influence from program influence is impossible with this design. We can make our concerns explicit by casting them as a question: "What assurance do we have with this design that the high employee motivation wasn't caused in whole or in part by the co-occurring pay raise (or additional extraneous influences)?" This design provides almost no assurance. Moreover, it does not include a comparison, a minimum requirement for a program assessment—definitely a design to be avoided.

One-Group Pre- and Postobservation Design

The second deficient assessment design addresses selection by observing employees before as well as after the program, so employees act as their own control. For example, employees may complete a motivation questionnaire both before and after attending sales training. Because the outcome is observed before and after the program, this is called the One-Group Pre- and Postobservation design and is depicted as

NRG O P O

Although employees are not randomly assigned to the training program, knowledge of their pretraining motivation level reveals if employee motivation was initially high, or if it increased because of

Mr. Green anticipates a superb assessment report. Coincidentally, he has pay raises in his hand for everyone.

the program. This design therefore reduces concern about selection, but it is susceptible to a host of other extraneous influences. Two sources of extraneous error arise with the addition of the preobservation. Added to alleviate the concern over selection, the preobservation still raises concerns over testing and instrumentation.

These are the types of extraneous error that accompany this design when employee motivation is observed both before and after sales training.

History
High employee motivation after training may be caused by a pay raise, new equipment, a new supervisor, or any other event that occurred between the pre-and post-observations and that influences employee motivation. The longer the interval between pre-and post-observations, the higher the risk of historical influences.

Maturation
High employee motivation after training may be caused by an increase in employee knowledge or skill, or any other internal process that naturally occurs with the passage of time between the pre- and postobservations and that influences motivation. The potential for maturation increases with the interval between pre- and postobservations.

Mortality
Motivation may increase because unmotivated employees dropped out between the pre- and postobservations, and only those motivated employees who stuck it out remained.

Testing
The experience of the preobservation may help employees perform on the postobservation. For example, employees may be alerted to what is being measured, or may learn what is valued, or may learn how to answer "correctly."

Instrumentation
Motivation may increase due to any changes in the observation procedures. The postobservation questionnaire may have been a cleaner copy than the initial questionnaire, making reading easier; the administrator of the post questionnaire may have inadvertently signaled employees what answers were expected; the post questionnaire may have contained different questions or been scored differently.

The causal link between the program and its outcome is confounded in the present design by a host of extraneous influences, too many to make this design acceptable for program assessment. Be aware that this design is too frequently used, and results based on it should be dismissed with the question, "What assurance do we have that the outcome wasn't caused in whole or in part by co-occurring extraneous influences like history, maturation, and so on?"

Nonequivalent Groups Observation Design

Another strategy to reduce extraneous error is to compare the program group to a similar group of employees who do not experience the program. For example, one group of employees may participate in a sales training program and then complete a questionnaire measuring motivation, while a similar, second group of employees does not participate in the sales training program but does complete the motivation questionnaire. The group that is exposed to the program is the program group, and the other is the control group. This design is called the Nonequivalent Groups Observation design and is depicted as

$$NRG_1 \ P \ O$$
$$NRG_2 \ \ O$$

The blank space indicates that employees in the control group performed their normal duties, while those in the program group attended sales training. Because employees are not assigned to groups randomly, the major extraneous influence in this design is selection, the possibility that the employees in the two groups were nonequivalent before the training. For instance, perhaps the employees volunteered for the training and they were actually more motivated than those who didn't volunteer but were assigned to the control group. Our concern is: "What assurance do we have that the outcome wasn't caused by the possibility that employees who received training were initially more motivated than those who didn't?" Whereas this design guards against the influences of history, maturation, and mortality, we will not dwell on these qualities. Instead, appreciate that the clear potential for initial differences between the groups mitigates against using this design. There is no assurance that the outcome would have been different in the absence of the training program. The possibility of initial differences between the groups looms large in this design, too large to recommend its use.

As a group, then, these designs—susceptible to extraneous error as they are—are inadequate for program assessment. Learning

Module 5.1 Assessment Design Exercise I invites you to become more familiar with the notation system for assessment designs and to practice recognizing potential sources of extraneous error. Please take time to carefully complete this Learning Module.

LEARNING MODULE 5.1: Assessment Design Exercise I

Instructions:

Diagram each program assessment described, using *RG/NRG* for random or nonrandom assignment of employees to groups, *P* for exposure to a program, and *O* for an observation of the outcome. Second, identify all sources of extraneous error that accompany each assessment and give an example of each. Finally, cast your concern for at least one source of extraneous error in each situation as a question. Answers to each situation are presented at the end of the chapter.

1. A large company instituted quality control circles in June of last year. In June of this year, employee morale was high, as indicated by a survey of a sample of employees. Managers declared that the institution of quality control circles was a success.
2. A large company established a three-week training program for its new employees. Fifteen new employees took a test of job knowledge and then attended the training program. A retest of the new employees indicated that their scores on job knowledge had substantially improved. From then on, the company required new employees to participate in the training program.
3. Managers in a manufacturing plant installed automated equipment into one of two intact units, both of which performed similar, manual work. The second unit continued processing materials manually as usual. A year later, the automated unit showed more production, and so the managers decided to automate the second unit.

END OF LEARNING MODULE 5.1

Deficient assessment designs preclude us from establishing a causal link between a program and its outcome. They are not recommended for program assessment, especially since better designs exist. Next we will consider two true assessment designs, both of which provide excellent protection against extraneous error. They are highly recommended and should be used whenever possible.

True Assessment Designs

In sharp contrast to the previous designs, true assessment designs control or rule out almost all extraneous influences. Evaluators should use true assessment designs whenever feasible. When one is not practical, however, the evaluator should not resort to a deficient assessment design. Instead, evaluators should use adaptations of true assessment designs, called quasi-assessment designs, discussed later.

Equivalent Groups Observation Design

This design features random assignment of employees to the program group and the control group. While employees in the program group participate in the program, employees in the control group perform their duties as usual. Then all employees complete the program outcome measure. For example, a set of employees, selected randomly, may receive sales training and then complete a questionnaire about their motivation level. A second set of employees, also selected randomly, receive no sales training (performing their usual duties) but complete the motivation questionnaire. The Equivalent Groups Observation design provides excellent protection against the types of extraneous error we have discussed and is depicted as

$$\begin{array}{lll} RG_1 & P & O \\ RG_2 & & O \end{array}$$

Random assignment of employees to groups prevents systematic, preprogram differences among employees in the two groups. Any initial differences are random and negligible. Chance ensures that highly motivated employees have an equal probability of being placed in either group. Equal probability of group membership makes the groups *equivalent* except for chance differences.

With a control group, the Equivalent Groups Observation design also guards against the extraneous influence of history, maturation, and mortality. Because these influences likely affect both groups, the groups remain essentially equivalent. Consequently, the evaluator can attribute any additional impact observed in the program group to the program. For example, if employees in both groups receive a pay raise, you can attribute higher motivation observed in the program group to the effectiveness of the program. The pay raise influences employees in both groups, keeping them equivalent. Fig. 5.2 assumes a pay raise coincides with a sales training program to illustrate that an extraneous influence affects both groups. The pay raise affects both groups, but the program affects only the program group. The large box represents the combined influence of the program and the pay raise. Since this box is larger than the influence of the pay raise by itself, you can conclude that the program accounts for its increased size.

The control group substantially guards against history, maturation, and mortality as long as they influence both groups. Should only employees in the program group receive a pay raise, however, the groups may no longer be equivalent, and we have no assurance that the observed high motivation is due to the training program. We call this local history, because only one group experienced it. Local maturation and local mortality can also occur, as when those in the program group mature or drop out in different proportion to the control group. All designs are susceptible to local history, so evaluators should always attempt to treat the program group and the control group similarly except for participation in the program. Given its strengths, evaluators should use the Equivalent Groups Observation design whenever possible.

A modification of this design is commonly used and is highly recommended when appropriate. The modified design compares the effects of two programs. For example, we might want to discover whether a sales training program or an incentive program creates

Figure 5.2
The Effect of Extraneous Error

	PROGRAM		OUTCOME	
RG_1	Training	*Pay Raise*	■	= Training + *Pay Raise*
RG_2		*Pay Raise*	▪	= *Pay Raise* Only

higher employee motivation. This modified design also provides excellent protection against extraneous error.

$$RG_1\ P_1\ O$$
$$RG_2\ P_2\ O$$

where P_1 represents the sales training program and P_2 represents the incentive program. Evaluators should use this modified design to compare the effectiveness of one program to another.

Equivalent Groups Pre- and Postobservation Design

This design assigns employees randomly to the program group and the control group and observes employees before and after the program. For example, an evaluator may ask one group to complete a questionnaire, attend safety training, and then complete the questionnaire again, and ask another group to complete the questionnaire twice but to perform their usual duties in place of attending the training. We depict this design as

$$RG_1\ O\ P\ O$$
$$RG_2\ O\quad\ O$$

The Equivalent Groups Pre- and Postobservation design guards against all extraneous influences, including testing and instrumentation, since their influences likely affect both groups. The evaluator should watch for local influences, such as if only one group receives a pay raise. This design provides a direct check for the preprogram equivalency of the two groups; the initial observations of the program group and the control group should be similar. Evaluators can attain additional precision by taking the preprogram observations into account in assessing the postprogram outcomes. This feature is described in Chapter 8.

Generally, evaluators prefer this design when they want additional statistical precision or when they want to assess gain scores (improvements between pre- and postobservations). Otherwise, they prefer the simpler but equally rigorous Equivalent Groups Observation design.

Evaluators should use the best assessment design possible within the constraints presented by organizational realities. Whenever possible, evaluators should assign employees to groups randomly to ensure that the groups are initially equivalent. However, organizational constraints sometimes preclude assigning employees to groups randomly, as when managers cannot afford for workers to forgo their normal duties to participate in the program. Sometimes, random assignment is possible but unethical, as when a program provides benefits that everyone should have. Consequently, the evaluator may have no control group or, having one, cannot assign employees to it randomly. But when organizational realities impinge on an assessment, the evaluator should not resort to a deficient assessment design; they are too vulnerable to extraneous error. Instead, evaluators should use adaptations of true assessment designs, called quasi-assessment designs.

Quasi-Assessment Designs

None of the quasi-assessment designs we will consider require random assignment of employees to groups, and one requires no control group. All, however, provide substantial protection against extraneous error. Because they are susceptible—as all design are—to local influences within one group, the evaluator must keep the environment, procedures, and events as similar as possible for both groups. Far superior to deficient assessment designs, evaluators should use quasi-assessment designs whenever true assessment designs are not feasible.

Nonequivalent Groups Pre- and Postobservation Design

This design uses two intact groups of employees, one as the program group and one as the control group. Both groups complete the program outcome measure before and after the program. For example, an evaluator may designate employees in Plant A as the program group and employees in Plant B as the control group. Employees in both plants complete the program outcome measure, then Plant A employees participate in the program while Plant B employees perform their usual duties. Finally, employees in both plants complete the program outcome measure again. We depict this design as

$$\begin{array}{llll} NRG_1 & O & P & O \\ NRG_2 & O & & O \end{array}$$

The Nonequivalent Groups Pre- and Postobservation design guards against the extraneous influences of history, maturation, mortality, testing, and instrumentation. As illustrated in Fig. 5.2, as long as extraneous influences affect both groups, the groups remain equivalent except for any initial differences. For example, whether or not the program is effective, having taken a test once may help employees in the program group the second time they take it. Also having taken it once, the control group, should also improve. When testing helps both groups, however, they remain essentially equivalent. Now if employees in the program group improve more than those in the control group, the evaluator can attribute this impact to the effectiveness of the program. The design protects against history, maturation, mortality, testing, and instrumentation by assuming they affect employees in both groups. The evaluator can attempt to account for initial group differences by conducting an analysis of covariance. This procedure is explained in Chapter 8.

To its credit, this design guards against extraneous error without random assignment of employees to groups. The next design we consider requires neither random assignment nor a control group, making it appealing for many assessment situations.

One-Group Multiobservation Design

This design is ideal when the evaluator can neither sample randomly nor form a control group. Even without these features, the design provides very good protection against extraneous error. This design observes a group of employees multiple times before and after the program. For example, an evaluator may ask managers to rate employee motivation monthly during the six months preceding and following a sales training program. This design is depicted as

$$NRG\ O_1\ O_2\ O_3\ O_4\ O_5\ O_6\quad P\quad O_7\ O_8\ O_9\ O_{10}\ O_{11}\ O_{12}$$

Each O represents an observation. Multiple observations do not prevent extraneous error, but they allow an evaluator to detect its presence. If a pay raise occurred in April (say at O_4) and increased employee motivation, its impact will be visible; motivation will jump at O_5. Conversely, if motivation remains constant between O_1 and O_6, no important extraneous influences occurred. Now if a jump in motivation occurs at O_7 and remains constant through O_{12}, we have considerable reason to believe that the training program caused the increase. Fig. 5.3 depicts three possible outcomes for this design: (a) no evidence of program impact, (b) evidence of impact of extraneous error, and (c) evidence of program impact. Dashed lines represent the level of employee motivation, beginning with January. The higher the line, the higher the motivation that month.

Note that the scores in part **a** of Fig. 5.3 are constant for all twelve months, showing no program impact. The scores in part **b,** however, jumped in April. Such a preprogram jump in motivation shows the presence of extraneous error, such as a pay raise. Finally, part **c,** in

Figure 5.3
Illustration of Three Possible Outcomes of This Design

(a) No Evidence of Program Impact
(Motivation remained constant all twelve months.)

(b) Evidence of Extraneous Error
(Motivation jumped in April, prior to the program.)

(c) Evidence of Program Impact
(Motivation jumped following the program.)

which motivation jumped just after the program, provides direct evidence that the program caused employee motivation to increase.

This design, however, does not guard against extraneous error that co-occurs with the program, such as a pay raise between O_6 and O_7. Whereas such events are unlikely when the interval is short, the evaluator should monitor this period for such influences. Requiring neither random assignment nor a control group, this design provides substantial protection against extraneous error. Evaluators should use this design whenever a comparison group is not available and multiple measures are possible. The next, and final, design we will discuss adds a control group to guard against extraneous error between O_6 and O_7.

Two-Group Multiobservation Design

This design adds a control group to the One-Group Observation design to protect against extraneous error that co-occurs with the program. For example, company managers may rate the motivation level of employees in Plant A monthly during the six months preceding and following a safety training program. In Plant B, managers do the same, except these employees do not attend the safety training program. This design is depicted as

$$\begin{array}{lllllllllllllll} NRG_1 & O_1 & O_2 & O_3 & O_4 & O_5 & O_6 & P & O_7 & O_8 & O_9 & O_{10} & O_{11} & O_{12} \\ NRG_2 & O_1 & O_2 & O_3 & O_4 & O_5 & O_6 & & O_7 & O_8 & O_9 & O_{10} & O_{11} & O_{12} \end{array}$$

In this design, one group is exposed to the program and one is not, and both are observed multiple times. The evaluator selects a control group that is similar to the program group. Now if a pay raise occurs at both plants between O_6 and O_7, the groups should remain similar. Whatever increase the pay raise caused in one group likely occurred in the other group. So if employees in the program group display higher motivation, the evaluator can attribute it to the effectiveness of the program, the only other difference between the two groups.

Multiple observations expose the influence of history, maturation, mortality, testing, and instrumentation. The evaluator can compare the preprogram observations of the program group to those of the control group to observe the influence of selection. If the two groups have similar preprogram observations, the evaluator would consider the groups equivalent, removing selection as a concern.

Fig. 5.4 illustrates three possible outcomes of this design: (a) no evidence of program impact, (b) evidence of extraneous error, and (c) evidence of program impact. Dashed lines reflect the level of

Figure 5.4
Illustration of Three Possible Outcomes of This Design

Upper dashes represent program group motivation.
Lower dashes represent control group motivation.

(a) No Evidence of Program Impact
(Motivation is constant in both groups.)

(b) Evidence of Extraneous Error
(Motivation jumped in May, prior to the program.)

(c) Evidence of Program Impact
(Motivation jumped after the program in the program group only.)

employee motivation, beginning with January. The higher the dash, the higher the level of employee motivation that month. The upper dashed line tracks the motivation level in the program group; the lower dashed line tracks the motivation level in the control group.

Part **a** of Fig. 5.4 shows no program impact because motivation is constant for both groups. Part **b** shows the presence of extraneous error because motivation jumped in May, before employees participated in the program. For example, a pay raise in May could have increased employee motivation. Finally, part **e** shows a program impact because motivation jumped after members in the program group received training, while motivation stayed low in the control group. Selection is not present since both groups have similar preprogram levels of motivation.

The Two-Group Multiobservation Design provides excellent protection against extraneous error without random assignment of employees to groups. The design is useful in many situations where use of a true assessment design is not feasible.

Quasi-assessment designs provide only slightly less protection against extraneous error than do true assessment designs and far more protection than do deficient assessment designs. Evaluators should use them whenever true assessment designs are not feasible. Learning Module 5.2 Assessment Design Exercise II will make you more familiar with the notation system for assessment designs and will help you recognize which assessment design an evaluator is using. Please complete the Learning Module carefully.

LEARNING MODULE 5.2: Assessment Design Exercise II

Instructions:

Please review Learning Module 5.1 Assessment Design Exercise I to reacquaint yourself with the notation system for assessment design and how it is applied. Then diagram and identify by name each assessment described below using *RG/NRG*, *P*, and *O* for random assignment of employees to groups, the program, and observation, respectively. Answers to this exercise are presented at the end of the chapter.

1. A newspaper publisher wanted to know if adding the reporter's name to the story would improve the perceived integrity of the paper. The publisher drew one hundred names randomly from the list of nonsubscribers. Fifty of these, chosen randomly, were mailed a newspaper with bylines on stories, a questionnaire, and a return envelope. The same

newspaper, with the bylines omitted, was mailed to the other fifty people, along with the same questionnaire and a return envelope.

2. The vice-president of a firm wanted to test the potential effectiveness of cellular car phones in the sales division. Technicians installed phones in the cars of half the sales force, selected randomly. The other half operated as they had in the past. Six months later, the vice-president compared the current volume of sales to the sales volume before installation of the cellular phones.
3. Managers at a large company became concerned with expenses due to worker injuries. They asked supervisors to record safety-related injuries at the end of every month, starting in January. At the end of June, management mounted an intensive, three-day safety awareness campaign. Following the campaign, supervisors recorded safety-related injuries each month for the remainder of the year.
4. Supervisors in the company in study number three (above) recorded safety-related injuries monthly during the six months preceding and following an intensive three-day safety awareness campaign. Assume, in addition, that supervisors in the company's other plant recorded similar statistics each month during the same period but did not mount a safety awareness campaign there for purposes of comparison.
5. Assume the supervisors in study number four (above) observed safety-related injuries only for the one month preceding and the one month following the safety awareness campaign. Further, supervisors in the company's other plant observed safety-related injuries for these same two months but mounted no safety awareness campaign there for purposes of comparison.

END OF LEARNING MODULE 5.2

We have explored a variety of assessment designs: deficient assessment designs, true assessment designs, and quasi-assessment designs. Fig. 5.5 presents a visual summary for easy reference. A program assessment design structures assessment activities so that

Figure 5.5
A Summary of Program Assessment Designs

Deficient Assessment Designs

One-Group Observation Design:	*NRG P O*
One-Group Pre- and Postobservation Design:	*NRG O P O*
Nonequivalent Groups Observation Design:	NRG_1 *P O*
	NRG_2 *O*

True Assessment Designs

Equivalent Groups Observation Design:	RG_1 *P O*
	RG_2 *O*
Equivalent Groups Pre- and Postobservation Design:	RG_1 *O P O*
	RG_2 *O O*

Quasi-Assessment Designs

Nonequivalent Groups Pre- and Postobservation Design:	NRG_1 *O P O*
	NRG_2 *O O*

One-Group Multiobservation Design:

$$NRG\ O_1\ O_2\ O_3\ O_4\ O_5\ O_6\ \ P\ \ O_7\ O_8\ O_9\ O_{10}\ O_{11}\ O_{12}$$

Two-Group Multiobservation Design:

$$NRG_1\ O_1\ O_2\ O_3\ O_4\ O_5\ O_6\ \ P\ \ O_7\ O_8\ O_9\ O_{10}\ O_{11}\ O_{12}$$
$$NRG_2\ O_1\ O_2\ O_3\ O_4\ O_5\ O_6\ \ \ \ \ O_7\ O_8\ O_9\ O_{10}\ O_{11}\ O_{12}$$

extraneous error is not mistaken for the impact of a program. When we minimize extraneous error, we can confidently attribute an observed program impact to the program.

Main Points of Chapter 5

- To conclude that a program caused an observed outcome, the outcome must occur after the program and cannot be caused by nonprogram influences, called extraneous error.
- Six common sources of extraneous error are history, maturation, mortality, selection, testing, and instrumentation.

- The degree to which extraneous error is intermingled with, and thus indistinguishable from, the impact of the program depends on the assessment design: What happens to whom and when.
- Deficient assessment designs provide inadequate control over extraneous error, and evaluators should avoid them.
- True assessment designs, employing random assignment of employees to a program group and to a control group, provide excellent control over extraneous error, and evaluators should use them whenever feasible.
- Quasi-assessment designs provide substantial control over extraneous error, and evaluators should use them whenever a true assessment design is not feasible.

ANSWERS TO LEARNING MODULE 5.1

1. The program in this study was quality control circles and the program outcome was employee morale. The steps to diagram an assessment design are to determine (a) the number of groups involved, (b) whether employees were randomly assigned to groups, and (c) the sequence of events. This study used one group of employees formed nonrandomly. Employees participated in quality control circles, then completed a morale questionnaire. The assessment used the One-Group Observation design, depicted as

   NRG P O

   This design is susceptible to the following types of extraneous error:

   History
   Perhaps a pay raise co-occurred with the quality circles, increasing morale.

   Maturation
   Perhaps morale improved as employees gained skill through practice.

   Mortality
   Perhaps unhappy employees left the quality circles, leaving only happy employees with high morale.

Selection

Perhaps these employees already had high morale

Regarding history we might ask, "What assurance do we have that the high morale wasn't caused by a pay raise (or new equipment, new supervisors, etc.) that co-occurred with the quality circles?" Because concerns about testing and instrumentation only arise with the presence of preprogram observations, they do not arise in this design.

2. In this assessment, the program was a training program for new employees, and the program outcome was a test of the employees' knowledge of job-related information. The design is the One-Group Pre- and Postobservation design, depicted as

   NRG O P O

   This design is susceptible to the following types of extraneous error:

   History

   Perhaps new employees received information outside the training that increased their knowledge.

   Maturation

   Perhaps during the three weeks of training new employees overcame new-job jitters.

   Mortality

   Perhaps the weakest employees quit during the three weeks of training.

   Testing

   Perhaps taking the test once helped employees take the test the second time.

   Instrumentation

   Perhaps the test changed in some way between administration.

3. The program in this study was the introduction of automated equipment, and the program outcome was employee productivity. The study used the Nonequivalent Groups Observation design:

$$NRG_1 \ P \ O$$
$$NRG_2 \quad\ O$$

This design is susceptible to selection, the possibility that the employees who began using the automated equipment were more productive workers than the employees who continued work as usual. They may have outperformed the other unit even without automated work.

ANSWERS TO LEARNING MODULE 5.2

1. Diagramming an assessment design requires that you determine the number of groups involved, whether the groups were selected randomly, and finally, the sequence of events that occurred. In this study, the program was the presence of bylines on newspaper articles. The program outcome was the perceived integrity of the newspaper. Two random groups of nonsubscribers received newspapers, one with bylines, one without. This study used the Equivalent Groups Observation design:

$$RG_1 \ P \ O$$
$$RG_2 \quad\ O$$

2. This assessment tracked the volume of sales (outcome) immediately before and after the installation of cellular car phones (program). It represents the Equivalent Groups Pre- and Postobservation design:

$$RG_1 \ O \ P \ O$$
$$RG_2 \ O \quad\ O$$

3. This assessment checked if a safety awareness campaign (program) could reduce work injuries (program outcome). Supervisors monitored work injuries monthly for six months before and after the campaign. This represents the One-Group Multiobservation design:

$$NRG \ O_1 \ O_2 \ O_3 \ O_4 \ O_5 \ O_6 \ \ P \ \ O_7 \ O_8 \ O_9 \ O_{10} \ O_{11} \ O_{12}$$

4. This assessment studied the impact of a safety awareness campaign on work injuries as did the previous study, except it added a control group. Thus we have the Two-Group Multiobservation design:

$$NRG_1\ O_1\ O_2\ O_3\ O_4\ O_5\ O_6\ \ P\ \ O_7\ O_8\ O_9\ O_{10}\ O_{11}\ O_{12}$$

$$NRG_2\ O_1\ O_2\ O_3\ O_4\ O_5\ O_6\ \ \ \ \ \ O_7\ O_8\ O_9\ O_{10}\ O_{11}\ O_{12}$$

5. In this assessment, supervisors observed work injuries for the month immediately before and after the safety awareness campaign, but a control group was still used. This is the Nonequivalent Groups Pre- and Postobservation design:

$$NRG_1\ O\ P\ O$$

$$NRG_2\ O\ \ \ \ O$$

Chapter Note

1. Thomas D. Cook and Donald T. Campbell, *Quasi-Experimentation: Design and Analysis Issues for Field Settings.* Chicago: Rand McNally, 1979; Donald T. Campbell and Jullian C. Stanley, *Experimental and Quasi-Experimental Designs for Research.* Chicago: Rand McNally, 1963.

6

Sampling Program Target Groups

Chapter Preview

This chapter examines how managers typically select members from a large group of employees to participate in program assessment. We will see how evaluators form random samples and how they determine the size of samples needed. We will also consider the degree to which evaluators can generalize sample results to the large group. We will discover that observations from sufficiently large, random samples can be generalized with confidence.

Learning Objectives

After reading Chapter 6, you should be able to:

- define the term *program target group* and identify the intended program target groups for a variety of programs
- appreciate that sampling is often more economical than observing an entire program target group
- define the term *random sample* and recognize whether a given selection procedure produces a random or a nonrandom sample
- form a random sample using a table of random numbers
- identify the degree to which various sampling procedures allow generalization to the program target group
- identify the sample sizes required for typical program assessments

The Focus of Chapter 6

The program assessment step discussed in this chapter, along with its corresponding component in the Scientific Model, is highlighted below.

The Steps of Program Assessment

1. Involve stakeholders throughout the assessment.
2. Specify the expected program outcome.
3. Establish a measure of the program outcome.
4. Plan a method of gathering data.
5. Collect the data.
6. Analyze the data.
7. Communicate the results.
8. Make program decisions.

The Scientific Model of Program Assessment

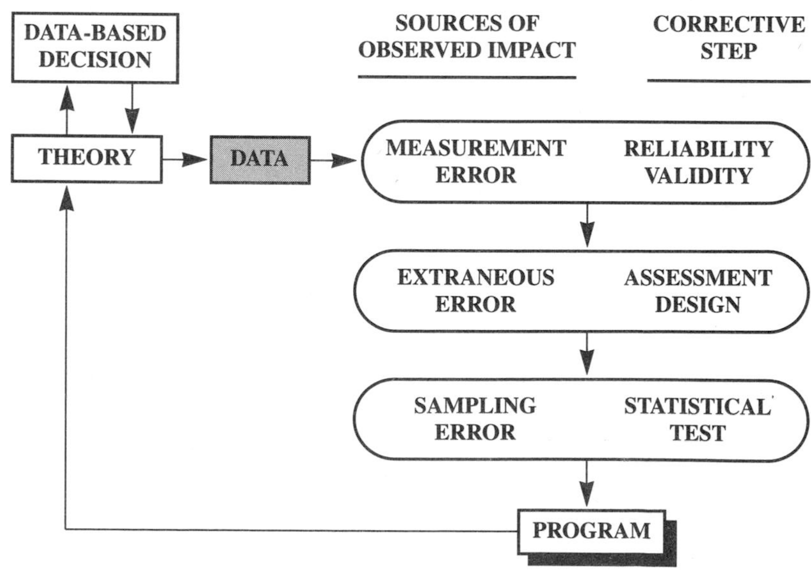

Gathering information about a program's impacts is an integral element of program assessment. Managers sometimes gather program data through direct observation, such as watching people's behavior, and more commonly, through indirect observation, such as administering questionnaires or conducting interviews. Gathering data by either method raises three questions:

1. How should the target group be defined?
2. How should the target group be sampled?
3. How many members of the target group should be sampled?

The first consideration is, what group of people makes up the program's intended target group? *Program target group* refers to the people that the program is intended to influence. The stated goal of a program often implies its intended target group. For example, the purpose of an orientation program is to help new employees adjust to a new job. This program's target group is new employees. The sample can be selected in a random or nonrandom way, as we will soon see.

The third consideration is, how many program target group members should we observe? Observing the entire target group might produce a complete picture of a program's effectiveness. We will discover, however, that observing all program recipients is often very costly, sometimes impossible, and usually unnecessary. Consider the costs of resources, time, and money in the following description of an attempt to observe a whole.

Every ten years, the United States Bureau of the Census undertakes a massive observation project—counting the population of the country. You may have resided in one of the 106 million households that received a questionnaire in the mail as part of the 1990 census. Your household may have been among the 63 percent that filled out and returned the questionnaire.

The second and more difficult phase of the project was to find and interview people in the households who did not respond. Operating out of 487 field offices across the United States, more than 200,000 enumerators, supported by another 115,000 support personnel, sought out those missed in the first phase.[1] For each percentage point of the population that did not return a questionnaire, the enumerators had to visit 950,000 additional households. All told, the enumerators faced the prospect of knocking on more than 35.2 million doors. The bureau's $2.6 billion budget for the ten-year census assumed a 70 percent return rate of questionnaires. Then Census Bureau director Barbara Bryan estimated that each percentage point shortfall in the targeted mail response rate increased follow-up costs by $10 million, for a total of $70 million.[2] The final U.S. census count was 248,709,873 people.[3] However, several sources (including the Government Accounting Office) estimated that from six million to 10 million people remained uncounted.[4] Despite the huge expenditure and the massive effort, everyone admits, even the Commerce Department, that the final count is wrong. Counting every citizen of the United States is expensive, labor intensive, and in the end, very difficult, if not impossible.

Sampling

All American companies employ far fewer people than the population of the United States, but obtaining program information can still be costly, labor intensive, difficult, and sometimes impossible. Observing all program recipients in even a medium-size company would be difficult. Some employees may be on sick leave or vacation. Some may have changed departments or departed. Others may return unusable questionnaires or none at all. We could try to observe every member of a program target group, but there is a much better way: Observe a sample of the whole.

According to the A. C. Nielsen Company, the most watched television show of all time was the "farewell" episode of *M*A*S*H* in 1983, viewed by 50,150,000 households. The next most-watched shows were the "Who Shot J. R.?" episode of *Dallas* in 1980, then *Roots, Part 8* in 1977, and then a succession of three Super Bowls.[5] To discover the number of households watching a show, the Nielsen Company provides an electronic people meter to each participating household. Each member of the household presses an assigned button when watching television. The people meter transfers data daily via telephone line to a computer in Florida for analysis.[6]

Networks value high ratings, using them to set prices they charge to advertisers for air time. For example, a thirty-second spot during the 1997 Super Bowl sported a $1.3 million price tag.[7]

Now consider this question: How many of the 92.1 million television households in the United States do you believe the Nielsen Company observed to attain their ratings? Every television household? How about 25 percent? That would be about 23 million households. Ten percent would be about 9 million households. You may be surprised that the ratings are based on a sample of .005 percent. That is 4000 of the possible 92 million households.[8] Do you imagine that .005 percent of all households is a big enough sample to support the rating results reported by Nielsen? This is an important question because just as the Nielsen Company observes a sample of television households, most companies observe a sample of employees to conduct program assessment. In both circumstances, researchers assume that sample results will mirror the whole, that they would obtain nearly the same results had they observed everyone. You needn't observe everyone if, with substantially less money, labor, and time, you can attain nearly the same results by observing a few. The Nielsen Company's own statistical analyses confirm that their sample size adequately represents the viewing public. A brief review of the results of a presidential campaign will illustrate this possibility.

During the 1992 election year, President George Bush, Bill Clinton, and Ross Perot squared off in three televised debates. They sometimes informed, sometimes entertained, and sometimes frustrated the viewing public as they attacked one another instead of the issues. The audience attending the debate at the University of Virginia persuaded the candidates to refocus on the issues. Afterward, each political camp tried to put the right "spin" on the ensuing poll results, claiming that Clinton "maintained his lead," Bush "closed the gap," and Perot's support "was underestimated."

Now that the election is over, we can examine how closely the preelection polls anticipated the actual vote tally. The Table 6.1

Table 6.1
Election Polls and the Actual Vote for 1992

Election Poll Results	Clinton	Bush	Perot
The *Washington Post* Poll	43%	35%	16%
Gallup for CNN/*USA Today*	43%	36%	15%
ABC News	42%	37%	17%
The Harris Poll	44%	39%	17%
The *New York Times*/CBS News Poll	43%	34%	15%
Gallup for *Newsweek*	41%	39%	14%
NBC News/The *Wall Street Journal*	43%	38%	11%
The *Los Angeles Times* Poll	44%	34%	18%
Actual Popular Vote	**43%**	**38%**	**19%**

summarizes several national polls conducted during the seven (the *Los Angeles Times* poll was during the ten) days before the November election.[9]

The poll results foresaw the election returns. Clinton garnered 43 percent of the popular vote, and five of the eight polls projected this exact result. All polls foretold Clinton's success within their plus or minus 3 (the *Washington Post* had plus or minus 4) margins of error. What's more, the polls performed nearly as flawlessly for President Bush. Although the polls underestimated Perot's support, they correctly placed him third, and only the NBC poll was markedly off. An unmistakable pattern emerges: The poll results accurately forecasted the election returns.

Now for the revealing part. How many people, would you imagine, pollsters needed to interview to secure results this accurate? None of the above polls involved more than 2000 participants. They achieved high accuracy with samples representing only .002 percent of the votes cast for the three candidates. We have the preferences of 101,133,038 voters delivered by fewer than 2000. Sampling thousands more people would substantially increase the cost (time, money, and energy) of the enterprise, while providing little more precision.

Similarly, managers seldom need to observe the entire program target group during program assessment. When conducted correctly, sampling usually costs less and sacrifices little precision. A few examples will underscore the impracticality of observing the whole. Imagine as an employee at the Campbell Soup Company your job is to test the tomato soup for taste. If you did not just sample, you would have to consume the entire batch. No soup would remain to be sold. What if the owners of Gallo Vineyards asked you to taste the harvest of Chablis wine for quality? Without sampling, you would consume all the wine. Oh, you will volunteer for the job? Well, then, imagaine the nurse drawing *all* of your blood for testing. Now you decline to volunteer? Not only is testing the whole often unrealistic, it is usually unnecessary. Sampling the whole achieves adequate precision.[10]

How closely sample results resemble the whole depends on how the members are selected. The best procedure produces a subset of people who are *representative* of the whole. The subset must be a miniature replica, a miniature edition, so to speak, of the whole. If the sample is representative of the whole, it can be interchanged with it, substituted for it, and managers can make decisions about program effectiveness from it. Now we'll see how to achieve representativeness.

Random Sampling

A sample is likely to be representative of the whole when its members are selected randomly. You should be able to recognize if a sample is random. Please complete Learning Module 6.1, Exploring Random Samples. It contains a definition of random sampling and will help you discern when a sample is and is not random.

LEARNING MODULE 6.1: Exploring Random Samples

Sampling is invaluable in program assessment because it is usually cheaper to observe a few program participants than all potential participants. For sample information to be useful, however, those observed must typify the whole. The surest way to attain representativeness is to select members of the sample randomly. This may seem odd at first, because we commonly think of randomness as scattered and unknown. How, you may wonder, could the unknown ensure something like representativeness? But scientists know a good deal about the collective behavior of random events, and this knowledge assures that selecting people randomly attains representativeness.

In our discussion of program assessment designs in Chapter 5, we used the terms random selection and random assignment without defining the word *random*. There we stressed that random sampling overcomes the source of extraneous error called selection. It is important to have a clear understanding of randomness. This Learning Module defines random sampling, but first two situations are presented. Please decide if the employees in each situation were selected randomly—that is, are these random samples?

Situation 1 To learn whether employees were satisfied with the new company cafeteria, a manager stood at the cafeteria door and gave every fourth employee a survey to complete as they exited the cafeteria.

Do you think this was a random sample? ___ yes ___ no

Consider another situation.

Situation 2 To assess the effects of a company program, a manager drew twenty-five names from the employee phone directory, a small but thick phone book. The manager

> opened the phone book, closed her eyes, dropped her finger on the page, and selected the employee nearest her finger. The manager repeated this process until twenty-five names were selected.

Do you think this was a random sample? ___ yes ___ no

Please recreate Situation 2 for yourself by selecting a word at random from this book. After reading these instructions, close the book, then open it again, close your eyes, drop your finger on the page, and observe the word nearest your finger. What is the word, and what page is it on?

Word: ______________ Page number: ______________

Was this word selected randomly from the words in the book?

Well no, actually, it was not. Nor was Situation 1 or 2 a random sample. Surprised? Before examining why this is true of all three situations, let's define random sampling.

For a sample to be random, *each person in the whole must have an independent and equally likely chance of being selected.*[11] The terms *independent* and *equally likely* are important. Independent means that the selection of one person can have no bearing on who else gets selected. For example, a person cannot be included just because she is a friend of someone already chosen. Her selection would not be independent of the selection of her friend. There can be no link between a selection and any previous selection. Equally likely means that no one can have a better chance of being selected than anyone else. For example, someone cannot be included just because she is cooperative or available. The uncooperative and unavailable must have the same chance of being selected as the cooperative and accessible. This issue is critical because it is the one most frequently violated. Every person in the whole must have an equal chance of being included in your sample.

With this definition of random in mind, let's reexamine the sampling situations, beginning with the word you selected from this book. Was your word selected randomly? First consider the issue of independence. For your word to be random, previous selections can have no influence on the word you selected. Since this was the only word you picked, that standard is upheld. Now consider whether all words in the book had an equal chance of being selected. Think about how you opened the book. Did every page have an equal likelihood of being picked? Here we encounter a problem. If you are like most people, you probably opened the book somewhere near its center. Did anyone open the book to its very first page and select the very first word? I am sure no one did. Neither, I imagine, did anyone open the book to its last page and select the last word. This doesn't seem random, does it—to open the book to some place deliberately? According to the definition of random sampling, the words on the book's first and last pages must have the same chance of being selected as the words in or near the middle. That's why your word is not random. When the book is opened near the middle, words on those pages have a much better chance of being selected than words near the front or back of the book. Some words had a better chance of being selected, and that's the opposite of randomness.

Here is a thought about the independence of your selection. If you were asked to select twenty-five additional words randomly, would you avoid opening it to exactly the same page twice in a row. Most people feel you must skip around. But now you are letting previous selections influence current selections, and you lose independence. The word right next to your initial selection must have an independent chance of being selected each time you close and open the book.

Look again at Situation 2. The manager chose names from the company phone directory. The sample selected in Situation 2 is nonrandom for the same reasons the word you chose is nonrandom. Likely, the manager repeatedly opened the phone directory near its center but avoided repeating the same page. By doing so, her previous selections influenced her current selections, and employees whose names were in the middle of the phone book had a better chance of being selected than employees whose names were at the beginning or the end of the phone book.

Can you see now why Situation 1 wasn't a random sample? Remember to search for the lack of independence or equality in the manager's selections. The first person to leave the cafeteria would be skipped (since the manager is waiting for the fourth person). We're in trouble already. The first person must have the same chance of being picked as the fourth person. This person may typically be the first to leave the cafeteria every day. As long as the manager counts to four, this person will almost never be given a survey. Moreover, the manager will bypass the three people directly behind anyone given a survey. These people are skipped merely because they were walking behind someone. Thus, the first selection influenced who was (actually, who was not) selected next. Also note that people who leave together are likely to have some connection. For example, they may be good friends, they may be in the same department, or they may all have a meeting to attend at that hour. It should be just as likely to select similar as dissimilar employees. Counting to four does not give each person an equal opportunity to be surveyed. Employees do not leave cafeterias randomly, and selecting every fourth one (or every third or every seventh one) does not change this.

Thus the employees were not selected randomly in either Situation 1 or Situation 2. The selections were neither independent nor equally likely. Now we'll examine procedures that do produce random samples.

END OF LEARNING MODULE 6.1

Forming Random Samples

Sampling is cheaper than observing the whole, and random samples, since they are representative of the whole, produce observations that mirror the whole. Random samples ensure that selections from the whole are independent and equally likely. A state lottery is a good example of random sampling. Every lottery player expects to have as good a chance to win as any other ticket holder. When and where customers buy a ticket and how officials conduct the drawing are not expected to influence the outcome. To preserve fairness, winning is due solely to chance.

I observed the workings of the Maryland State Lottery one day. Officials were televising the drawing from the state fair. Happening by, I asked if I could assist with anything. I felt very official when handed a clipboard and told, "Fine, you can be our witness today." The witness, I learned, helps monitor the fairness of the lottery drawing. I was surprised by the number of steps they asked me to perform to insure that the drawing was fair. First, the director shuffled nine playing cards and placed them facedown on a table offstage. He then told me to point to any four of the cards. I did, and I felt really part of the Lottery, except I had no idea why I was selecting cards on a table when the machines were onstage. The director turned the four cards faceup, and I learned that this determined the order in which the machines would be placed for the Pic 4 drawing. The director reshuffled the cards. This time he told me to point to three cards, thus determining the order of the machines for the Pic 3 drawing. I felt even more honored, but my card pointing wasn't over. "Why this time?" I asked. They explained, "This one determines which canister of balls will be placed in each machine." I was impressed. Randomness was assured at every juncture. Pushing the point, I asked if they confirm that the balls in each machine weighed the same. Again they were ahead of me. Drawing officials weigh all balls digitally and use only those weighing between 2.4 and 2.6 grams. By law, the balls must weigh between 2.3 and 2.9 grams to preserve randomness statistically.[12]

As I climbed onto the stage, toting a clipboard, a crowd formed. The machines were arranged as dictated by the numbers on the cards I selected, and the balls, propelled by air, were flying around in each machine. However, to the crowd's dismay, and my surprise, this wasn't the drawing. This was the pretrial. Four times we went through the motions of a real drawing. My job was to record the numbers on the balls that popped up for each machine. This, they informed me, checks whether a machine produces the same number too often before the actual drawing occurs. If a machine produces the same number four times in a row it gets replaced by a backup machine waiting offstage. People watched attentively: Numbers were being called out, so something was going on. I had the clipboard and looked important. My fifteen minutes of fame ended, however, when I was ushered offstage and the real drawing began. The lights and TV cameras were on, and the TV and state fair celebrities took center stage. Even the Farm Queen was onstage to help. Then it was all over. Torn tickets littered the ground, and my importance vanished, although my responsibilities did not. After the official drawing, four more drawings were conducted. These were the posttrials. Again it was ensured that no machine produced a number too frequently. Even after the drawing, randomness was important. I recorded the numbers for each machine in relative silence (since the crowd had moved on to the carnival rides). One post note: As a gesture of gratitude for acting as a witness that night, I received a one-month lottery subscription and won $36!

Forming a random sample for a program assessment is simpler than assuring randomness in a state lottery, where the appearance and the actuality of randomness are equally important. This is fortunate because few organizations can spare the resources to etch employee names on little balls, make sure they are of equal weight, and propel them about in a machine so that one pops out at a time. Similarly, putting all employee names in a hat is unnecessary and should be avoided. Imagine cutting each employee's name out of the phone book, ensuring that each sliver of paper is equal in size, weight, and

Little Stanley suspects Big Al stuffed the drum full of 9s from the labels of those 9 Lives Cat Food cans

shape. More telling, it is almost impossible to mix paper slips well enough to assure random selection.[13]

Random selection is precisely and efficiently attained with computer-generated random numbers available in a Table of Random Numbers. The computer generates the numbers so that any number between zero and nine is equally likely to appear in every table location. Consequently, any number obtained from the table is random. To form a sample using the Table of Random Numbers, assign each employee a number in sequence (1, 2, 3, etc.), then select those employees whose numbers you encounter in the table. Learning Module 6.2, Forming a Random Sample describes the Table of Random Numbers and presents guidelines for its use. Please complete the Learning Module carefully, as later discussions assume you have mastered the basic skill of forming a random sample of employees.

LEARNING MODULE 6.2: Forming Random Samples

Take a moment to look at the Table of Random Numbers in Appendix A. Part of the table appears here.

Table of Random Numbers

		Column				
		1	2	3	4	5
Line	1	1368	9621	9151	2066	1208
	2	5953	5936	2541	4011	0408
	3	7226	9466	9553	7671	8599
	4	8883	3435	6773	8207	5576
	5	7022	5281	1168	4099	8069

The numbers on top of each column label the columns, the numbers to the left of the vertical line label the rows. This lets us refer to a specific location in the table. For example, the number 9466 is at line 3 of column 2. This number, or any portion of it, is a random number, as is every other number in the table. Second, the numbers in the table contain four digits for our convenience. Since a table containing a solid mass of numbers would be overwhelming, spaces between columns were added to improve readability. Third, understand that every single digit in every location in the table is random. The very first digit in the table underscores this in an interesting way.

Locate the digit in the upper left corner of the table, column 1, line 1. The table begins with a 1! Now is that any way to begin a table of random numbers? Ironically, it is, because the computer gave every digit between zero and nine the same chance of appearing in the table first. It just happened that when all numbers faced an equal chance, a 1 appeared. Remember, according to the definition of *random,* it is vital that the number 1 have the same chance of appearing first as any other number. Now notice that the number to the immediate right of the 1 is a 3. A 1 had just as much chance to appear in this location as did the 3. This important feature holds throughout the table: In every single-digit location in the table, every number between 0 and 9 had an equal chance of appearing. Because every single-digit number is random, so too is every pair, every threesome and so on.

The final characteristic of the table may surprise you. You may select a number from the table by closing your eyes and dropping your finger anywhere on the page. Remember that blindly opening a phone directory in this way is not random because most people select toward the middle of the phone book. Phone books do not list names randomly, but because every number in every location in the Table of Random Numbers is random, it is fine to drop your finger in the center of the table. It doesn't matter because the numbers in the middle of the table are just as random as the numbers in the corners. This brings us to some welcome news: No matter how you proceed—across or downward—you cannot get a nonrandom number from this table.

Now let's see how to use the Table of Random Numbers to form a random sample of employees. Say a company wants to select five employees randomly to form a quality circle that will meet weekly to review recent company problems and suggest possible solutions. We need both a numbered list of the nonmanagerial employees, presented below, and a Table of Random Numbers.[14]

Company Employees

01. Ackerman, Barbara	11. Hales, Kenny	21. Meredith, Leo
02. Bevard, June	12. Hopple, Lynn	22. Mitchell, Samuel
03. Emge, Raymond	13. Ingle, Kirk	23. Moody, David
04. Flowers, Lori	14. Jackson, Brenda	24. Owen, Judith
05. Folger, Russell	15. Jacobson, Thomas	25. Peterson, Jeri
06. Fuller, Robert	16. Lee, Donald	26. Roberts, Byron
07. Gompper, Carol	17. Lopes, Linda	27. Sasselli, David
08. Green, Jackie	18. Lynch, Lauren	28. Small, Elaine
09. Griffith, William	19. Markland, Andora	29. Welch, Matthew
10. Hanson, Jennifer	20. Martino, Gina	30. Willoughby, Bruce

Table of Random Numbers

		Column				
		1	2	3	4	5
Line	1	1368	9621	9151	2066	1208
	2	5953	5936	2541	4011	0408
	3	7226	9466	9553	7671	8599
	4	8883	3435	6773	8207	5576
	5	7022	5281	1168	4099	8069

To secure a random sample, you use two sets of numbers: those that number each employee and those in the Table of Random Numbers. Enter the Table of Random Numbers, and move through its numbers until you encounter one that matches an employee's number. In the present case, move through the Table of Random Numbers until you encounter any table number between 01 and 30. Then assign to the quality control circle the employee whose number matches the table number. Repeat this process, assigning to the quality control circle each employee whose number matches a number encountered in the Table of Random Numbers until you have assigned five employees.

Let's try it. When I closed my eyes and aimed at the table, my finger landed on the number 2541. Please find this number in line 2 of column 3. Since 2541 is much larger than 30—the number of employees in the list—I will use 25, the first two digits of the number. Truncating the number is perfectly acceptable and a common practice. I do, however, need to use a two-digit number. One-digit numbers only go up to 9, and thus we would never select employees with numbers above that. Since employee number 25 is Jeri Peterson (please verify this for yourself), I assigned her to the quality control circle. The next number I encountered in the table was 95 (directly below the 25). Please take a moment to find it in the table (line 3 column 3). Since this number exceeds 30, the number of employees in the list, I bypass it. This is common practice. The number below it, 67, exceeds 30, so I bypassed it, too. However, next I encountered the number 11, which belongs to Kenny Hales, so he became the second member of the quality control circle. Since I have now reached the bottom of column 3, I moved my finger to the top of column 4. Beginning a new row is common practice. Here I found the number 20 (please verify—line 1, column 4). Gina Martino is employee number 20, so into the quality circle she goes. Moving on, I bypassed the remaining numbers in column 4 because all exceeded 30. At the top of column 5, I found the number 12. This is Lynn Hopple's number, so she becomes the fourth member of the circle. Finally, I encountered the number 04, which means that person number 4, Lori Flowers, is the fifth and last employee to join the group.

Thus you form random samples by selecting those employees whose numbers match the numbers encountered as you move through the Table of Random Numbers. I would like to explain three topics that may have occurred to you as you followed the example. First, although I initially dropped my finger in the center of the table (line 2, column 3), you can enter the table anywhere. Second, you may have worried that the company phone book lists employees in alphabetical order. This is not a problem. It's the order of the numbers in the table that is important, that is random. Employee names can be in any order. Third, you may have wondered why I moved down instead of across the table. Good point. Because every number in the table is random, I could have moved left to right instead. You can go in any direction. Three rules, however, do matter:

Rule 1 Use table numbers as wide as the number of digits in the last employee's number.

Rule 2 Bypass table numbers that exceed the number of employees.

Rule 3 Bypass table numbers encountered more than once.

For example, for 30 (and up to 99) employees, use table numbers two digits wide, including a preceding zero for numbers less than 10 (e.g., 06 to match employee 6). For up to 999 employees, use table numbers three digits wide, with 0 preceding numbers from 10 to 99 (e.g., 075 to match employee 75), and two zeros preceding numbers less than 10 (e.g., 006 to match employee 6). Bypass table numbers that exceed the total number of employees, in other words, that exceed the number of the last employee, and bypass repetitive table numbers. If we had a total of 60 employees instead of 30, for example, I would have selected employee number 40 upon encountering this number in the table at line 2, column 4. But I would skip the number when it appears again in line 5 in the same column, because that person is already in the quality control circle.

The procedures above work well for any numbered list of employees. When operating from a nonnumbered or long list of people, such as a phone book, you may match table numbers with page numbers initially instead of employee numbers. First, check the page number of the last page of the phone book, and select the first number encountered in the Table of Random Numbers that is this size or smaller. Turn to that page of the phone book. Next, use the table to select among the columns on the page of the phone book. Finally, you can use the table to select a name from this column. Using successive random numbers as we have to "narrow the field" is allowable, provided that the pages contain equal or nearly equal numbers of names. Although this procedure uses three table numbers to select each person, this goes quite fast. If employee names are in a computer database, the computer can select employees randomly even more quickly.

Evaluators sometimes do not have access to employee names. The manager who wished to survey cafeteria goers, for example, cannot know who will visit the cafeteria on a particular day. The manager, however, could count cafeteria tables, provided they have the same number of chairs, and then single out an employee whose cafeteria table and chair match successive numbers encountered in the Table of Random Numbers.

The above procedures are well suited for obtaining a random sample for a descriptive survey of a large target group, say to discover how registered voters will vote in an upcoming election. You can also use the procedures to form a random sample to compare it to a preexisting norm. For example, a manager might want to know how a sample of company employees performs on conflict resolution ability compared to how managers score nationally.

END OF LEARNING MODULE 6.2

Random Assignment to Groups

Even when they are selected from a whole randomly, employees should be assigned to groups randomly. The first step allows generalization of the results to the whole; the second step ensures that members of the program group and the control group are initially comparable. Moreover, even when employees are not a random sample of the whole, as when they are hand picked by managers or when they volunteer, an evaluator can instill an important element of randomness. Whenever possible, the evaluator should assign hand picked or volunteer employees to the program group and the control group randomly. This important step is called *random assignment* to groups. Because random assignment to groups gives each employee an independent and equally likely chance to be in either group, the groups are comparable except for chance differences. Consequently, we can use probability theory to estimate random sampling error. Although the employees may not represent the whole, the groups—due to random assignment to groups—are comparable to each other. Any initial difference between the program group and the control group is due solely to chance. Because evaluators so often have access to employees who are not representative of the whole, they should assign them randomly to groups whenever possible.

Random assignment to groups may be impossible when the evaluator only has access to intact groups, such as work groups or employees on the same shift or floor. Even here, the evaluator can assign intact groups to the program group and the control group. This retains randomness, although the data analysis should treat each intact group's average as if it were an individual's score.

Randomness is essential to making groups equivalent initially. When sampling the whole randomly is not feasible, as often happens, you should make every attempt to assign what employees you do have to the program group and the control group randomly. Learning Module 6.3, Random Assignment of Employees to Groups, outlines typical ways of assigning employees to the program group and the control group using the Table of Random Numbers.

LEARNING MODULE 6.3: Random Assignment of Employees to Groups

Forming random samples requires additional steps when a program assessment compares a program group to a control group. You could assign an employee to one or the other group according to whether the number encountered in the Table of Random Numbers is even or odd. But this can produce more people in one group than the other, just as flipping a coin thirty times can produce more heads than tails. Moreover, although not required, there are advantages to having an equal number of employees in each group.[15] The procedures to form equal-sized groups depend on whether the evaluator knows the number of people who will participate in the program assessment.

You can form equal-sized groups once you know the number of people who will participate in the program assessment. The procedure consists of four steps:

Step 1 Create a sequentially numbered list of the employees.

Step 2 Separately, create a list of random numbers by drawing numbers from the Table of Random Numbers. Draw as many random numbers as there are employees. The random numbers should be the same width as the number of digits in the number of the last employee. Bypass repetitive table numbers.

Step 3 Write each employee's name next to the random number in the separate list that matches his or her initial number.

Step 4 Divide the list of random numbers at the midway point. Assign the employees in the top half to the program group and the employees in the bottom half to the control group.

If you don't know the number of participants initially, as when volunteers arrive at a specified time, Steps 1 through 4 must be completed after they arrive. This is how you would assign eight employees randomly to a program group and a control group.

First, I assigned successive numbers to each employee (Step 1).

Company Employees

1. Ackerman, Barbara
2. Bevard, June
3. Emge, Raymond
4. Flowers, Lori
5. Folger, Russell
6. Fuller, Robert
7. Gompper, Carol
8. Green, Jackie

Then I selected eight numbers from the Table of Random Numbers (Step 2).

Table of Random Numbers

		Column				
		1	2	3	4	5
Line	1	**136**8	9621	9151	2066	1208
	2	**5**953	5936	2541	4011	0408
	3	**72**26	9**4**66	9553	7671	8599
	4	**8**883	3435	6773	8207	5576
	5	7022	5281	1168	4099	8069

I began in the upper left corner of the table and proceeded downward, searching for single-digit numbers between 1 and 8. I used numbers one digit wide because the total number of participants (eight) is one digit wide. I bypassed repetitive table numbers and numbers that exceeded 8. I boldfaced the numbers I encountered in the table:

Column of Random Numbers
1
5
7
8
3
2
6
4

Next, I wrote each employee's name next to the random number that matched his or her initial number (Step 3).

Column of Random Numbers	Names
1	Ackerman, Barbara
5	Folger, Russell
7	Gompper, Carol
8	Green, Jackie
3	Emge, Raymond
2	Bevard, June
6	Fuller, Robert
4	Flowers, Lori

Finally, I divided the list at the midway point and assigned the employees in the top half to the program group and the employees in the bottom half to the control group (Step 4).

Column of Random Numbers	Names/(Program Group)
1	Ackerman, Barbara
5	Folger, Russell
7	Gompper, Carol
8	Green, Jackie

Column of Random Numbers	Names/(Control Group)
3	Emge, Raymond
2	Bevard, June
6	Fuller, Robert
4	Flowers, Lori

You would follow the same steps for a large number of participants, where the number sought from the table is as wide as the total number of participants, and employee numbers are preceded by zeros as needed (e.g., for up to 99 participants, employees 1 through 9 become 01 through 09). We have seen that you can use the Table of Random Numbers to assign employees randomly to groups. The return for the effort is that the groups will be comparable except for differences due to chance.

END OF LEARNING MODULE 6.3

Nonrandom Sampling

Sampling employees randomly within organizations is sometimes impractical, as when important work would remain undone if key employees attended a program. In response, managers often adopt procedures that result in nonrandom samples. Managers often assume incorrectly that such samples are random. The reader should avoid these procedures when planning a program assessment and interpret results from such samples with caution. Mathematicians simply know of no way to determine the probable inaccuracies of nonrandom samples; mathematicians cannot anticipate how the results of a nonrandom sample will differ from the whole. Consequently, generalizations from nonrandom samples to the whole contain an unknown amount of error, and thus do not meet the standards of the scientific method of decision making. Interpret with caution any report that extrapolates to the whole from a nonrandom sample. Next, you are alerted to three ways managers form nonrandom samples: informed choice, intact groups, and volunteers. Try to recognize why they are nonrandom procedures as you review each method.

Based on their knowledge of members of a program's target group, managers sometimes hand pick employees for a sample. They select employees that are "good examples" of the topic under study, or they pick employees they consider "typical" of employees generally. Relying on a manager's judgment produces informed but not random choices. Several nonchance factors influence choices of who is "good" for a study or who is a typical employee. For example, managers know some employees better than others, or they may evaluate positively employees similar to themselves. Influenced in unmonitored ways by such influences, a collection of informed choices are not predictable as is a collection of random choices. Not amenable to mathematical description, generalizations to the whole would contain unknown error.

Using an intact group is a common but nonrandom means to secure a sample of employees. Rather than selecting employees throughout the organization, some managers use the members of an existing unit, department, work group, or hospital ward. Using an intact group is convenient, but employees within a department are often more similar to each other than to employees in general and thus they are not representative of the whole. These differences are undeterminable, and any errors in generalization cannot be assessed. When using an intact group is the only viable way to obtain a sample, the researcher should treat the intact group as one person. That is, the scores from the group should be averaged and the average used as a single data point.[16] Now the sample size is one (one intact group), and additional intact groups need to be selected randomly to enlarge the sample. In this way, the sample consists of intact groups selected randomly, and the sample size is the number of intact groups (not the cumulative number of employees within the intact groups). Using intact groups is an expensive alternative to random sampling and should give way to random sampling whenever possible.

Finally, managers often secure samples by asking for volunteers. Whether the invitation is oral or written, the manager must depend on who is willing to participate. Volunteers however, may differ from typical employees in motivation, ability, or desire for upward mobility.[17] When such nonrandom influences remain unmonitored, as usually happens, they remain beyond the explanation of mathematics, and errors accompanying generalization to the whole cannot be assessed.

Generalizing Sample Results

Observing all members of the program target group is usually difficult and seldom advisable. Sampling a program target group saves time, energy, and money. Moreover, observations from random samples will resemble what you would have observed of the whole. This enables a manager to generalize the results from random samples to the larger program target group.

The method of sampling limits the degree to which results can be generalized. The sampling procedures we have discussed—random sampling of a whole, sampling randomly a convenient subset of the whole, random assignment of employees to groups, and nonrandom sampling—afford successively less ability to generalize to the program target group.

When they sample the whole randomly, managers can generalize observed program impacts to the program target group generally. Managers seldom sample a nationwide target group, however. More typically they draw a random sample in a single company, the one conducting the program assessment. In this case, the manager can generalize an observed program impact to the employees of the company. Generalization is limited because the sampling procedure only ensured that the sample was representative of employees of this company. Because similar programs often exist at other companies, managers sometimes generalize results from a single company to the full program target group. They base such generalizations on nonmathematical grounds. For example, they may argue that this company is similar to other companies, and thus the results would apply there, too. Additionally, they may cite research with similar findings. Replication is persuasive. Researchers have conducted hundreds of studies on typical organizational programs: quality circles, employee training programs, managerial style. As assessments find similar program impacts on diverse subsets of the whole, we have more reason to generalize those findings.

When they initially select employees on some nonrandom basis, but then randomly assign the employees to groups, managers can generalize assessment results to that set of employees only. However, managers, often generalize beyond this limited set of employees on nonstatistical grounds: They may argue that these employees are similar to other employees and they may cite other assessments with similar findings.

When employees are neither selected nor assigned to groups randomly, no mathematical basis exists to generalize the program group findings beyond the employees in the program group itself. Because probability theory does not apply to nonrandom events, there is no way to distinguish nonrandom sampling error from the impact, if any, of the program. The findings may not even hold for the employees in the control group. Nor is there a basis to suggest that the employees are similar to the full program target group or that other studies replicate the present study. Use great caution in interpreting the findings of a program assessment that lacks the benefit of randomization.

Sample Size

The degree to which a sample will be representative of the whole depends on its size as well as whether it is drawn randomly. Other things equal, the larger the random sample, the more likely it will be representative of the whole. Increments in sample size, however, quickly reach a point of diminishing return. Because random samples of even moderate size are representative of the whole, increasing the sample size adds little additional accuracy. There simply remains little accuracy to add. This is fortunate because obtaining large samples is costly. The small gain in representativeness is seldom worth the effort and expense of securing a larger sample. Remember that the news service polls predicted accurately that then Governor Clinton would receive 43 percent of the popular vote in the presidential election of 1992 with sample sizes less than .002 percent of the voters. Sampling more people adds cost without concomitant gains in accuracy. That is why the Nielsen Ratings Company samples about .005 percent of the American TV households to determine national viewing habits. Asking more people wouldn't add appreciably to the representativeness of their findings. We are going to discover that:

- Large, descriptive surveys seldom require samples larger than 2400 members of the target group.
- Program assessments that compare a program group to a control group often require no more than 64 employees in each group.
- Program assessments that compare a program group to a national norm often require no more than 32 employees in the program group.

These are impressively small numbers. By convention, and absent other considerations, evaluators can use these sample sizes in program assessment. The following sections explain how these sample sizes were determined, and how to determine sample sizes for special cases.

Descriptive Surveys

National surveys, such as voting polls and Nielsen surveys, attempt to gather information about the characteristics of the whole. They do not make explicit comparisons, either to established norms or to comparable groups. Lacking a comparison, national surveys are marginally useful for program assessment. They serve here to introduce the terms and steps we need to determine sample size for comparing a program group to a control group or to a national norm. The steps for determining sample size for such comparisons will be presented after we examine descriptive surveys.

The sample size for descriptive surveys depends on four interconnected factors:[18]

1. The confidence level with which generalizations to the whole are made
2. The acceptable margin of error
3. The size of the target group
4. The diversity of target group.

We will consider each factor in turn.

Confidence Level. Confidence level is the assurance we desire that the sample results will mirror what would be observed of the whole. By convention, a 95 percent confidence level is usually chosen. This means that over the long run, we expect to observe our survey result 95 out of every 100 times. That is a high level, indicating that the survey obtained results that reflect those of the full target group. Sometimes researchers want to be 99 percent confident that results from a sample reflect what would be observed of the whole. Higher confidence requires a larger sample size.

Margin of Error. Margin of error is the degree that sample results resemble what would be observed of the whole. For example, most presidential election polls have a margin of error of ±3 percent. The interval formed by adding and subtracting 3 points to and from the poll result will likely include the result you would have obtained by surveying the whole. If you had adopted the 95 percent confidence level, you could summarize the survey results as follows: I am 95 percent confident that the results of surveying the whole fall within ±3 percentage points of the poll results. If you want, you can use a ±2 margin of error but still with a 95 percent confidence level. Now you can expect sample results to be closer to the whole (within ±2 instead of within ±3) with the same amount of confidence. Thus you can decide both how confident you want to be that the results of the sample resemble what would be observed of everyone and how close to that the results should be. The first decision reflects the confidence level; the second reflects the margin of error. Smaller margins of error require larger sample sizes.

Let's review the difference between *confidence level* and *margin of error.* Their definitions are similar, but they refer to different decisions. The confidence level reflects how much assurance you want that the sample results will resemble what would be observed of everyone. The margin of error reflects how much resemblance you want. One asks, "How important is it to be close?"; the other asks, "How close do you want to be?" Suppose I offer you a ride home from work, and I tell you I am 95 percent confident I can get you *close* to your destination. How close you ask? Well that's another question. I am confident I can get you within one mile. Having fulfilled your workout quota for the week, you ask if I can get you closer? My confidence level reflects my knowledge of my car, the city, and how much gas I have, and I know I can get you close to home. Despite *my* confidence, however, one mile away is not close enough for *you.* Both are chosen for a survey: how much assurance you want of being close and how close you want to be.

Size and Diversity of the Target Group. Two additional factors determine sample size: the size and the diversity of the whole. We will consider them together since both pertain to the target group. In the Gallup polls we read in our newspapers, the entire U.S. adult population is the whole. Typically, managers only wish to draw conclusions about employees in their organization. Here the whole is simply the number of people the company employs. Other things equal, the larger the whole, the larger the sample size required to ensure representativeness.

Diverse wholes require larger sample sizes to reflect the diversity; homogeneous wholes require smaller samples, as similarity is easy to detect. For example, a small sample can better detect a lead when voters heavily favor one candidate than when voters are split evenly among the candidates. And because of the low diversity among viewers, small samples will more easily reflect viewing habits on Super Bowl Sunday than on a typical viewing day.

In sum, we need a larger sample size for higher confidence levels, smaller margins of error, and large or diverse wholes. Now we can be specific about the sample sizes required to be representative of the whole for various combinations of these factors. Appendix 3 presents the sample sizes needed to conduct descriptive surveys when the target group is diverse and the survey items are answered yes or no.[19] Table 6.2 presents the top portion of the table in Appendix 3. This portion identifies samples sizes required for very large (population infinity) and diverse wholes. The margins of error are listed across the top line. Sample sizes to insure a 95 percent confidence level are in bold type. To use Table 6.2, you need to specify the confidence level and the margin of error you wish your survey to have. For example, a manager may wish to survey a large and diverse whole at the 95 percent confidence level and with a margin of error of ±3 percentage points. The manager would need a sample size of 1067 to be 95 percent confident that a survey of the whole would be as close as plus or minus three percentage points of the sample result. (Please examine Table 6.2 and verify this for youself.) A margin of error of ±2 requires a sample of about 2400 people, at the 95 percent confidence level. Thus most national polls survey between 1000 and 2000 people.

Appendix 3 also includes sample sizes for smaller size wholes. A 5000 member agency needs to survey 879 employees for a 95 percent confidence level and a ±3 margin of error.

Observations that are representative of a larger whole, while useful in presidential elections, stop short of the needs of program assessment. Recall that program assessment requires a comparison, whether to a comparable group, to an established norm, or to previous performance. The sample sizes in Appendix 3 are used to describe a target group as a whole, not to compare it to a comparable group, norm, or previous performance. Without comparison, we have a piece of information with no way to know if it represents a program impact, and if it does, how much of an impact it represents.

Table 6.2
*Survey Sample Sizes for **95 percent (Bold)** and 99 percent Confidence Levels*

	Margin of Error				
POPULATION	±1	±2	±3	±4	±5
Infinity	**9604**	**2401**	**1067**	**600**	**384**
	16587	4147	1843	1037	663

Program Assessment

Five interconnected factors determine the sample sizes needed for program assessments that contain a comparison:[20]

1. The confidence level that sample results mirror the whole
2. The statistical power to detect an impact of given size
3. The size of program impact considered important to detect
4. The size of the target group
5. The diversity of the target group.

Confidence level and the size and diversity of the target group were discussed in the previous section where we used them to obtain sample sizes for descriptive surveys. Confidence level is our assurance over the long run that comparisons made with samples emulate comparisons made with the whole. Researchers use a 95 percent confidence level by convention. The size of the target group is usually presumed to be large for program assessments. The scientific community prefers broad statements of program impact over statements limited to a single department, or company.The diversity of the whole, while a factor, works behind the scenes. Because it appears in the numerator and the denominator of the equation that determines sample sizes, the diversity of the whole "cancels out" as a consideration. If a large whole is assumed, the evaluator needs to preselect only the confidence level (of the factors we have already encountered) to determine sample size.

Two factors besides confidence level must be considered: statistical power, which is the likelihood that a comparison will detect a program impact (assuming one exists), and the size of the program impact. With inadequate statistical power, a program impact can remain undetected. Low statistical power makes it difficult to distinguish a program impact from sampling error. By convention, researchers seek a statistical power of 80 percent. This means that in the long run, we can distinguish a program impact from sampling error 80 in every 100 times.

Finally, the size of the program impact is important, either to a practical, real-world application, such as an increase in organizational productivity, or to substantive progress in theory building. In disease prevention, researchers value even small program impacts. For a costly program, on the other hand, managers may value only a large program impact. To decide the impact size of interest to them, evaluators consult relevant theory, past research, and their own experience in organizations.

Jacob Cohen defined small, medium, and large impacts from his review of previous theory and research in several disciplines.[21] Small impacts are illustrated by the difference in average height (about ½ inch) between 15- and 16-year-old girls, medium impacts by the difference in average height (about 1 inch) between 14- and 18-year-old girls, and large impacts by the difference in average height between 13- and 18-year-old girls. We will see examples of impact sizes more pertinent to program assessment in Chapter 7 when we consider how to interpretet the importance of assessment results. Here we will use Cohen's conventions for small, medium, and large impacts to determine sample size.

Comparison of the Program Group to a Control Group. The most common design in program assessment involves a comparison between a program group and a control group. Cohen presents tables to determine sample sizes for various combinations of confidence level, statistical power, and the size of program impact considered important. Sections of Cohen's tables for small, medium, and large program impacts are presented in Appendix 4 and in Table 6.3.[22]

The table shows the number of people needed in each group, the specified number in the program group, and the same number in the control group. To obtain the required sample size, enter the table with the desired confidence level, the desired level of power, and the size of the program impact of interest. By convention, researchers use the 95 percent confidence level and statistical power of 80 percent to detect a medium-size impact.[23] For example, a manager may wish to

Table 6.3
Per Group Sample Sizes for ***95 percent (Bold)*** *and 99 percent Confidence Levels*

	PROGRAM IMPACT		
POWER	Small	Medium	Large
70%	**310** 482	**50** 79	**20** 32
80%	**393** 586	**64** 95	**26** 38
90%	**526** 746	**85** 120	**34** 48

determine whether employees with training outperform employees without training with 95 percent confidence and 80 percent power to detect a medium-size program impact.

That is: Confidence level = 95 percent
Statistical Power = 80 percent
Program Impact Size = Medium

This requires a sample size of 64 persons in each group. (Please see Table 6.3 and verify this for yourself.) At the 99 percent confidence level, 95 persons are needed in each group. As you can see, sample sizes for group comparisons are a lot smaller than those for descriptive surveys.

Occasionally, circumstances limit the size of the program group, such as when there are resources to train only 50 employees. You can use information from Table 6.3 in the following formula to determine the size of the control group that would compensate for the smaller program group:[24]

$$n_U = \frac{n_K n_T}{2n_K - n_T}$$

where n_U = the unknown size of the control group
n_K = the known size of the program group
n_T = the sample size recommended in the table

To illustrate the procedure, consider a manager who wants to compare a program group to a control group at the 95 percent confidence level, with 80 percent statistical power and for a medium-size program impact.

That is Confidence Level = 95%
Statistical Power = 80%
Program Impact Size = Medium

Normally this set of conditions requires a sample size of 64 people in each group. Suppose that the Program accommodates only 50 people. We would solve for n_U, the control group sample size, using $n_K = 50$ (the known size of the program group), and $n_T = 64$ (the sample size of each group recommended in Table 6.2 had there been no restrictions on the size of the program group), as follows:

$$n_U = \frac{(50) \times (64)}{(2 \times 50) - 64} = \frac{3200}{100 - 64} = \frac{3200}{36} = 89$$

The control group needs 89 people to make up for the limit of 50 people in the program group.

Comparison of the Program Group to a Norm. Sometimes evaluators compare a program group to an established norm, say whether following conflict resolution training company employees exceed the knowledge of employees nationally. Smaller sample sizes suffice when comparing a group to a whole.

Cohen has created tables to determine sample sizes for various combinations of confidence level, statistical power, and impact size. Sections of Cohen's tables for small, medium, and large program impacts are presented in Appendix 5 and in Table 6.4.[25] The table identifies the number of people needed in the program group; the group for which the norm exists is treated as the whole.

To obtain the required sample size, enter the table with the confidence level, power level, and impact size of interest. By convention, researchers use the 95 percent confidence level with 80 percent statistical power to detect a medium-size impact. For example, a manager may want to determine if, after conflict resolution training, employees scored higher than the national norm as reported in the materials accompanying a standardized test of conflict resolution. The manager wants to detect a medium program impact at the 95 percent confidence level with statistical power of 80 percent.

Table 6.4
*Program Group Sample Sizes for **95 percent (Bold)** and 99 percent Confidence Levels*

	PROGRAM IMPACT		
POWER	Small	Medium	Large
70%	**159** 247	**26** 40	**11** 17
80%	**201** 300	**32** 48	**13** 20
90%	**269** 381	**43** 61	**18** 25

That is Confidence Level = 95 percent
Statistical Power = 80 percent
Program Impact Size = Medium

The sample size needed for these conditions is 32.

We have shown how to determine the sample sizes for descriptive surveys, comparisons of the program group to a control group and comparisons of the program group to an established norm. Adopting a 95% confidence level and ±2 margin of error by convention, descriptive surveys need 2401 people. Adopting by convention a 95 percent confidence level, statistical power of 80 percent, and a medium-size program impact, comparisons of a program group to a control group need 64 people in each group. Finally, comparisons of a program group to a norm require 32 people in the program group at 95 percent confidence level with 80 percent statistical power for a medium-size program impact. Researchers depart from these conventions if warranted by theory or previous research. Adequately large, random samples assure evaluators they will detect a program impact if it exists.

Main Points of Chapter 6

- The program target group is the group of people for whom a program was designed.
- Sampling a program target group saves time, energy, and money, and random sampling ensures that the sample is representative of, and thus interchangeable with, the program target group.
- A random sample gives each person in the program target group an independent and equally likely chance of being selected.
- To form a random sample, select people from the program target group whose numbers match the numbers encountered in the Table of Random Numbers.
- Managers often use procedures that produce nonrandom samples, including using a handpicked sample, an intact group, and volunteers.
- Whether random or nonrandom initially, employees should be assigned randomly to the program group and to the control group, whenever possible.

- Evaluators can generalize the results of a random sample to the whole. Evaluators can generalize results of a random sample of a subset of the program target group (e.g., a single company) to the subset. Random assignment of a nonrandom set of employees to groups allows generalization to employees in the program assessment. Nonrandom samples allow no generalizations.
- By convention, sample sizes of 2401 are usually adequate for descriptive surveys. Comparisons between a program group and a control group require about 64 people per group, and comparisons of a program group to a norm require a program group of 32.

Chapter Notes

1. Census and you. U.S. Department of Commerce (Bureau of the Census). August 1990, Vol. 25, No. 8, pp 1+. In Social Issues Resources Series. Vol. 5, Article 14, *Population.*
2. *Congressional Quarterly Almanac.* 101st Congress, 2nd Session, 1990, pp 415–416.
3. *Congressional Quarterly Almanac.* 102nd Congress, 1st Session, 1991, p. 181.
4. *Congressional Quarterly Almanac.* 1991, p. 180.
5. The super bowl and the small screen. The *Sun* [Baltimore]. January 29, 1993, Vol. 312, No. 64, p. 6C; A. C. Nielsen Company, Public Relations Department, Telephone Interview, May 1998.
6. Alan D. Fletcher and Thomas A. Bowers, *Fundamentals of Advertising Research.* Belmont, CA: Wadsworth, 1988, p. 249.
7. Millie Takaki, *Sheet.* January 16, 1998, v. 39, n. 3, p. 1(3).
8. Roger D. Wimmer and Joseph R. Dominick, *Mass Media Research.* Belmont, CA: Wadsworth, 1991, p. 283.
9. The *Washington Post.* No. 334, November 3, 1992, p. A8; The *New York Times.* Vol. CXLII, No. 49,138, November 2, 1992, p. A12; The *New York Times.* Vol. CXLII, No. 49,141, November 5, 1992, p. A1; The *Sun* [Baltimore]. Vol. 165, No. 140, November 2, 1992, p. 11A.
10. Fletcher and Bowers, p. 63.

11. More generally, random sampling is "A method of drawing samples such that each and every distinct sample of the same size *N* has exactly the same probability of being selected." William L. Hays and Robert L. Winkler, *Statistics: Probability, Inference, and Decision*. Volume 1. New York: Holt, Rinehart, and Winston, 1970, p. 243.
12. Mr. Jim Cadden, Drawings Manager, Maryland State Lottery, August 29, 1992. Personal Interview.
13. Paul A. Games, *Elementary Statistics: Data Analysis for the Behavioral Sciences*. New York: McGraw-Hill, 1967, p. 216.
14. Actually, some of these names are members of my family who wanted me to "wiggle" their names in somewhere in the book.
15. Compared to samples of unequal size, samples of equal size yield greater statistical power to detect a program impact and are more robust to violations of the assumption of equal spread of scores, $s_P^2 = s_C^2$, which underlies the *t*-test (Jacob Cohen, *Statistical Power Analysis for the Behavioral Sciences*. New York: Academic Press, 1969, p. 57; Gene V. Glass and Julian C. Stanley, *Statistical Methods in Education and Psychology*. Englewood Cliffs, NJ: Prentice-Hall, 1970, p. 279).
16. E. F. Lindquist, *Design and Analysis of Experiments in Psychology and Education*. Boston: Houghton Mifflin, 1953, pp 74–75.
17. Robert Rosenthal and Ralph Rosnow, The volunteer subject. In *Artifact in Behavioral Research*. New York: Academic Press, 1969, p. 111.
18. Mary John Smith, *Contemporary Communication Research Methods*. Belmont, CA: Wadsworth, 1988, pp 223–224.
19. Sample sizes presented in Appendix 3 for infinite populations were derived using the formula:

$$n = \frac{(\pm Z_\alpha)^2 (pq)}{(\pm ME)^2}$$

where Z_α is 1.960 for the 95 percent and 2.576 for the 99 percent confidence levels, p and q estimate the proportion of the program target group responding yes or no, set at .5 and .5 respectively, and ME is the specified margin of error, here ranging from ±1 to ±5. The sample sizes for smaller populations were derived using the formula:

$$n' = \frac{N n}{N + n}$$

where *N* is the smaller population size and *n* is the sample size for an infinite population for the specified confidence level and margin of error, derived from the first formula (Smith, p. 224).

20. Jacob Cohen, *Statistical Power Analysis for the Behavioral Sciences*. New York: Academic Press, 1969, p. 50.
21. Cohen, pp 22–24.
22. Cohen, p. 53.
23. Jacob Cohen, Some statistical issues in psychological research. In B. B. Wolman (Ed.), *Handbook of Clinical Psychology*. New York: McGraw-Hill, 1965, p. 57.
24. Cohen, *Statistical Power Analysis for the Behavioral Sciences*, p. 57.
25. Sample sizes presented in Appendix 5 were derived using the formula:

$$n = \frac{n_{.10}}{100\, d^2} + 1$$

where $n_{.10}$ is the necessary sample size for a specied confidence level and desired power for small ($d = d_3' \sqrt{2} = .28$), medium ($d = .71$), and large ($d = 1.13$) effect sizes. Cohen, *Statistical Power Analysis for the Behaivoral Sciences*, pp 51, 59, 61–62.

7

Controlling Sampling Error

Chapter Preview

In this chapter, we will discover that random sampling error and the observed impact of the program are intermingled initially. After examining three pieces of information related to any set of scores, we will acquire tools that distinguish the impact of a program from the impact of random sampling error. These tools also indicate the strength of the relationship between the program and the outcome measure. We will be able to conclude that a program is effective, with known level of confidence in our decision.

Learning Objectives

After reading Chapter 7, you should be able to:

- appreciate that random sampling produces random sampling error that can be mistaken for a program impact
- define the mean, standard deviation, and degrees of freedom of a set of scores
- define the terms *Program t value* and *Table t value* and identify how each is obtained
- describe the purpose and the steps of the t test
- conduct a t test and interpret its results
- determine the strength of relationship between a program and its outcome measure
- specify when to use t' and df' in place of t and df

The Focus of Chapter 7

The program assessment steps discussed in this chapter, along with their corresponding components in the Scientific Model, are highlighted below.

The Steps of Program Assessment

1. Involve stakeholders throughout the assessment.
2. Specify the expected program outcome.
3. Establish a measure of the program outcome.
4. Plan a method of gathering data.
5. Collect the data.
6. Analyze the data.
7. Communicate the results.
8. Make program decisions.

The Scientific Model of Program Assessment

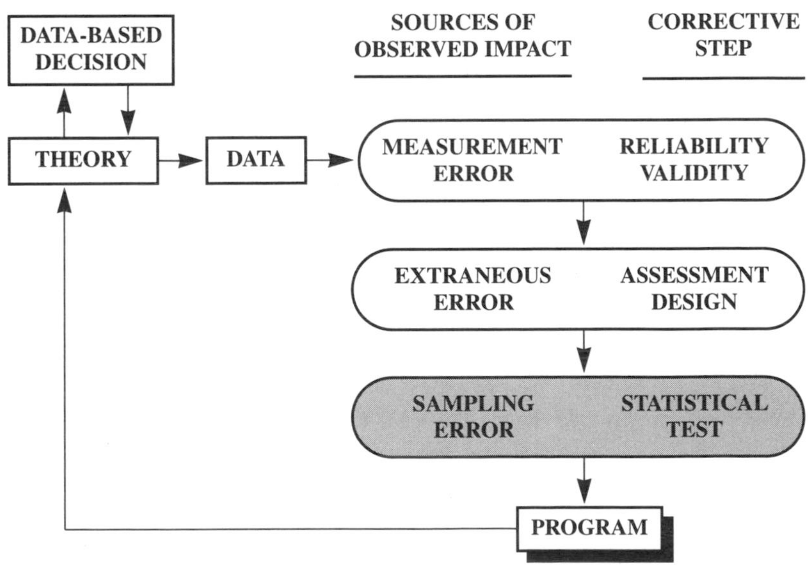

Program assessment seeks to determine whether a program has its intended impact on its target group. To save time, energy, and money, evaluators usually observe the impact of the program on a sample of the program target group, although the manager's primary interest remains the whole, how the program would impact the program target group generally. The evaluator seeks to learn the improvement anticipated in all employees from observing the program's impact on some of them.

Rarely, however, do samples mirror the whole exactly. Due to the sample's limited size, the characteristics of some people in the target group will be underrepresented by those in the sample. This difference—the departure of sample results from what would be observed of everyone—is called sampling error. In general, sampling a whole always produces sampling error, as does assigning employees randomly to groups, where the difference between the groups represents sampling error.

To illustrate this, imagine a program target group of ten people (the target group is deliberately small so it is easy to examine). The scores from a questionnaire administered to each person are presented in Table 7.1. For comparison purposes, I formed a sample by selecting five persons (persons 2 through 5 and person 10) randomly from the target group, and the scores of this sample are in Table 7.1 as well. The average of the scores in the five-person sample ($16 \div 5 = 3.2$) departs from the average of the scores of the target group as a whole ($30 \div 10 = 3$). This small difference $(3.2 - 3) = .2$ represents random sampling error, the expected departure of sample results from what would be observed of everyone.

Sources of Random Sampling Error

Random sampling error in program assessment stems from three sources. First, random sampling error arises when we draw a sample randomly from a whole. Large, descriptive surveys, such as the Gallup Poll and preelection polls use this method. Here, random sampling error marks the degree to which the answers from the few differ from what would be observed of everyone. Second, error arises when we draw a random sample from a whole and divide it in two parts, where one sample receives the program and the other sample acts as a control group. Here, any preprogram difference between the two groups reflects random sampling error. That is, the groups should be initially comparable except for chance differences. Finally, when a random sample of the whole is unavailable, as when we must rely on

Table 7.1
Target Group Scores and Sample Scores

Person	WHOLE	SAMPLE
1	3	
2	2	2
3	4	4
4	2	2
5	5	5
6	2	
7	3	
8	4	
9	2	
10	3	3
Total	30	16
Average	(30 ÷ 10) = 3	(16 ÷ 5) = 3.2

volunteers to participate in our study, we should whenever possible assign these people at random to the program group and to the control group. Called random assignment to groups, this important step ensures that the program and control groups are similar initially. Again, any pre-program difference between the two groups reflects random sampling error.

Visualizing Random Error

Ironically, whereas we cannot predict an individual random event, the behavior of a collection of random events is patterned. For example, we cannot know beforehand if a flipped coin will land heads or tails, but we know that a coin flipped many times will result in heads about half the time. Thousands of coin tosses form a pattern: About half will be heads. Similarly, if I place a book on the floor and drop a coin from waist high onto the book, I cannot predict in which direction and how far the coin will bounce. The bounce of an individual coin is unpredictable; it might land on the book or bounce some distance. In contrast, if I drop many coins, one at a time, on the book from waist high, a pattern forms. A cluster of coins will lodge close to the book, while a few will bounce or roll further.

Random sampling error works the same way: A collection of random errors forms a pattern. We can illustrate that a collection of random errors forms a pattern by referring again to the example of dropping many coins, one at a time, on a book from waist high. Let's say you did this, too. If you think of the book on the floor as a target you were trying to hit, then the distance from the book that each coin falls is error. If you dropped each coin in essentially the same manner, the error is random. Thus, quite literally, the spread of the coins about the book represents random error, for if there were no error, the coins would stack up in a single pile ready for a coin wrapper and you would be famous if you could repeat this feat on television. But alas, coins bounce and roll, and the bounce and roll represents error because we were aiming at the book.

If we drop many coins, one at a time, most of them would cluster near the book and only a small percentage would land far away. If we kept track, we could say how many inches away from the book 95 percent of the coins fell. For example, when I dropped 100 pennies one at a time from waist high (don't laugh, it was so I could write about it), 95 percent of them fell within a sixteen-inch circumference around the book, as illustrated in Fig. 7.1.

Because I was aiming at the book, the distance of each coin from the book represents random error. Collectively, 95 percent of the random error fell within sixteen inches of the book. In other words, we can expect sixteen inches of random sampling error 95 percent of the time. It is useful to know how much random sampling error is expected. Fortunately, even though a single instance is unpredictable, a collection of random error is patterned, and this pattern is knowable.

The Effects of Random Sampling Error

Although it minimizes error, random sampling does not eliminate it, and what remains can be mistaken for a program impact. Initially, random sampling error is intermingled with, and indistinguishable from, the impact of the program. Here is an example: Imagine that the average motivation score for the sixteen randomly selected salespeople who received a company's sales training program was 4.3, while the average score of the salespeople in the control group was 3.2. These results are depicted below.

	Average Motivation
Program Group	4.3
Control Group	3.2

Figure 7.1
Portrayal of One Hundred Dropped Coins

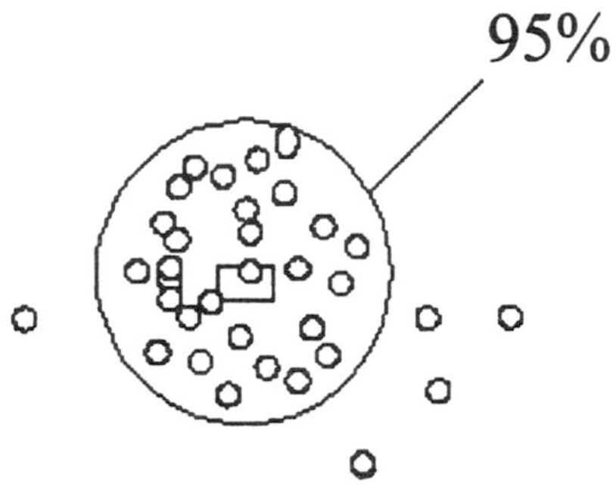

The nonzero difference (4.3 − 3.2 = 1.1) in motivation signals an apparent program impact. The term *apparent* acknowledges that the difference between 4.3 and 3.2 can reflect random sampling error, the effectiveness of the program, or both. The difference may be due to sampling error because anytime you sample, the sample results usually differ somewhat from what would be observed of everyone. The average motivation level of all salespeople, had they received training, would likely differ slightly from 4.3. Similarly, the average motivation level of all salespeople, had they not received training, would likely differ slightly from 3.2.

Because random sampling error influences the results of both groups, it affects the difference between them (i.e., 4.3–3.2) as well. Thus, random sampling error is embedded within the apparent program impact, as is the impact of the program, if any. Moreover, the influences of random sampling error and the program are initially intertwined, indistinguishable from each other. As both a sample and the group that received the program, the program group result reflects both random sampling error and program impact. How much of one or the other it contains is unclear initially. This raises the danger that we might mistake the influence of random sampling error for the influence of the program. Fig. 7.2 illustrates this concern.

Fig. 7.2(a) shows an apparent program impact. It reflects both random sampling error and program impact combined. We don't know how much of (a) is due to the program and how much is due to sampling error. Fig. 7.2(b) illustrates that random sampling error (represented by the dark box) can mask program impact (the white

Figure 7.2
The Role of Random Sampling Error

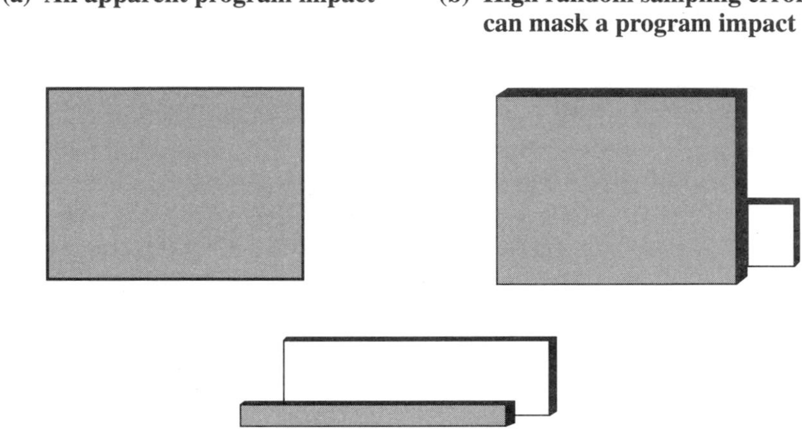

box), while Fig. 7.2(c) illustrates that low random sampling error usually reveals program impact. Upon observing an apparent program impact, however, we face the situation in Fig. 7.2(a).

Mathematicians have derived a way to determine whether an apparent program impact reflects random sampling error or the program. When an apparent program impact exceeds that expected from random sampling error, it can be attributed to the program. This requires three pieces of information drawn from the scores of the employees in the sample: the mean, the standard deviation, and the degrees of freedom.

The Mean

The mean of a set of scores is the sum of the scores divided by the number of scores summed. For example, the mean of the four numbers 3, 2, 3, and 4 is $(3 + 2 + 3 + 4) \div 4 = (12 \div 4) = 3$. Although this is the familiar average we learned as youngsters, the term *mean* is preferred because in mathematics the word *average* is actually a more general term, encompassing three measures of central tendency: the mean, the median, and the mode. We will only use the mean. The mean is commonly abbreviated as $\bar{X}$ (pronounced "ex bar") and we will use this notation frequently. For any set of scores, the formula for the mean is

$$\bar{X} = \frac{\Sigma X_i}{n}$$

where n is the number of scores in the group and Σ is the Greek letter sigma and instructs you to sum the scores. ΣX_i is simply shorthand for $X_1 + X_2 + X_3 + \ldots + X_n$, and saves writing it out.

The mean locates the typical score on a program outcome measure. When comparing a program group to a control group, you need the mean of the scores of the employees in the program group and separately, the mean of the scores in the control group. When comparing a program group to a norm or quota, you need the mean of the scores of the employees in the program group only and then you compare it to the value of the national norm.

A preliminary step in analyzing program assessment data is to look for a difference between the means of the program group and the control group (or between the program group mean and the national norm) for an apparent program impact. Any difference signals an apparent program impact. Earlier we saw an apparent program impact reflected in the difference between the means of employees in the sales training program ($\bar{X} = 4.3$) and those in a control group ($\bar{X} = 3.2$), with those receiving training apparently having higher motivation. The apparent program impact is the difference between the means, or , $(\bar{X}_P - \bar{X}_C)$, where $\bar{X}_P$ is the mean of the program group and $\bar{X}_C$ is the mean of the control group.

The apparent program impact may be due to the program or to the random sampling error produced by observing a portion, rather than all, of the program target group. The second piece of information needed to judge whether a program impact exceeds the impact expected from random sampling error is the standard deviation.

The Standard Deviation

The *standard deviation* identifies the degree to which a set of scores is spread out or dispersed. More precisely, it indicates the average degree to which the scores are dispersed around the mean. Whereas the mean locates a common or typical employee score on the outcome measure, the standard deviation indicates how spread out or dispersed the scores are on the average from this common or typical score. The standard deviation is usually abbreviated as s, and its formula is

$$s = \sqrt{\frac{\sum (X_i - \overline{X})^2}{n - 1}}$$

where n is the number of scores, and $\Sigma(X_i - \overline{X})^2$ is shorthand for summing the squared differences between each score and the mean—that is, $(X_1 - \overline{X})^2 + (X_2 - \overline{X})^2 + (X_3 - \overline{X})^2 + \ldots + (X_n - \overline{X})^2$. The standard deviation is readily attained by computer. It is enough for us to appreciate that the formula produces a single value that reflects the average spread of the scores around the mean. Two elements of the formula are important. First, notice that the mean is subtracted from each score, thereby identifying the score's distance from the mean. Second, division by $n - 1$ gives the average amount that the scores are dispersed around the mean.

Two minor points will also be mentioned. First, although we usually divide by n to obtain an average, we divide by $n - 1$ in the formula for the standard deviation. Mathematicians have shown that this step provides a more accurate estimate of the standard deviation of the program target group.[1] Although we divide by $n - 1$ instead of n, we will still be correct to view the standard deviation as an average, the average spread of the scores around the mean.

Second, to accommodate a property of the mean, the $(X - \overline{X})$ differences are squared, and, as the last step of the formula, the square root is taken. Because the mean locates the center or balance point of the scores, some deviations from this center will produce negative values and some will produce positive values, which together balance out to zero. We can easily illustrate that the mean is a balance point with a small set of data. Consider the three numbers 5, 10, and 15. Their mean is $(5 + 10 + 15) \div 3 = (30 \div 3) = 10$. Now subtract the mean from each number:

Person	**Score**	$(X - \overline{X})$
1	5	$5 - 10 = -5$
2	10	$10 - 10 = 0$
3	15	$15 - 10 = 5$
		Total = 0

The first number lies below the mean by -5, and the third number lies above the mean by $+5$. The middle number is right at the mean and doesn't deviate from it. Notice that adding the three deviations, -5, 0, and $+5$ totals zero. Because the mean is the balance point of the scores, those below it always cancel out those above it.

This occurs for any set of scores. Squaring each difference produces all positive values and produces a nonzero total when they are summed. The nonzero total is used to reflect the spread of the scores around the mean. In effect, taking the square root as the last step of the formula undoes the earlier squaring. The important point to remember is that the difference between each score and the mean is included in the formula and then averaged to obtain the standard deviation, the average spread of the scores around the mean.

To visualize standard deviation, please complete Learning Module 7.1, The Standard Deviation. The steps clarify the meaning of the average spread of scores around the mean.

LEARNING MODULE 7.1: The Standard Deviation

Step 1 Get seven coins (the same denomination if you wish).

Step 2 Get a ruler, yardstick, or tape measure.

Step 3 Place a book on the floor.

Step 4 Stand near the book and drop all the coins from waist high so that they fall on the book at the same time. Please do this now, or as soon as you can. Reading about the standard deviation is helpful, but seeing it for yourself is much more informative.

Step 5 Now look at the coins. (Hopefully none disappeared under a couch or down a heat vent.) They should be dispersed, scattered. Appreciate that employee scores on an outcome measure will also be dispersed. The next step asks you to determine *how* dispersed the coins are.

Step 6 Without moving the coins or the book, measure the distance in inches from the closest edge of each coin to the closest edge of the book. Remember, please do not move the coins. Record the distances on a sheet of paper. Record zero inches for any coins that stayed on top of the book. When I did this, I got two zeros (good coins), 1, 3, 4, and 10 inches, and 24 inches for one particularly rambunctious coin. I imagine your results were similar.

Let's interpret what we've found so far. Each score you recorded is a distance between a coin and the book, a deviation. Think of the book as the mean. Now each score is the distance from a coin to the mean. Obtain the average spread of your coins by summing your scores and dividing by seven, the number of coins. My average was 42 ÷ 7 = 6. On the average, my coins spread out six inches around the mean.

Finally, just look at the coins scattered on the floor. (I hope you didn't move them. If you did, put 'em back quickly while no one's watching). What you see on the floor—coins scattered around a book—is similar to the idea of spread in the standard deviation. Like you did for your coins, the standard deviation averages the distances that scores depart from the mean (although the distances are first squared so they don't total zero).[2]

END OF LEARNING MODULE 7.1

You need the mean and the standard deviation to judge whether a program impact exceeds the impact expected from random sampling error. The third element is called degrees of freedom.

Degrees of Freedom

The amount of random sampling error accompanying a sample of the whole varies with the number of people observed. Intuitively this makes sense, for large samples should reflect the whole more accurately than small samples. More precisely, the amount of random sampling error varies with what are referred to as degrees of freedom. Other things equal, the higher the number of degrees of freedom, the smaller the amount of random sampling error.

We use *degrees of freedom* instead of the sample size due to two factors, one stemming from the definition of random sampling and the other from the formula for the standard deviation.[3] The definition of random sampling stipulates that every member of the program target group must have an independent and equally likely chance of being selected. The term *independent,* you may recall, means that the selection of one employee can have no influence on the selection of additional employees. Correspondingly, degrees of freedom refers to the number of scores obtained from employees that are independent of, or indeterminable from, the scores of other employees in the sample. The degrees of freedom will be the number of employees in the sample if no employee score can be determined from other employee scores. Random sampling insures this initially.

The degrees of freedom would remain the same as the sample size except for a provision contained in the formula for the standard deviation. This provision makes it possible for one employee score to be determined from the other employee scores. Consequently, the degrees of freedom associated with the standard deviation is one less than the sample size. The size of the sample is usually abbreviated as n, for number of people, and the term *degrees of freedom* is usually abbreviated *df*. Thus, $df = n - 1$ for any random sample as soon as you compute its standard deviation. Be assured that no score is eliminated; all are used in computing the mean and standard deviation. However, the number $n - 1$ determines the amount of random sampling error expected when you sample a whole instead of the number n.

Why the standard deviation lowers the degrees of freedom by one can be illustrated with a small set of data. Let's say I have a set of five scores that sum to 15, and I show you all of the scores except one. For example, I may withhold Jim's score from you as depicted below.

$$2 + 4 + 2 + 4 + (\textit{Jim's Score}) = 15$$

Can you say what Jim's score must have been? The first four scores sum to 12 (Please verify this for yourself). If the first four scores sum to 12 and all scores sum to 15, Jim's score must be 3 because $(12 + 3) = 15$. Notice that once you know that the scores sum to 15, Jim's score is no longer indeterminate, no longer free to vary. It has to be 3. No other number would make all five scores sum to 15. Once the sum is known, the degrees of freedom—the number of scores that are free to vary—are lowered by one, because at least one score can be determined from the others.

Let's see if this also occurs for the mean of a group of scores, of which the sum is a part. Instead of telling you that the five scores sum to 15, this time I've indicated that the mean of the five scores is 3.

$$\frac{2 + 4 + 2 + 4 + (\textit{Jim's Score})}{5} = 3$$

Do you see that Jim's score must be 3? That is, $(2 + 4 + 2 + 4 +$ Jim's score of $3) = 15$ and $(15 \div 5) = 3$. Because no number other than 3 will solve the equation correctly, Jim's score must be 3 and is determined by the other scores once the mean is known. As for the sum, knowing the mean of a set of scores allows one score to be determined from the others.

Finally, let's see how this relates to the formula for the standard deviation.

$$s = \sqrt{\frac{\Sigma(X_i - \overline{X})^2}{n - 1}}$$

The loss of one degree of freedom when calculating the standard deviation stems from the $(X_i - \overline{X})$ portion of the formula, which instructs us to subtract the mean $(\overline{X})$ from each score (X_i). This step requires that the mean be calculated before additional portions of the formula can be performed—that is, we must know the value of the mean before we can subtract it from each score. As we have already seen, once we know the mean, at least one score can be determined from the others. The calculation and then subsequent use of the mean lowers the degrees of freedom by one because now at least one employee score can be determined from the others. If we used n instead of $n - 1$, we would overstate the number of scores that are free to vary and thus underestimate—because larger samples have less sampling error—the amount of random sampling error that accompanies our sample.

With this in mind, let's look at the degrees of freedom associated with two common types of program assessment. When a program group is compared to a control group, the standard deviation of each group is calculated, and there is one less degree of freedom for each group. The comparison combines the degrees of freedom so that $df = (n_P - 1) + (n_C - 1)$, where n_P is the number of persons in the program group and n_C is the number of persons in the control group. The somewhat simpler and algebraically equivalent formula $df = n_P + n_C - 2$ is more commonly used, however. You might want to satisfy yourself that each formula yields the same result when $n_P = 10$ and $n_C = 10$. Each formula should produce a value of eighteen degrees of freedom.

When a program group is compared to a norm, the formula for the degrees of freedom is $df = n_P - 1$, one less than the number of persons in the program group. The degrees of freedom are associated with the standard deviation of the program group only.

In either case, the amount of random sampling error that arises from sampling a whole depends on the number of degrees of freedom. As df increases, random sampling error decreases. Using degrees of freedom ensures that we determine the amount of random sampling error that accompanies a sample based on the number of scores that are actually free to vary. Together with the mean and the standard deviation, the degrees of freedom are needed to distinguish the impact of the program from that of random sampling error.

The t test

A difference between the means of the program group and the control group signals an apparent program impact. We say apparent because two factors—the effectiveness of the program and the influence of random sampling error—combine to produce this difference. Ruling out random sampling error as the sole cause of an apparent program impact allows a powerful conclusion: The effectiveness of the program caused the impact. Now we'll examine a procedure that can distinguish between random sampling error and a program impact. Initially, we will examine how to address random sampling error when comparing a program group to a control group. Later we will examine the very similar procedure for comparing a program group to a norm or quota.

Comparing a Program Group to a Control Group

Both the program and random sampling error "contribute" to an apparent program impact. Because their contributions are initially indistinguishable from one another, the genuine danger arises that evaluators will mistake the influence of random sampling for the effectiveness of the program. Be aware that random sampling error can masquerade as program impact. Because random sampling always produces random sampling error, we need a way to discern whether there is a program impact as well.

The solution is to conduct a t test. In a t test, we compare the impact of the program and random sampling error combined to the impact of random sampling error by itself. When the impact of the program and random sampling error combined exceeds the impact of random sampling error by itself, you may conclude that there is a program impact.

The t test compares two t values. The Table t value, which mathematicians derived years ago and is obtained from a Table of t values, reflects the impact of random sampling error by itself. The Program t value, which we must calculate from the scores of the employees in the program and control groups, reflects the impact of the program and random sampling error combined.

The Table t Value. The Table t value reflects the impact of random sampling error by itself. To appreciate why, recall the difference between an individual random event and a collection of random events. Although individual random events are not predictable, a

It is always hard to think of what to wear to a Masquerade Party.

collection of random events forms a pattern. When I dropped those coins, 95 percent landed within sixteen inches of the book. In aiming at the book, I created a condition where error was in operation. Here, the distance between each coin and the book represents error, with 95 percent of the cumulative error occurring within sixteen inches.

By the same token, random sampling error forms a pattern. To see the pattern, we set up a mathematical condition where only random sampling error operates. Instead of coins, however, we observe a collection of t values, where the departure of any t value from zero represents error. Where the coins targeted the book, the t values target in on zero. If no error exists, all t values equal zero. Short of this, departures from zero represent random sampling error, because that is the only influence in operation.

Let's be more specific about how to set up a condition where only random sampling error operates. Imagine that we draw two random samples from the same large whole and compute the mean ($\overline{X}_1$ and $\overline{X}_2$) of each sample. Because the samples were drawn from the same whole, $\overline{X}_1$ should equal $\overline{X}_2$, except for random sampling error. Literally, the degree to which $(\overline{X}_1 - \overline{X}_2)$ departs from zero represents error. Additionally, the dispersion—or more accurately, the standard deviation—of a collection of $(\overline{X}_1 - \overline{X}_2)$ values represents error, for if there were no error, all $(\overline{X}_1 - \overline{X}_2)$ values would equal zero, and they would have no scatter. That is, the degree to which the standard deviation of a collection of $(\overline{X}_1 - \overline{X}_2)$ values departs from zero also represents error. A t value is the ratio of these two indices of error: the difference between two means, $(\overline{X}_1 - \overline{X}_2)$, in the upper portion or numerator of the t, and the standard deviation of a collection of $(\overline{X}_1 - \overline{X}_2)$ values, represented as $s_{\overline{X}_1 - \overline{X}_2}$, in the lower portion or denominator of the *t*. The formula for *t* is

$$t = \frac{\overline{X}_1 - \overline{X}_2}{s_{\overline{X}_1 - \overline{X}_2}}$$

The degree to which *t* departs from zero represents error. In this manner, a collection of $(\overline{X}_1 - \overline{X}_2)$ values can be transformed to a collection of t values, which forms a pattern much like that in Fig. 7.3, where the baseline is composed of the various t values.

This is the t distribution, well known among mathematicians. It represents a pile of error, since only error is operating. As can be seen, a vast number of t values forms a symmetrical curve, with its highest point at $t = 0$. Because the area under the curve will be exactly 1, we can locate the point above and below zero that includes

Figure 7.3
A Collection of t Values

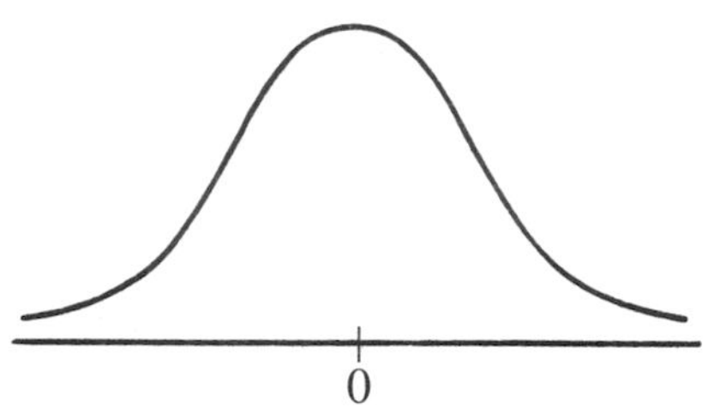

95 percent of the area under the curve. This will be the t value that marks a distance above and below zero between which lies 95 percent of the area under the curve and beyond which lies less than 5 percent of the area under the curve. The Table of t values contains just such t values, ones that mark 95 percent of cumulative random sampling error.

We transform the $(\bar{X}_1 - \bar{X}_2)$ values to t values because, although $(\bar{X}_1 - \bar{X}_2)$ itself is an index of error, and a collection of $(\bar{X}_1 - \bar{X}_2)$ values represents the accumulation of error, the distance above and below zero that includes 95 percent of the cumulative error will vary, depending on how dispersed scores are in the large whole. Forming a ratio with $s_{\bar{X}_1 - \bar{X}_2}$ standardizes the point above and below zero that includes 95 percent of the cumulative error, regardless of how dispersed scores are in the whole. This is convenient because 95 percent of the cumulative error will lie at the same distance for all wholes. To determine this distance we need only know the number of scores in the samples that were free to vary. That is, the amount of random sampling error depends on the degrees of freedom of the two samples $(n_1 + n_2 - 2)$. The Table of t values presents the amount of random sampling error for various size samples based on their degrees of freedom. Remember this: A Table t value reflects the impact of random sampling error by itself; it in no way reflects the impact of a program. Mathematicians derived these t values years ago under conditions where only error could operate, and they have been available in a Table of t values ever since.

Appendix 2 contains a Table of t values.[4] Please take a minute to find the table and look it over. Part of the Table of t values is in Table 7.2.

The left column of the table contains degrees of freedom, abbreviated *df*. Degrees of freedom refers to the number of scores that are indeterminable from the others $(n_P + n_C - 2$ for a program group

Table 7.2
Table of t Values

	Probability Level	
df	**.05**	**.01**
1	12.706	63.657
2	4.303	9.925
3	3.182	5.841
4	2.776	4.604
5	2.571	4.032
6	2.447	3.707
7	2.365	3.499
8	2.306	3.355
9	2.262	3.250
10	2.228	3.169

and a control group). The middle column of the table contains t values that mark 95 percent accumulation of random sampling error. Equivalently, and more commonly, the percentage is expressed as a probability. In this sense, the middle column contains t values that mark the amount of random sampling error expected with probability of .95. As indicated by the heading of the middle column, random sampling error greater than that indicated by the t value is expected with probability less than .05. Literally, each t value marks the distance above and below zero beyond which random sampling error falls with probability less than .05. Correspondingly, the right column of the table contains t values that mark a 99 percent accumulation of random sampling error, the amount expected with probability .99. As the column heading indicates, random sampling error greater than that indicated by the t value is expected with probability less than .01.

For example, for two random samples of size six, $df = n_1 + n_2 - 2 = 6 + 6 - 2 = 10$. For $df = 10$, the t value in the middle column is 2.228. Please verify this for yourself. The probability is less than .05 that random sampling error falls beyond a distance of 2.228 above or below zero as illustrated in Fig. 7.4. Error larger

Figure 7.4
Distance Above and Below Zero at 95 Percent Probability

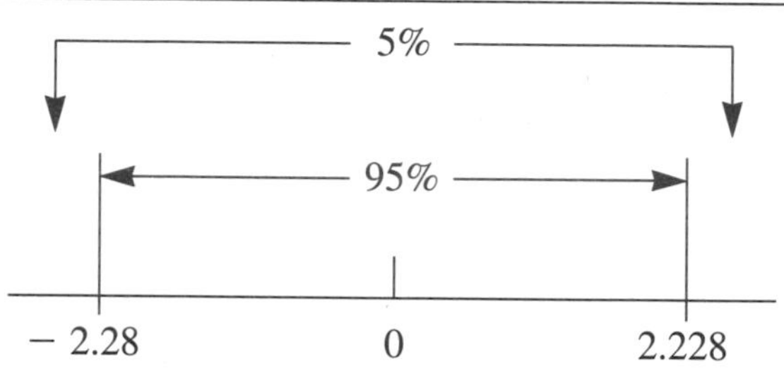

than this is rare. Meanwhile, 2.228 is the amount of random sampling error expected 95 percent of the time for two samples each of size 6.

Let's see what the t value is at the .01 level of probability. For $df = 10$, the t value in the Table at the .01 probability level is 3.169. Random sampling error falls beyond a distance of 3.169 above and below zero with $p < .01$. Error larger than this is extremely rare.

To determine if there is a program impact, it is very useful to know the point above and below zero beyond which 5 percent or 1 percent of random sampling error falls. First, however, we have to become familiar with a second t value, one obtained from the data collected in a program assessment.

The Program t Value. The Program t value reflects the combined impact of the program and random sampling error. To obtain the program t value, evaluators analyze the scores of the employees in the program and control groups. The formula to calculate the Program t value requires three pieces of information from the program and control group scores: their means, standard deviations, and degrees of freedom. Because computer programs can efficiently calculate the program t value, its formula is presented here only to highlight its components. Be warned, though, that the formula looks formidable. To maintain your focus as you read the description of the formula, keep this important point in mind: The Program t value, calculated from the scores of the employees in the program and control groups, reflects the combined impacts of the program and random sampling error. The formula for the Program t value is

$$t = \frac{\bar{X}_P - \bar{X}_C}{\sqrt{\frac{(n_P - 1)s_P^2 + (n_C - 1)s_C^2}{n_P + n_C - 2}\left(\frac{1}{n_P} + \frac{1}{n_C}\right)}}$$

where n_P and n_C are the number of employees, $\bar{X}_P$ and $\bar{X}_C$ are the means, and s_P and s_C are the standard deviations of scores from the program group and the control group, respectively. Although this is a complicated formula, the computer efficiently performs the calculations, yielding a single value. This frees us to focus on the meaning of its terms and how we will use the end result.

Let's examine the key features of the formula. First, verify for yourself that the formula contains the means, standard deviations, and degrees of freedom of the program group and the control group. The means are in the numerator of the equation, where one mean is subtracted from the other. A nonzero difference between the means signals an apparent program impact. The word *apparent* signifies that the difference could reflect random sampling error rather than the impact of the program. Whereas we cannot distinguish the impact of random sampling error from that of the program at this point, it is enough to know that the numerator of the formula for the Program t value contains the impact of the program and random sampling error combined.

The standard deviations (s_P and s_C) are in the denominator of the equation, as are their respective degrees of freedom ($n_P - 1$ and $n_C - 1$) and their combined degrees of freedom ($n_P + n_C - 2$). Each standard deviation is squared and then multiplied or "weighted" by its degrees of freedom, while taking the square root of the denominator in effect "undoes" the squaring. The final term in the denominator involves the sample sizes, which also acts to weight the standard deviations. Squaring, weighting, and taking the square root are performed for somewhat technical reasons—essentially to ensure that the Program t value is derived on the same basis as the Table t values. Explaining these reasons would detract from the important feature that the standard deviations appear in the denominator of the formula for the Program t value. This denominator is the weighted average of the combined spread of the scores in the program and the control groups. It estimates the standard deviation of a collection of $(\bar{X}_1 - \bar{X}_2)$ values. As such, the denominator reflects random sampling error, but because it does not contain the difference between the means, it does not reflect the impact of the program.

Both the numerator and the denominator of the formula for the Program t value incorporate an important element of spread: The numerator indexes the spread of the means (how far apart they are) by subtracting one from the other, and the denominator, containing standard deviations, indexes the combined spread of the scores around their respective means. These two indices of spread estimate random sampling error, except the numerator also reflects the impact, if any, of the program. That is, if the program group and the control group were drawn from the same large whole, then $(\overline{X}_P - \overline{X}_C)$ should equal zero, except for random sampling error and the effect if any of the program. Additionally, the standard deviation of a collection of $(\overline{X}_1 - \overline{X}_2)$ values (represented as $s_{\overline{X}_1 - \overline{X}_2}$) should equal zero, except for random sampling error. In this sense, the formula for the Program t value reduces to the same form as that for the Table t value, namely

$$t = \frac{\overline{X}_1 - \overline{X}_2}{s_{\overline{X}_1 - \overline{X}_2}}$$

The only difference is that the numerator of the Program t reflects the impact of random sampling error and the program combined, whereas the numerator of the Table t value represents the impact of random sampling error only.

The Comparison. Derived from probability theory, each Table t value indicates the amount of random sampling error expected for various size samples. Calculated from the scores of the employees in the program and control groups, the Program t value also reflects random sampling error but increased by whatever impact the program has. An effective program "separates" the means of the program and control groups, increasing the Program t value.

More specifically, both the Table t value and the Program t value contain two indices of random sampling error—one in the numerator, embodied as the spread between the means, and one in the denominator, based on the spread of the scores around their respective means. The difference is, the numerator of the Program t is enlarged by whatever impact the program has, whereas the Table t reflects random sampling error only. We can depict this important principle as

Table t Value	**Program t Value**
$\frac{RSE}{RSE}$	$\frac{P + RSE}{RSE}$

where each *RSE* is an independent estimate of random sampling error, and *P* is the impact, if any, of the program. Two things show clearly: Random sampling error occurs in the numerator and denominator of both t values, and only the Program t is inflated by whatever impact the program has, as indicated in its numerator by $P + RSE$. This important condition—that the Table t value reflects random sampling error only, whereas the Program t value reflects both random sampling error and the influence of the program—forms the basis of the t test.

There is one final important point: Because their formulas contain $(\overline{X}_1 - \overline{X}_2)$, both the Table t value and the Program t value can be negative in value. Because the Table t value marks the point above and below zero beyond which random sampling error occurs with probability .05 or .01, the point below zero will be a negative number. For convenience, only the positive values are listed in the Table since both values are the same except one is positive and one is negative.

The Program t value will be negative whenever the mean of the program group is smaller than the mean of the control group. If $\overline{X}_P = 3.00$ and $\overline{X}_C = 3.50$, then $(\overline{X}_1 - \overline{X}_2) = (3.00 - 3.50) = -.50$. A negative result is desirable whenever a low score indicates a good outcome, such as absenteeism, dissatisfaction, number of errors, or response time. You want outcomes like these to be lower in the program group. On the other hand, when a high score indicates a good outcome, as it would for employee morale, then a negative Program t value indicates a potentially harmful program, one that produced poorer results than occurred in the control group. Thus when conducting a t-test, you must know whether a low or high score indicates a good outcome and which group had the higher mean. When you expect a lower score in the Program Group, as for absenteeism, look for a negative Program t value.

Here are two reminders:

- Evaluators find the Table t value in the Table of t Values, and it reflects the impact of random sampling error by itself.
- Evaluators calculate the Program t value from the scores of employees in the program and control groups, and it reflects the impact of the program and random sampling error combined.

To conduct a t test, compare the Program t value to the Table t value. Because the table lists only positive values, compare the absolute value of the Program t value to the Table t value. The absolute value of a number is simply the number with a positive sign—

the absolute value of both −5 and 5 is 5. Absolute values are always positive numbers. Two vertical lines around the number indicate absolute value: $|-5| = 5$. In comparing the Program t value to the Table t value, we will use the abbreviation |Program t value| to mean the absolute value of the Program t value. However, use the absolute value of the Program t value only long enough to compare it to the Table t value. All other times, a negative Program t value should have its negative sign. This is important in computing, reporting and interpreting the results of a t test.

The t test has two decision rules:

- If |Program t value| exceeds the Table t value, the program had an impact beyond that expected from random sampling error.
- If |Program t value| equals or is less than the Table t value, the program may or may not be effective, you cannot say either way.

We can shorten these rules further by using the mathematical abbreviations > for exceeds or "is greater than," and ≤ for "less than or equal to." In these terms, when |Program t value| > the Table t value, you can conclude that the program created the program outcome, with $p < .05$ or $p < .01$ risk that you would be wrong in this conclusion, depending on which column of the Table of t Values you used. Conversely, if |Program t value| ≤ the Table t value, you can reach no firm conclusion, the program may or not be effective. You cannot conclude that the program is effective because the Program t value may reflect random sampling error. Nor can you conclude that the program is ineffective because a better study—larger sample sizes or smaller standard deviations—may detect a program impact. The program's impact, if any, is masked by the impact of random sampling error.

State the conclusion of a t test using the name of the program and the program outcome, in past tense. If assessing whether an incentive program increased productivity, for example, and you found that |Program t value| > the Table t value, you would write the following conclusion:

- Employees who participated in an incentive program displayed higher productivity than employees who did not participate in an incentive program.

On the other hand, if you found that |Program t value| ≤ the Table t value, you could conclude the following:

- We cannot say whether or not employees who participated in an incentive program displayed higher productivity than employees who did not participate in an incentive program.

Now let's conduct a t test for our example in which a manager assessed the impact of a sales training program on the motivation level of the sales force. The mean motivation of the sixteen employees in the program group was 4.3, and the mean motivation of the sixteen employees in the control group was 3.2, signaling an apparent program impact. We need to conduct a t test to determine if the apparent program impact is typical of that produced by random sampling error or whether it represents the impact of the training program as well.

We need three pieces of information from the scores in each group to calculate the Program t value: the means, standard deviations, and degrees of freedom. As previously noted, the means are 4.3 and 3.2, and let's say the standard deviations obtained by computer are 1.60 and 1.55 for the program group and the control group, respectively. Finally, since there are sixteen employees in each group, $df = 16 + 16 - 2 = 30$. Given these values, the computer produced a Program t value of 1.80, reflecting the impact of random sampling error and the program combined.

Next, we should determine the Table t value for $df = 30$ to ascertain the amount of random sampling error expected for samples of this size. Consult the Table of t values in Appendix 2 or the relevant portion of the table presented in Table 7.3. Trace down the column headed *df* (degrees of freedom) until you come to the number 30. Now trace across to the right and find the number 2.042, the boldfaced value in the table. This is the amount of random sampling error you can expect 95 percent of the time. More random sampling error than this is rare, arising with probability less than .05 as indicated by the heading of the column.

Now the pivotal question is, does |Program t value| exceed the Table t value (e.g., does 1.80 exceed 2.042)? It does not, and consequently, no conclusion can be drawn either way about the effectiveness of the program. Because it does not exceed 2.042, an apparent program impact represented by 1.80 is typical of the impacts of random sampling error expected 95 percent of the time. There are two possibilities: There may be no program impact, only random sampling error, or there could be a program impact that is obscured by random sampling error. For example, larger sample sizes may reduce the sampling error enough to detect it. So this t test should have the

Table 7.3
Table of t Values

	Probability Level	
df	**.05**	**.01**
⋮	⋮	⋮
22	2.074	2.819
23	2.069	2.807
24	2.064	2.797
25	2.060	2.787
26	2.056	2.779
27	2.052	2.771
28	2.048	2.763
29	2.045	2.756
30	**2.042**	2.750

following conclusion: We cannot say whether or not employees who participated in the sales training program had higher motivation than employees who did not.

One final point. The evaluator should specify the probability level (.05 or .01) before data analysis, based on how important it is to be 95 percent confident or 99 percent confident in the correctness of the decisions to be made. For example, if a program is very costly to implement, an evaluator may want a 99 percent level of confidence and would use the right-hand column in the Table of t values, headed .01. In the absence of such considerations, evaluators adopt the .05 level of probability, by convention.

This is a good point to stop and summarize the logic underlying the t test. The t test compares two t values. The Program t value, computed from the scores of the employees in the program and control groups, reflects the combined impact of random sampling error and the program. The Table t value, found in the Table of t Values, reflects the impact of random sampling error by itself. When the absolute value of the Program t value exceeds the Table t value, you can

In this corner, weighing 390 lbs, The Influence of the Program and Random Sampling Error Combined. And in the far corner, at 90 lbs, The Influence of the Program by itself.

conclude that the program has an impact with probability less than .05 or .01 of being mistaken in your conclusion. Otherwise, you can make no firm conclusion.

Learning Module 7.2, Conducting t tests, gives you practice conducting t tests and explains a few special situations that can arise. Completing this Learning Module carefully should be a high priority. Feel free to review the previous material as you complete the Learning Module.

LEARNING MODULE 7.2: Conducting t tests

This learning module describes four program assessment situations and provides sufficient information for you to conduct a t test on each. Your task is to supply any missing information in each situation and conduct a t test. State the conclusion of the t test in terms of the effects, if any, that the program had on the outcome measure. For example, your result might be: "Employees who received safety training had fewer accidents than employees who did not receive training." If the Program t value did not exceed the Table t value, your statement would be: "It cannot be concluded whether employees who received safety training had fewer accidents than employees who did not receive training."

The information in the suggested answers following each situation is cumulative, containing suggestions that could be useful in the next situation. After you have completed Situation 1, read its suggested answer, then complete Situation 2 and read its suggested answer, and so on.

Situation 1

A manager wanted to see if company secretaries would be more satisfied with new word processing software when used by itself or when used with voice recognition capability. The computers of 17 secretaries, chosen randomly, were upgraded with the new word processing software and voice recognition capability. The computers of the 15 remaining secretaries were upgraded only with the new word processing software. All secretaries received individual instruction in the use of their computer's new features. Four months later, all secretaries completed a survey about their satisfaction with their computer's new features. Partial results of the analysis are presented below. Please supply the degrees of freedom, the Table t value, and a conclusion based on the t test.

WITH VOICE RECOGNITION	**WITHOUT VOICE RECOGNITION**
$n_P = 17$	$n_C = 15$
$\overline{X}_P = 3.30$	$\overline{X}_C = 3.08$

Program t = 2.12

df = Table t = (at .05)

Conclusion:

Answer to Situation 1

An initial step is to visually examine ($\overline{X}_P - \overline{X}_C$) for an apparent program impact. The difference between the means is 3.30 − 3.08 = .22 on a five-point scale, showing an apparent program impact. The means differ by more than one-fifth step on a five-point scale. The question is, does this difference exceed that expected by random sampling error? The t test addresses this question. The t test compares two t values, the Program t, calculated from the data and representing the combined impact of the program and random sampling error, and the Table t, derived from probability theory and representing the impact of random sampling error by itself. If the absolute value of the Program t value exceeds the Table t value, that is if |Program t value| > the Table t value, you can conclude that the program had an impact; otherwise, you can make no conclusion either way. The conclusion should be stated in terms of the impact of the program on the program outcome.

You may have noticed that the program group contained two more secretaries than did the control group and wondered if this presents a problem. Unequal sample sizes do not present a problem when comparing means because the sum of each set of scores is divided by its sample size. This makes the means directly comparable, even if the sums are not.

The Program t value obtained by computer is 2.12, and $df = n_P + n_C - 2 = (17 + 15 - 2) = 30$. For 30 degrees of freedom, the Table t value at the .05 level of probability is 2.042. This number is found in the Table of t Values by tracing down the column headed *df* until you find the number 30. Now move right on the same line to find 2.042 in the column headed .05. The Program t value exceeds the Table t value, that is, |2.12| > 2.042, indicating that the apparent program impact is

Table 7.4
Effect of Voice Recognition (VR) on Satisfaction of Secretaries

	n	$\overline{X}$	*s*	*t*
With VR	17	3.30	.294	2.12*
Without VR	15	3.08	.293	

$^*p < .05$

greater than that expected from random sampling error alone. We can conclude that the program had an impact. The conclusion, however, should be stated in terms of the effect of the program on the outcome measure: The word processor with voice recognition produced higher secretary satisfaction than the word processor without voice recognition. Evaluators often summarize the results of a t test as is done in Table 7.4. The t value in Table 7.4 is the Program t value (including the minus sign when it is negative). If the Program t value had not exceeded the Table t value, the letters *ns* (for nonsignificant) replace the asterisk.

Situation 2

Of forty-two clerical typists reassigned to one of two typing pools, twenty-one, selected randomly, were assigned to the first typing pool. This group was allowed to select the starting time of their eight-hour work day, but it had to be between 6:30 and 10:00 A.M. Moreover, they could change their starting time every three months if they chose. The remaining twenty-one clerical typists were assigned to the second typing facility. They began their eight-hour work day as usual, at either 8:00 or 8:30 A.M., as set by their supervisor. A manager wanted to learn if the time flexibility would increase productivity as measured by the number of pages produced per hour by each employee. Partial results of the analysis are presented below. Please supply the degrees of freedom, the Table t value, and a conclusion for the t test.

FLEX TIME **NORMAL TIME**

$\overline{X}_P = 15.6$ $\overline{X}_C = 15.0$

Program t = 2.021

df = Table t =
(at .05)

Conclusion:

Answer to Situation 2

Here the program is flextime, allowing employees to choose when their work day begins. The outcome measure is productivity, the number of pages produced by each employee per hour. The difference between the means (15.6 − 15.0 = .6) is small (6 tenths of a page). The question is, does this difference exceed that expected by random sampling error. It is so small it may not. To find out, we need to compare the Program t value to the Table t value.

The Program t value produced by computer is 2.021. You had to look at the description of the situation to see that the sample sizes were twenty-one in each group. Accordingly, $df = 21 + 21 - 2 = 40$, and the Table t value at the .05 level of probability is 2.021. What can we conclude when the Program t value is equal to the Table t value? Being equal does not *exceed.* Unless |Program t| exceeds the Table t value, you cannot conclude whether the program had an impact. State your position in terms of the program and its outcome measure: It cannot be determined if flextime increased productivity.

Situation 3

A manager surveyed the satisfaction of twenty-five clients, selected randomly, who were serviced by a unit of the organization that used quality control circles, and another twenty-five clients, selected randomly, who were serviced by a similar unit of the organization that used MBO (management by objectives). The clients responded to questions on a five-point scale, where 5 indicates high satisfaction with service. Please supply the degrees of freedom, the Table t value, and a conclusion for the t test.

QC	**MBO**
$n_{QC} = 25$	$n_{MBO} = 25$
$\bar{X}_{QC} = 3.27$	$\bar{X}_{MBO} = 3.16$

Program t = 1.05

$df =$ Table t = (at .05)

Conclusion:

Answer to Situation 3

This Program Assessment compared two programs to each other, rather than a program to a control group. The manager wanted to discover whether quality circles or management by objectives produced higher client satisfaction. The t test that compares one program to another proceeds exactly as when comparing a program group to a control group. The apparent program impact (3.27 − 3.16 = .11) is small, however, and may not exceed that expected from random sampling error. The Program t value is 1.05, and $df = 48$. What is the Table t value at the .05 level for $df = 48$? You probably noticed that the degrees of freedom in the Table of t Values skip from 40 to 60, and 48 is in between. What should you do? When this happens, use the smaller *df* (in this case 40). Using the larger degrees of freedom would inappropriately base the t test on a larger sample size than you had. Because the t values for 40 and 60 degrees of freedom are very close (2.021 and 2.000, respectively), using the smaller degrees of freedom seldom changes the outcome of the t test. When it does, you can find a more detailed Table of t Values. For $df = 40$, the Table t value is 2.021. Now what is the result of the t test? The Program t value (1.05) does not exceed the Table t value (2.021). Your position must be that you cannot conclude whether quality control circles or management by objectives produced higher client satisfaction.

Situation 4

The human resources officer of an organization wanted to discover if comprehension is higher when employees receive personal instruction (PI) than when they listen to instructional tapes (IT) in their car during commutes. Twenty-four randomly selected employees received training by a personal instructor, and another twenty-four randomly selected employees received instructional cassette tapes to play in their car. All employees completed a one-hundred-item examination. Please supply the degrees of freedom, the Table t value at the .01 level of probability, and a conclusion for the t test.

PERSONAL INSTRUCTION	**INSTRUCTIONAL TAPES**
$n_{PI} = 24$	$n_{IT} = 24$
$\bar{X}_{PI} = 79.4$	$\bar{X}_{IT} = 84.2$

Program t = −2.99

df =

Table t =
(at .01)

Conclusion:

Answer to Situation 4

This program assessment also compares the effectiveness of two programs: personal instruction versus instructional tapes. The outcome measure is employee comprehension, with a high score indicating high comprehension. An apparent program impact exists, but to the evaluator's surprise, favoring the second program, instructional tapes. Verify for yourself that the mean for the second program is larger than the mean of the first program. One should always inspect the means before interpreting the results. The Program t value is −2.99, and the Table t value at the .01 level of probability for $df = 46$ is 2.704 (based on $df = 40$ and using the column headed .01, as instructed). You no doubt noticed that the Program t value is a negative number. This can occur because the formula for the t value subtracts one mean from the other mean. The result will be negative whenever the first mean is smaller then the second mean, as it is here. To address this possibility, we use the absolute value of the Program t value and proceed as usual. The absolute value of −2.99 is 2.99, and 2.99 exceeds 2.704. Therefore, we should conclude that instructional tapes produced higher employee comprehension than personal instruction. Remember that we use the absolute value of the Program t value only to compare it to the Table t value. The Program t value is still negative and should be reported as such. Reporting the negative Program t value will signal the reader that the first mean is smaller than the second mean. Remember also that the interpretation of the Program t value depends both on which group has the larger mean and on whether a high or a low score reflects effectiveness. In the present case, a high score is good, signaling higher comprehension. The second program was the more effective because it had the higher mean. Conversely, had the outcome measure been rate of errors, for which a low score is good, we would have concluded that the first program, personal instruction, with its lower mean, is the more effective program. Therefore, always draw conclusions from a t test based both on which group has the higher mean and whether a high or low mean is good. This advice holds whether the Program t value is positive or negative.

Summary

The suggested answers to the program assessment situations presented seven guidelines to help you conduct a t test appropriately.

1. Means based on unequal sample sizes are still directly comparable.
2. When *df* lies between two *df* values in the table, use the smaller *df*.
3. To conclude there is a program impact, the Program t value must exceed, not just equal, the Table t value.

4. Compare one program to another the same way you compare a program group to a control group.
5. When a Program t value is negative, its absolute value must exceed the Table t value.
6. Base conclusions from a t test both on which group has the higher mean and whether a high or low mean is good.
7. State the conclusion of a t test in terms of the impact of the program on the program outcome.

END OF LEARNING MODULE 7.2

Significant and Important Program Impacts. When |Program t value| > the Table t value, the results of the t test are statistically significant. A significant t test simply means that the Program t value exceeds the Table t value at a specified probability, say .05. In turn, we can conclude that the program impact is no longer apparent; it is real, more than expected from random sampling error. But because the results of a t test are significant does not mean that they are important.[5] Important results interest decision makers. For example, a program impact of two steps on a five-point scale of job satisfaction would interest most decision makers. In contrast, finding that satisfaction improved from 2.55 to 2.60 on a five-point scale would impress few decision makers. Yet, with large enough sample sizes, a t test can distinguish program impacts this small from random sampling error. Appreciate that program impacts large and small can produce significant t tests, and by itself the t test sheds no light on the magnitude of the results—and thus on their practical importance to decision makers—other than to indicate that they exceed random sampling error at a specified level of probability. This raises the issue of how to judge when results are important.

To gauge the importance of the results of a t test, transform the Program t value to a correlation coefficient with the following formula:

$$r = \sqrt{\frac{t^2}{t^2 + df}}$$

where r is a special case of the Pearson correlation, called the point biserial correlation, and df and t are the degrees of freedom and the Program t value from the t test, respectively.[6] This correlation reflects the relationship between (a) employee absence or membership in the program and (b) the level of the outcome. When comparing two programs, the correlation reflects the relationship between (a) employee membership in one program or the other and (b) the level of the outcome. Cohen has identified correlations associated with small, medium, and large effect sizes from research findings in a variety of fields.[7] These are the effect sizes used to determine adequate sample sizes as discussed in Chapter 6. Unless theory or previous research suggest specific criteria, use the following correlations, designated weak, moderate, and strong, as general guidelines for interpreting the importance of results

	Weak	**Moderate**	**Strong**
r	**.10**	**.24**	**.37**

where larger correlations suggest more important results. While these correlations seem small, Cohen reminds us that it is the separation between the program group mean and the control group mean that is weak, moderate, or strong.[8]

The results of meta-analyses show the practical importance of even moderate relationships. In a meta-analysis, the researcher examines the body of research on a relationship of interest and applies specific procedures to the correlations reported in those studies. The goal is to derive the actual relationship based on this body of evidence. Correlations between most organizational variables are often moderate in size. Table 7.5 gives several examples.

Although most of these relationships are moderate, our practical experience suggests they are important. You should transform any significant t test to a correlation to discover the strength of the relationship between the program and its outcome measure, and by that its importance. Conversely, do not transform a nonsignificant t test.

Let's review the t tests in Learning Module 7.2 with an eye toward the importance of their results. The t test in Situation 1 was statistically significant, and its value *r* is

$$r = \sqrt{\frac{(2.12)^2}{(2.12)^2 + 30}}$$

$$= \sqrt{\frac{4.49}{4.49 + 30}}$$

$$= \sqrt{\frac{4.49}{34.49}}$$

$$\sqrt{.13}$$
$$= .36$$

A correlation of .36 suggests a moderate relationship between secretaries having or not having voice recognition and their level of satisfaction. This impact would interest most decision makers. Since the t tests in Situations 2 and 3 were not statistically significant, their t values should not be changed to *r* values. Finally, the correlation for the t test in Situation 4 is .40, suggesting a strong relationship between employees receiving personal or audio instruction and employee comprehension. Please verify this for yourself with a calculator. The formula uses the actual *df* and the program t value. Decisions makers may decide to favor the lower costs of audio instruction over the more expensive personal instruction, given this strong relationship.

Table 7.5
Relationships Found Through Meta-Analyses

r	Relationship	Number of Indices	Number of Studies	Total Sample
−.11	Employee lateness and general job satisfaction	15	15	3767
−.29	Employee lateness and organizational commitment[9]	8	8	3140
.255	Rehearsal and mental performance	62	35	3214
.364	Rehearsal and physical performance[10]	39	Overall	Overall
.27	Employee work experience and subsequent job performance[11]	44	22	25,911
.31	Employee job satisfaction and employee job performance[12]	20	20	3140
.33	Absence and turnover[13]	33	17	5316
.55	Quality of boss-employee working relationship and employee job performance[14]	12	12	1909

It's been four days and Stan hasn't remembered—You can't judge the importance of a t until you convert it to an r value.

Assumptions of the t test. Finally, we should consider any assumptions made about the data when we compare a program group to a control group. We will also note what to do when the data do not meet these assumptions. The assumptions ensure that the Program t value is derived on the same basis as the Table t values. Otherwise, comparisons to the Table t values can produce incorrect conclusions.

The first assumption is that the data are drawn from people in a random sample of the whole or from people assigned randomly to groups. The laws of probability theory are founded on this assumption. The procedures to form a random sample in Chapter 6 satisfy this assumption.

The second assumption is that the scores on the outcome measure are normally distributed. Among other characteristics, a normally distributed distribution is bell shaped and symmetrical. The normality assumption ensures the independence of the indices of random sampling error in the numerator and in the denominator of the formula for the Program t value, as required by the properties of the t distribution.[15]

The third assumption is that the spread of the scores is the same within all treatment populations. The assumption of equal spread is needed because the denominator of the formula for the Program t value "pools" the spread of the scores from each group to form a combined average spread of the scores. Whereas using the combined spread is statistically superior to using individual indices of spread,[16] when pooled, it can be shown that the t test actually divides s_P^2 by n_C and divides s_C^2 by n_P.[17] This presents no problem as long as $s_P^2 = s_C^2$ and thus the assumption of equal spread. When s_P^2 doesn't equal s_C^2, the Program t value is no longer distributed as *t* and comparisons to the Table *t* Values can produce incorrect conclusions.

Fortunately, statisticians have ample evidence that reasonably large and equal, or nearly equal, sample sizes insure that we can proceed confidently with a t test even when the normality assumption or equal-spread assumption is grossly violated.[18] Sample sizes recommended in Chapter 6 yield sample data for which we can safely ignore these two assumptions. When one sample size is markedly different from the other, say one is 20 and one is 60, or when both are small, say each is less than 20, then violating these assumptions can produce incorrect conclusions when using the Table of t Values.

When sample sizes are markedly unequal or less than 20, evaluators should use t' (t prime) in place of the usual Program t value and df' in place of df.[19] In all other respects, we conduct the t test as before. Referred to as the Behrens-Fisher t test with Welch's solution for degrees of freedom, the formula for t' divides each standard deviation by its own sample size. This modification of the t is quite tolerant of even gross violations of the assumptions underlying the t test, even with small or unequal sample sizes.[20] Both t' and df' are efficiently obtained by computer. Moreover, researchers can use t' instead of t for all t tests, with little loss of power but with substantial safeguard against violation of the assumptions underlying the t test.

Although it doesn't produce an exact solution in either case, it is sensible to treat t' as if it were the conventional t when determining an appropriate sample size and when determining the importance of a significant test. That is, use the procedures discussed in Chapter 6 for sample size, and transform t' to an r in the usual way to assess its importance.

To find an application of t', we have only to return to Learning Module 7.2. The sample sizes in Situation 1 are unequal and less than 20. We need to be concerned about violating the assumptions of the t test here and should use t' and df' in place of t and df. Let's see how this would work. Assume the computer results found that $t' = 3.01$ and $df' = 22$. Now you proceed as you would with any t test. For $df' = 22$, the Table t value at the .05 level of probability is 2.074. Since $|3.01| > 2.074$, you can conclude that the apparent program impact exceeds that expected from random sampling error, and thus, that secretaries were more satisfied with word processors with voice recognition than without it. For $t' = 3.01$ and $df' = 22$, $r = 0.54$, suggesting a strong relationship between use of voice recognition technology and secretary satisfaction.

Finally, we will examine the t test for comparing a program group to a norm or quota. The procedure is quite similar to comparing groups.

Comparing the Program Group to a Norm

Sometimes the objective of a program assessment is to compare the program group to a norm or quota. For example, an evaluator may want to compare a group of supervisors who have received training in conflict resolution to the national norm for this skill.

Although the formulas for df and the Program t value differ slightly, we conduct the t test to compare a program group to a norm the same way that we compare a program group to a control group. The formula for degrees of freedom is based on the number of people in the program group and is simply $n_p - 1$. We assume the national norm group is based on a whole, not a sample, and thus it requires no degrees of freedom.

In the formula for the t test, the norm or quota replaces the mean of the control group and an apparent program impact is shown by ($\overline{X}_P$ − norm). The formula for the Program t value for comparing a program group to a national norm is

$$t = \frac{\overline{X}_P - norm}{\sqrt{\frac{s_P^2}{n_P}}}$$

where n_P is the number of employees in the program group and $\overline{X}_P$ and s_P are the mean and standard deviation, respectively, of the program group scores. Since the computer can efficiently compute the value of the Program t value, we present it here only to highlight a few of its features. The numerator contains the apparent program impact as ($\overline{X}_P$ − norm), and the denominator contains the average spread of the scores around the mean of the program group. The numerator and denominator represent two, independent indices of random sampling error where the index in the numerator is "inflated" by whatever impact the program has. We can represent the Program t as

$$\frac{P + RSE}{RSE}$$

where *P* refers to the impact of the program (in this case training) and each *RSE* refers to independent estimates of random sampling error. The impact of both the program and random sampling error are initially intertwined and indistinguishable.

Let's see how to conduct a t test for comparing a program group to a norm. Assume you have seen it reported that the national norm of conflict resolution skills for supervisors is 65 out of a possible score of 100, based on a standardized test of conflict resolution skills. After training in conflict resolution techniques, 25 supervisors, selected randomly from the supervisors at a large agency, completed the standardized survey of conflict resolution skills. The mean of their scores was 70, with a standard deviation of 3.60.

We want to know if the training program increased the supervisors' skills above the national norm? There is an apparent program impact, indicated by ($\overline{X}_P$ − norm) = (70 − 65) = 5. The Program t value, obtained by computer, is 6.94. For $df = n_P - 1 = (25 - 1) = 24$, the Table t value at the .05 level of probability is 2.064 (please verify this for yourself). The Program t value (6.94) exceeds the Table t value (2.064) at the .05 probability level. We can conclude that the conflict resolution training increased the supervisors' skills in conflict resolution above the national norm.

A significant t test indicates that the program impact exceeds that expected from random sampling error but sheds no light on whether the outcome is an important one, one that would interest decision makers. Unfortunately, there is no counterpart in correlation for this t test, and thus there is no statistical way to interpret the importance of a significant result. Instead, this determination must be based on the researcher's knowledge of theory, previous research, and experience.

Finally, we will consider any assumptions about the data when we compare a program group to a norm or quota. The assumptions ensure that we derive the Program t value on the same basis as the Table t values. Otherwise, comparisons of the Program t value to the Table t value can produce incorrect conclusions.

We make two assumptions about the data. The first assumption is that the sample of the program target group is random, as required by probability theory. The second assumption is that the data are normally distributed, forming a symmetrical, bell-shaped curve. This ensures the independence of the estimates of random sampling error in the numerator and the denominator of the formula of the Program t value.

Fortunately, the t test for comparing a program group to a norm is tolerant of even gross departures from the normality assumption with samples larger than thirty.[21] Researchers who use the tables presented in Chapter 6 to determine sample size can proceed with confidence.

Main Points of Chapter 7

- Random samples, while representative of the whole, do not mirror it exactly. The departure from what would be observed of everyone is called random sampling error.
- Whereas random sampling minimizes random sampling error, it does not eliminate it, and evaluators can mistake the remaining error for a program impact.
- Three pieces of information about the scores are needed to distinguish a program impact from random sampling error:

The mean identifies the typical employee score on the outcome measure; the standard deviation identifies the average spread of the scores around the mean; degrees of freedom is the number of scores that are independent of one another.

- A t test distinguishes a program impact from that of random sampling error by comparing two t values.
- The Table t value is derived from probability theory and reflects the impact of random sampling error by itself.
- The Program t value is calculated from the scores of the employees and reflects the impact of random sampling error and the program combined.
- The program has an impact beyond that expected from random sampling error if |Program t| > the Table t, with .05 (or .01) risk of a wrong decision.
- Transforming a statistically significant Program t value to an r value to gauge the strength of the relationship between the program and the outcome measure.
- Using t' and df' provides confidence that the Table t value is appropriate when sample sizes are markedly unequal or less than 20.
- Except for the computation of df and the Program t value, the t test for comparing a program group to a norm parallels that for comparing a program group to a control group.

Chapter Notes

1. Summing the squared deviations from the mean, $\Sigma(X - \bar{X})^2$, as is done in calculating the standard deviation, produces a smaller value than summing the squared deviations from any other number, such as the median. Due to random sampling error, the mean of the sample is likely to be different than the mean of the program target group, and summing the squared deviations from this different value would produce a larger value. Thus $\Sigma(X - \bar{X})^2$ will be smaller than Σ(X − *the program target audience mean*)^2, and thus underestimate the standard deviation of the program target group. Dividing by $n - 1$ instead of n enlarges the sample standard deviation enough to make it a better estimate of the standard deviation of the program target group. See Paul

Games, *Elementary Statistics: Data Analysis for the Behavioral Sciences.* New York: McGraw Hill, 1967, p. 143.

2. I should note two minor sources of inaccuracy contained in our coin demonstration, but they needn't detract from its visual usefulness. First, we summed distances instead of squaring them, as specified in the formula, and second, our coins scattered in any direction, whereas employee scores scatter above and below the mean in a linear fashion. But the visual image of scattered coins is useful to triggering a memory of the central feature of the standard deviation, that it reflects the average degree to which scores scatter around the mean.
3. Gene V. Glass and Julian C. Stanley, *Statistical Methods in Education and Psychology.* Englewood Cliffs, NJ: Prentice Hall, 1970. p. 295.
4. Table t values are presented for a nondirectional (two-tailed) t test. A directional (one-tailed) t test, wherein the probability level is doubled based on a theoretical prediction, is less robust to violations of assumptions that underlie the t test and preclude interpreting results in the unpredicted direction. See Glass and Stanley, *Statistical Methods in Education and Psychology.* Englewood Cliffs, NJ: Prentice-Hall, 1970, pp 289, 295.
5. Paul A. Games and George R. Klare, *Elementary Statistics: Data Analysis for the Behavioral Sciences.* New York: McGraw-Hill, 1967, pp 422–24.
6. Herbert Friedman, Magnitude of experimental effect and a table for its rapid estimation. *Psychological Bulletin,* 1968, *70,* 245–251.
7. Jacob Cohen, *Statistical Power Analysis for the Behavioral Sciences.* New York: Academic Press, 1969, pp 22–25.
8. Cohen, p. 24.
9. Meni Koslowsky, Abraham Sagie, Moshe Krausz, and Ahuva Dolman Singer, Correlates of employee lateness: Some theoretical considerations. *Journal of Applied Psychology,* 1977, *82,* 79–88.
10. James E. Driskell, Carolyn Cooper, and Aidan Moran, Does mental practice enhance performance? *Journal of Applied Psychology,* 1994, *79,* 481–492.

11. Miguel A. Quiñones, J. Kevin Ford, and Mark S. Teachout, The relationship between work experience and job performance: A conceptual and meta-analytic review. *Personnel Psychology*, 1995, *48,* 887–910.
12. M. M. Petty, Gail W. McGee, and Jerry W. Cavender, A meta-analysis of the relationships between individual job satisfaction and individual performance. *Academy of Management Review*, 1984, *9*, 712–721.
13. Atul Mitra, G. Douglas Jenkins, Jr., and Nina Gupta, A meta-analytic review of the relationship between absence and turnover. *Journal of Applied Psychology*, 1992, *77*, 879–889.
14. Charlotte R. Gerstner and David V. Day, Meta-analytic review of leader-member exchange theory: Correlates and construct issues. *Journal of Applied Psychology*, 1997, *82*, 827–844.
15. William L. Hays and Robert L. Winkler, *Statistics: Probability, Inference, and Decision,* vol. 1. New York: Holt, Rinehart and Winston, 1970, p. 337.
16. Hays and Winkler, p. 324.
17. Paul A. Games, Lecture material, The Pennsylvania State University, 1974.
18. B. J. Winer, *Statistical Principles in Experimental Design.* 2nd ed., New York: McGraw-Hill, 1971, pp 37–38; C. A. Boneau, The effects of violations of assumptions underlying the t test. *Psychological Bulletin*, 1960, *57*, 49–65.
19. Winer, p. 42.
20. Paul A. Games, Lecture material, The Pennsylvania State University, 1974.
21. Games, p. 306.

8

Matching Tests and Designs

Chapter Preview

In this chapter, we revisit assessment designs and t tests. Assessment design, you will remember, controls extraneous error, and the t test addresses random sampling error. We will identify designs for which the t test is appropriate and introduce more general procedures for the remaining designs. We will also examine a few additional designs.

Learning Objectives

After reading Chapter 8, you should be able to:

- identify assessment designs for which the t test is appropriate
- explain why other designs require more general procedures
- identify the steps to conduct an analysis of covariance
- identify the steps to conduct an analysis of time-series data
- identify the steps to conduct an analysis of variance
- identify the steps to conduct the Bonferroni t test
- identify the steps to conduct Hotellings T^2 test
- identify which procedures are appropriate for each assessment design

The Focus of Chapter 8

The program assessment step discussed in this chapter, along with its corresponding component in the Scientific Model, is highlighted below.

The Steps of Program Assessment

1. Involve stakeholders throughout the assessment.
2. Specify the expected program outcome.
3. Establish a measure of the program outcome.
4. Plan a method of gathering data.
5. Collect the data.
6. Analyze the data.
7. Communicate the results.
8. Make program decisions.

The Scientific Model of Program Assessment

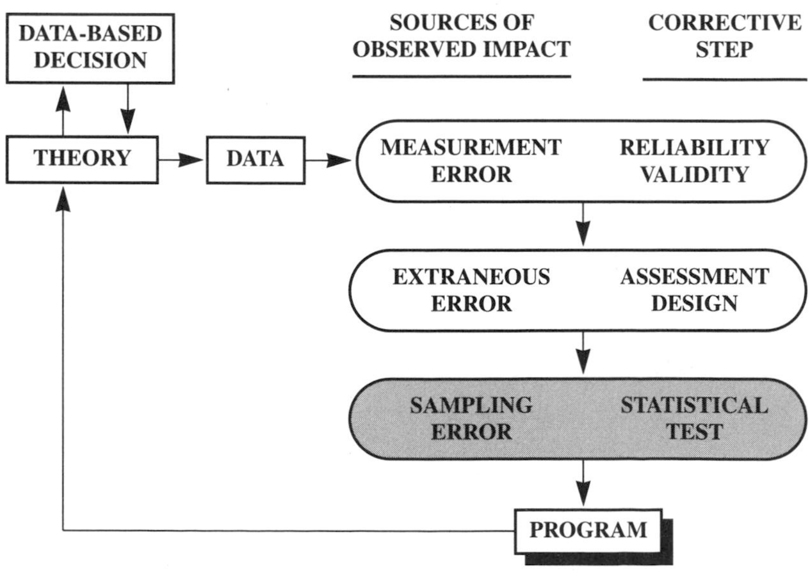

In Chapter 7, we used the t test to determine whether the impact of a program exceeded that expected from random sampling error. We applied the t test to compare the mean of a program group to the mean of a control group, to the mean of a second program, or to a norm or quota. The t test requires random assignment of employees to groups, such as we find in the true assessment designs discussed in Chapter 5. We will now see that more general procedures should be used for true assessment designs that have pretests. Nonetheless, because true assessment designs provide excellent protection against both extraneous error and random sampling error, they are highly recommended and should be used whenever feasible.

As we know, forming a control group or randomly assigning employees to groups is not always practical. Providing substantial protection against extraneous error, quasi-assessment designs meet this need. Without the benefit of random assignment, however, analysis of data from quasi-assessment designs also requires more general procedures.

Moreover, evaluators sometimes want to compare the effectiveness of multiple programs. For example, an assessment may compare the amount of learning that occurred within three training formats: full interactive format, where employees interact directly with the presenter, video conference format, where employees in a remote location interact with the presenter via interactive television, and video playback format, where employees watch a video of the training program. The evaluator may want to compare the amount of learning that occurred in each method to the others, producing three comparisons:[1]

Full Interactive	vs.	Video Conference
Full Interactive	vs.	Video Playback
Video Conference	vs.	Video Playback

One option is to conduct three t tests, one for each comparison. However, applying the t test more than once inflates α, the significance level, beyond the level specified for each test. For example, if set at .05 for each comparison, α may actuality exceed this amount after all three tests are completed. Table 8.1 shows that a .05 α level quickly swells above .05 if we conduct multiple t tests, even though α is held at .05 in each individual test.

Multiple t tests quickly inflate alpha.[2] Nonetheless, conducting a set of t tests is appropriate when evaluators have specific, theoretical predictions to test. Called planned comparisons, these t tests

Table 8.1
Effects of Multiple t tests on the Probability Level α = .05

# t tests	1	2	3	4	5	6	7	8
α	.05	.0975	.1426	.1855	.2262	.2649	.3017	.3366

examine only the theory-predicted comparisons. Even if additional comparisons could be made, they are not if not specified by theory. For example, a theory may predict that

1. More learning occurs in full interactive than in video conference format
2. More learning occurs in video conference than in video playback format

The evaluator would test these two predictions. The evaluator would not test the remaining comparison—video conference versus video playback—even if the means looked different. Such "after the fact" tests capitalize on chance, giving greater likelihood of finding a significant difference than specified for each test as Table 8.1 shows.

More general procedures are required in the absence of specific, theoretical predictions, especially when the evaluator would be interested in all differences that may exist. The procedures search for differences anywhere among a set of means while holding α at a specified level.

Evaluators sometimes want to assess a program's impact on multiple program outcomes. For example, compared to video playback, the evaluator may expect full interactive training to produce both higher learning and higher satisfaction with the training session. Again, more general procedures are required to analyze multiple program outcomes.

Fortunately, the logic of the more general procedures often parallels that of the t test. That is, we compare a Program value to a Table value, the former representing the effects of the program and random sampling error combined, the latter representing the effects of random sampling error only. If the Program value exceeds the Table value, we attribute the impact to the Program instead of chance. Thus, the more general procedures require little in the way of learning fundamentally new ways of thinking about data analysis.

True Assessment Designs

Because they randomly assign employees to groups, true assessment designs are amenable to powerful statistical procedures to distinguish the influence of the program from that of random sampling error. The simplest of these designs, discussed next, uses the t test.

Equivalent Groups Observation Design

This design assigns employees randomly to one group that receives the program and one group that does not, and both groups are observed on the outcome measure after the program:

$$\begin{array}{lll} RG_1 & P & O_1 \\ RG_2 & & O_2 \end{array}$$

As we saw in Chapter 7, we conduct a t test on the scores in O_1 and O_2 and transform a significant outcome to an r value to determine its practical importance.

We can also compare the effectiveness of onc program to another:

$$\begin{array}{lll} RG_1 & P_1 & O_1 \\ RG_2 & P_2 & O_2 \end{array}$$

For example, we could compare a monetary incentive (P_1) to a release time incentive (P_2) to discover which motivates employees to higher productivity. We would again conduct a t test on the scores in O_1 and O_2.

This simple design guards against both extraneous error and random sampling error and is highly recommended whenever employees can be assigned randomly to groups.

Equivalent Groups Pre- and Postobservation Design

This design assigns employees randomly to one group that receives the program and one group that does not, and the outcome measure is observed before and after the program:

$$\begin{array}{llll} RG_1 & O_1 & P & O_2 \\ RG_2 & O_3 & & O_4 \end{array}$$

The addition of a pretest provides two possible advantages over the simpler, previous design. First, it allows one to gauge whether more improvement occurred in the program group than in the control group. To do this, the evaluator computes a difference score ($d = O_1 - O_2$) for each employee before conducting the t test. Specifically, for each employee in the program group, a new score is computed, called *d*, by subtracting the person's score in O_2 from his or her score in O_1. In the same manner, a *d* score is computed for each employee in the control group. Then the t test is conducted on the two sets of difference scores. This analysis attempts to determine whether more change occurred among employees in the program group than in the control group. The results of this t test are reported in the usual way, and significant results are transformed to an *r* value to assess practical importance.

Unfortunately, change scores are substantially less reliable than the original measures. More specifically, the measurement reliability of change scores is the square of the reliability of the original measures. So, for original measures whose measurement reliability is $r = .90$, the reliability of change scores drops to $r = .81$. Ensuring proper reliability can be difficult for the types of program outcomes we typically want to measure. Using change scores is inadvisable for measures whose measurement reliability is less than $r = .90$.

A second possible advantage of using pretests is that evaluators can attempt to remove any pretest differences between employees from the posttest measures. Although initial differences should be due to random sampling error, their effects can be removed from the program effects. As long as pretest measures are moderately correlated with the posttest measures, this step reduces the denominator of the statistical test, making the test more powerful, more likely to detect a small program impact. The statistical procedure is called analysis of covariance.

Analysis of covariance removes pretest variation from the posttest measures, leaving a set of residual measures at the posttest devoid of the influence of the pretest. You can think of this step as the creation of a new posttest score for each employee, a residual score that is "purified" of pretest differences. Now the residual measures for the program group are compared to those in the control group. Although most easily understood as a two-step procedure, this is done in one set of computations. The mathematical computations yield a single value, called an F value, with which we can conduct a statistical test similar in logic to conducting a t test. After controlling for initial pretest differences, the Program F value is

$$F = \frac{MS_B}{MS_W}$$

where MS_B (mean squares between) reflects the average spread of means from each other, and MS_W (mean square within) represents the average combined spread of scores within groups, much as was the case in computing t. As usual, we have an estimate of random sampling error, except it is increased by the impact of the program, if any.

Appendix 8 presents Table F values associated with $p <.05$ and $p <.01$. These F values represent the influence of random sampling error. The F test, however, has two sets of degrees of freedom, one for the numerator, df_N, and one for the denominator, df_D. The formula for each set of degrees of freedom varies according to the application. In analysis of covariance, $df_N = k - 1$, and $df_D = n_1 + n_2 - k$, where k is the number of groups. In the present case, we have $k = 2$ groups, the program group and the control group, and $df_N = 2 - 1 = 1$. If each group contained sixteen employees, $df_D = 16 + 16 - 2 = 30$. The Table F value at the .01 level for $df_N = 1$ and $df_D = 30$, is 7.56. Please consult Appendix 8 to verify this for yourself. If the Program F value exceeds the Table F value, you can conclude that the program had an impact beyond that expected by chance.

The F test was described in some detail because of its wide applicability. The F test can compare the means of any number of groups using logic similar to the t test. F and t are related such that $t^2 = F$. The t test is the special case of the F test for two means, where df_N of the F test is equal to 1. For example, the Table t value for $\alpha = .01$ and $df = 30$ is 2.75, and this value squared—$2.75 \times 2.75 = 7.5625$—is the same as the Table F value for one and 30 degrees of freedom before rounding. But where the t test is limited to comparing two means, the F test can compare any number of means. The F test is applicable to a wider range of assessment situations, including analysis of covariance.

These two designs provide excellent protection against extraneous error. The first design is simple and affords excellent protection against both extraneous error and random sampling error. The addition of pretests in the second design helps those interested in change scores, as long as the measure of the program outcome is highly reliable ($r \geq .90$). The pretests also allow one to remove from the posttest measures the effects of initial differences between members of the program group and the control group using analysis of covariance.

Quasi-Assessment Designs

When the constraints of the assessment setting prevent assigning employees to groups randomly or prevents forming a control group, quasi-assessment designs provide substantial protection against extraneous error. Gauging sampling error is more problematic, however, because the t test assumes data are generated by a random process. In the absence of randomization, procedures that attempt to distinguish program impacts from sampling error are more complex and sometimes offer no exact solution.

Nonequivalent Groups Pre- and Postobservation Design

This design is similar to the preceding design, except it lacks random assignment of employees to groups:

$$\begin{array}{llll} NRG_1 & O_1 & P & O_2 \\ NRG_2 & O_3 & & O_4 \end{array}$$

Employees are assigned to groups by some nonrandom process. For example, employees may have selected group membership themselves, may have been assigned to groups by a manager, or may have been part of an intact group, such as a department, and the entire department formed the group. Lacking random assignment, this design is vulnerable to the extraneous influence of differential selection, the possibility that initial, systematic differences exist between employees in the program and the control groups. If employees differ before the program, differences after the program cannot be attributed confidently to the program.

Evaluators commonly analyze data from this design in either of two ways. First, some compute and analyze change scores, the difference between each employee's pre- and postscore. Second, some conduct analysis of covariance in which pretest differences are removed from posttest scores. You might recall that both approaches are also applied to the Equivalent Groups Pre- and Postobservation design discussed earlier. However, these procedures are problematic in the present design, lacking random assignment as it does. Unfortunately, neither these two approaches, nor any of the statistical procedures considered thus far, ensure unbiased solutions for this design. No known, single procedure provides an exact solution in this design.[3]

Many researchers have attempted to compensate for the possibility of differential selection, only to admit the inexactness of their approach.[4] One reasonable strategy suggests that evaluators conduct multiple types of analyses in an attempt to "bracket" the actual solution.[5] These researchers hope that the answer will lie within a specified interval. Even here, they urge that statements of caution accompany any conclusions. Thus this design provides adequate protection against extraneous error, but it has no exact solution to address random sampling error.

One-Group Multiobservation Design

This design observes a nonrandom group of employees multiple times before and after the program:

$$NRG\ O_1\ O_2\ O_3\ O_4\ O_5\ O_6\ P\ O_7\ O_8\ O_9\ O_{10}\ O_{11}\ O_{12}$$

The objective is to determine if there is a difference between the series of preprogram and postprogram observations, indicating a program impact. This is accomplished with a t test. Before the t test is performed, the evaluator must address the dependencies that characterize observations over time. That is, observations collected at regular intervals tend to be more similar to adjacent than to nonajacent observations. This similarity is called dependency. The t test does not address the dependencies within observations collected over time.

The solution is to treat the entire series of observations as the product of a single source of influence—error—and then account for the systematic portion of that error so that any remaining error is unsystematic. Because it is unsystematic, this residual error represents random error. This random error will meet the independence of errors requirement of the t test and statistical testing can proceed.

To conceptualize the set of observations as the product of error, we momentarily ignore the presence of the program and assume that the series of observations is a realization of an ARIMA model (autoregressive integrated moving average).[6] The presence of the program is considered after the series is conceptualized as a realization of the ARIMA model.

In its simplest form, the ARIMA model describes a stationary process with no depencencies in the data.[7] A stationary process has no trend, no systematic rise or fall over time. Fig. 8.1(a) portrays a series of observations with an upward trend, and Fig. 8.1(b) portrays a series of observations with no trend. Random error follows the no-trend pattern in Fig. 8.1(b). As an initial step, the evaluator should remove any trend in the series of observations through a simple transformation of the data, called distancing. The distancing procedure subtracts the first observation from the second, the second from the third, the third from the fourth, and so on, forming an adjusted series of observations. This step produces a series with no trend.[8]

Data collected at intervals can contain two forms of dependency called autocorrelation and moving average.[9] Autocorrelation exists if an observation can be predicted in part from the preceding observation. A moving average exists if an observation can be predicted in part from the error associated with the previous observation.

Figure 8.1
Time Series With and Without Trend

(a)

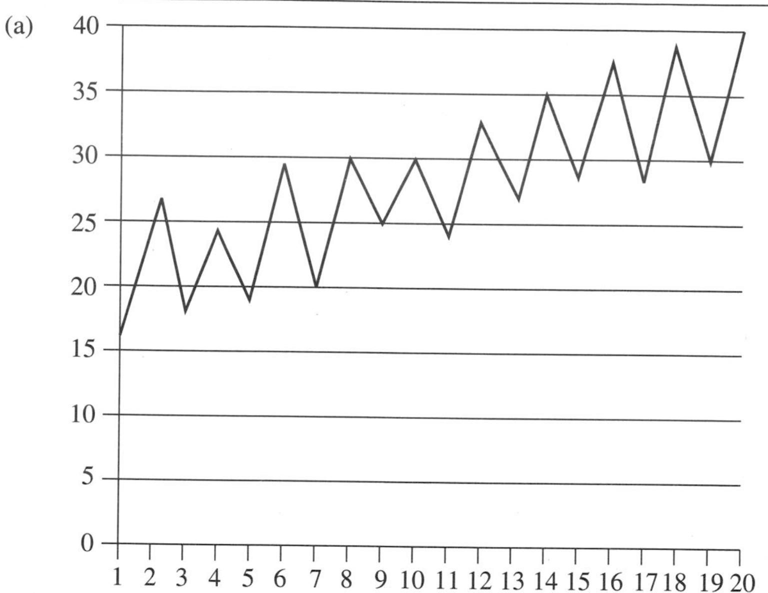

(b)

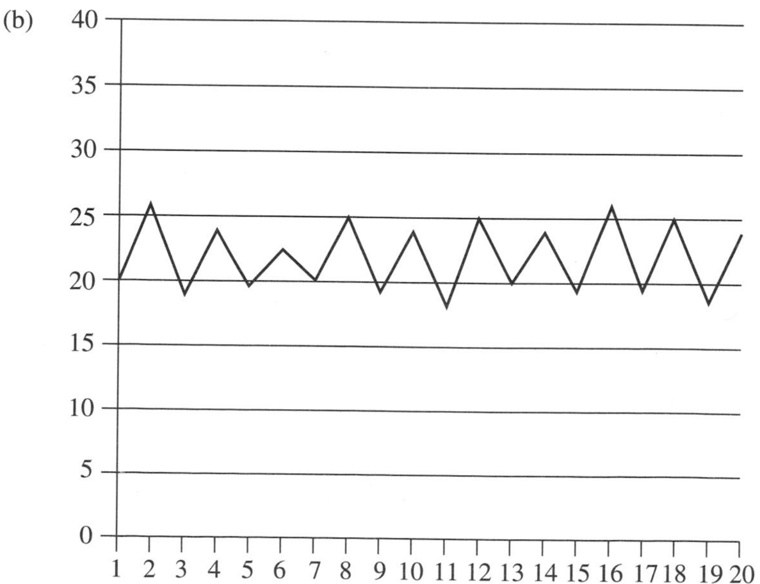

Fig. 8.2 contrasts the situations where observations and errors are independent and dependent.

Fig. 8.2(a) illustrates the situation where a given observation—observation six (O_6)—is independent of both the preceding observation and the error associated with the preceding observation. This is usually the case with nontime series data and meets the requirements of the t test. Fig. 8.2(b) illustrates autocorrelation, and Fig. 8.2(c) illustrates a moving average. In the first case, observation six can be predicted in part from observation five. In the second case, observation six can be predicted in part from the error associated with observation five. One or the other of these forms of dependency usually characterizes time series data. The objective is to identify which form of dependency exists in the series of observations collected in a program assessment. Once identified, the ARIMA model would reflect the systematic portion of error in the data, and the remaining error would be random error that could be used in a t test.

To discover which form of dependency is present, the evaluator first proposes that no dependencies exist and then completes a set of calculations by computer and inspects the results for patterns known to indicate the presence of autocorrelation or the presence of a moving average. When inspection of the computer results suggests

Figure 8.2
Autocorrelation/Moving Average

(a) Independent Observations and Errors

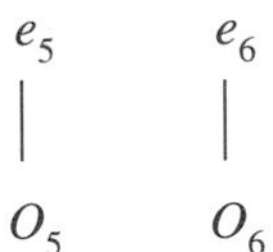

(b) Autocorrelation

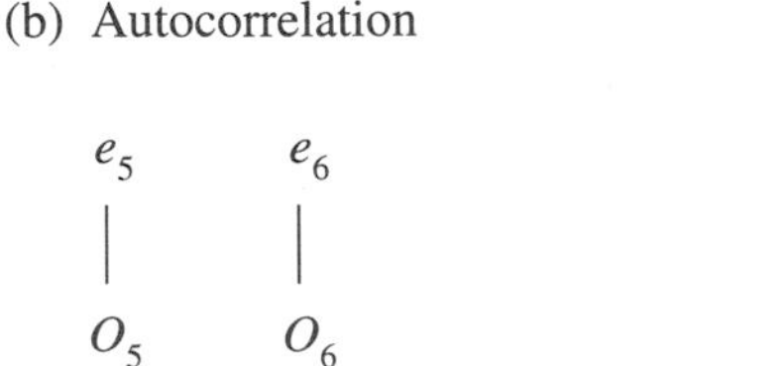

(c) Moving Average

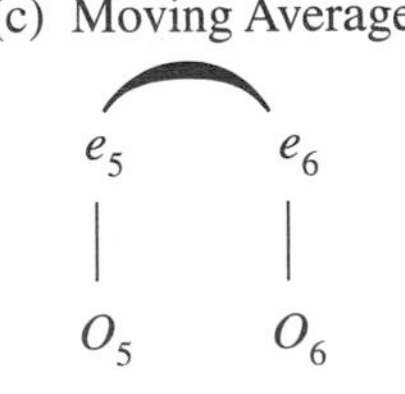

one or the other form of dependency, the evaluator respecifies the ARIMA model to this effect and again completes the computer analysis and inspects the results to verify that the model correctly describes the dependencies in the data. Through this analysis-inspection procedure, the evaluator arrives at an ARIMA model that accurately describes the data.

The ARIMA model accounts for the serial dependencies in the data, where the series is assumed to reflect error. Any unexplained, remaining error is free of dependencies as required by the t test, and attention turns to assessing the program impact. The evaluator now conducts a t test to discover if the jump in the postprogram observations exceeds jumps expected from random error. If a significant jump is detected, additional tests can determine if the jump is abrupt or gradual, permanent or diminishing.

Application of the ARIMA model prior to conducting t tests provides a viable approach to analyzing data from the One-Group Multiobservation design, with one important provision: Confident use of the ARIMA model requires observations for at least fifty points in time. Obtaining fifty observations is sometimes possible, as for measures collected weekly or monthly. More typically, evaluators are able to obtain a total of twelve observation points. Here, the dependencies in the serial observations are problematic for traditional significance tests, including those more general than the t test. Treat with caution conclusions from tests on fewer than 50 observations. Thus, while affording substantial protection against extraneous error, the One-Group Multiobservation design protects against random sampling error, but only for lengthy series.

Two-Group Multiobservation Design

Adding a control group to the previous design, the two-group multiobservation design provides additional protection against extraneous error. Because they likely affect both groups, extraneous influences, except local history, raise little concern. The design can be depicted as

$$NRG\ O_1\ O_2\ O_3\ O_4\ O_5\ O_6\ P\ O_7\ O_8\ O_9\ O_{10}\ O_{11}\ O_{12}$$
$$NRG\ O_1\ O_2\ O_3\ O_4\ O_5\ O_6\quad O_7\ O_8\ O_9\ O_{10}\ O_{11}\ O_{12}$$

At first blush, it might seem that analyzing data from this design would follow the tack just described for the One-Group Multiobservation design, only extended to two groups. That is, we could consider each series as error, fit a ARIMA model to the systematic portion of error in each series so that remaining error is random, suitable for statistical tests. However, analysis of multiseries data is problematic. A set consisting of two observation series has a complicated structure, a structure guaranteed to be nonnormal in some cases, and a structure as yet not modeled satisfactorily for statistical testing.[10] Thus, whereas the Two-Group Multiobservation design provides good protection against extraneous error, there is no clear way to address random sampling error.

Table 8.2 summarizes the strengths and weaknesses of the assessment designs we have considered. True assessment designs provide excellent protection (indicated by ++) against both extraneous error and sampling error. Quasi-assessment designs provide substantial protection (indicated by +) against extraneous error but provide mixed protection against sampling error. The One-Group Multiobservation design requires fifty or more observations to accurately model the dependencies in the data. The remaining quasi-assessment designs do not avail themselves to statistical testing, although some researchers use multiple methods to "bracket" the exact solution in the Nonequivalent Pre- and Postobservation design. Accordingly, this design was assigned one negative sign (−). Deficient assessment designs protect against neither extraneous error nor sampling error (indicated by −−).

Table 8.2
Strengths and Weaknesses of Assessment Designs

TRUE ASSESSMENT DESIGNS	Extraneous Error	Random Sampling Error
Equivalent Groups Observation Design	++	++
Equivalent Groups Pre- and Postobservation Design	++	++
QUASI-ASSESSMENT DESIGNS		
Nonequivalent Pre- and Postobservation Design	+	−
One-Group Multiobservation Design	+	+
Two-Group Multiobservation Design	+	−−
DEFICIENT ASSESSMENT DESIGNS		
One-Group Observation Design	−−	−−
One-Group Pre- and Postobservation Design	−−	−−
Nonequivalent Groups Observation Design	−−	−−

Additional Designs

Sometimes evaluators want to determine the impact of a program on more than one program outcome or the impact of multiple programs on a single outcome. Requiring random assignment of employees to groups, the procedures for these designs share the logic of the t test. That is, the evaluator compares a statistic representing program impacts and random sampling error combined to a Table value representing the influence of random sampling error only. Statistics that exceed the Table value indicate significant program impacts.

Multiple Programs

Useful as it is, the t test compares only two means at a time. To compare three or more programs, we would have to conduct multiple t tests. However, doing so risks inflating α beyond the level specified in each test. As we saw earlier in Table 8.1, three comparisons inflate from .05 to .1426. Instead, data from multiple programs are analyzed using analysis of variance procedures. The F test used in analysis of variance holds ∞ at the specified level while testing for differences among any number of means. Fortunately, the F test shares the logic of the t test, and its formula, although more general to include any number of means, is similar in form. That is, like the Program t value, the Program F value contains two estimates of random sampling error, one in its numerator, inflated by the impact of the program, and one in its denominator. This F value is compared to a Table F value that reflects the influence of random sampling solely. If the Program F value exceeds the Table F value, you may conclude that the observed spread among the means exceeds that expected by chance variation. Some combination of the programs created this difference, although the F test does not specify which. To discover where differences lie requires followup tests, adaptations of t tests specifically designed to fix ∞ for multiple tests.

Let's illustrate the principles of analyzing data from multiple programs. An evaluator wishes to compare employee satisfaction with three training formats: full interactive format (FI), where employees interact directly with the presenter; video conference format (VC), where employees in a remote location interact with the presenter via interactive television; and video playback format (VP), where employees watch a video of the training presentation. We have three programs, decreasing successively in personal contact. The evaluator theorizes that employees will express successively less satisfaction as the personalness of training decreases. To test this expectation, the evaluator asked seventy-five employees to meet for an initial briefing and to receive a packet of material. Employees then dispersed to separate areas according to the code on their packets. The evaluator had precoded the packets using a random procedure to insure that twenty-five employees would regather for training in each of three separate areas. The areas were set up for full interactive, video conference, or video playback training format. Employees completed a satisfaction questionnaire at the conclusion of the training. The resultant means and standard deviations of each group are presented below for a fictitious set of data.

Training Format	n	$\bar{X}$	s
Full Interactive	25	4.20	.805
Video Conference	25	3.90	.820
Video Playback	25	3.00	.875

In analysis of variance, the evaluator computes the following F value from the data:

$$F = \frac{MS_B}{MS_W}$$

where MS_B, pronounced mean squares between, reflects the average spread between the means, and MS_W, pronounced mean squares within, reflects the average, combined spread of the scores within the groups.

As did the Program t value, the Program F value contains the mean of each group in the numerator, where their degree of spread about their own mean (i.e., about the mean of the means) is determined. In determining the amount of spread among the means, the numerator of the F test computes the mean of the group of means, then subtracts it from each mean. Once the mean of the means is known, one mean is no longer free to vary, and there is a loss of one degree of freedom. Knowing the mean of the means allows the mean of one group to be determined from knowledge of the other means. Consequently, the numerator of the F test has $k - 1$ degrees of freedom (where k is the number of groups). Of course, all means are used in the analysis, but we use $k - 1$ instead of k to determine the amount of random sampling error associated with k number of means.

The denominator of the F test contains the standard deviation of each group, where each is weighted by its degrees of freedom and averaged. The degrees of freedom for the denominator of the F test combines the $n - 1$ degrees of freedom of each standard deviation, yielding $k(n - 1)$ degrees of freedom, where k again is the number of groups. However, the equivalent and simpler expression $N - k$ is used, where N is the sum of the individual sample sizes ($N = n_1 + n_2$ and so on). Thus $df_N = k - 1$ denotes the degrees of freedom of the numerator of the F test and $df_D = N - k$ denotes the degrees of freedom of the denominator. In our example, we have three groups, each containing twenty-five employees. Thus, $df_N = (3 - 1) = 2$, and $df_D = (75 - 3) = 73$.

To conduct the F test, the evaluator uses the computer to compute MS_B/MS_W, yielding a single F value. This Program F value is compared to the Table F value obtained from the Table of F values using $df_N = k - 1$ and $df_D = N - k$. A Table of F values is presented in Appendix 8. The Program F value reflects the influence of random sampling error and the program combined. The Table F value reflects the amount of random sampling error expected with k number of groups and N total sample size.

If the Program F value does not exceed the Table F value, you cannot conclude whether or not employees were more satisfied with video playback, video conference, or full interactive formats of training. Conversely, if the Program F value exceeds the Table F value, you may conclude that there is a difference in employee satisfaction for some combination of the training formats. At this point, you can't say exactly where differences may lie, but you know that the spread of the means exceeds that expected from chance variation.

Table 8.3 summarizes an analysis of variance for the effects of three training formats—full interactive, video conference, video playback—on satisfaction with the training. *SS* (sum of squares) is the *MS* before it is divided by its degrees of freedom. Remember, the F value is the result of dividing MS_B by MS_W. This F value is compared to the Table F value for $df_N = k - 1$ and $df_D = N - k$. The Table F value at the .05 level for $df_N = 2$, and $df_D = 72$ is 3.925. Please consult the Table of F values in Appendix 8 to verify this for yourself. Remember to drop to the smaller degrees of freedom when the table does not contain the one you seek. Because the Program F value (14.03) exceeds the Table F value (3.925), we may conclude that there is a difference in employee satisfaction for some combination of the training formats. We know, however, that significant results are not necessarily important. For example, large sample sizes can detect very small impacts. To gauge the practical importance of F test results, convert the Program F value to an η value (η is the Greek letter eta), where

$$\eta = \sqrt{\frac{df_N(F)}{df_N(F) + df_D}}$$

As $r_{\text{point-biserial}}$ did for two groups, η reflects the relationship between the variation in the program outcome and employee membership in multiple groups. In the present situation, $\eta = .53$, indicating that employee satisfaction with training was related to whether employees experienced video playback, video conference, or full interactive format. Cohen presents values of η for weak, moderate, and strong relationships.[11]

	Weak	**Moderate**	**Strong**
η	.10	.24	.37

In our example, $\eta = .53$ represents a strong effect size for training format. Evaluators sometimes report η^2, which is interpreted as the proportion of variation in the program outcome accounted for by variation in group membership. In the present case, $\eta^2 = .28$, which indicates that training format accounts for 28 percent of the variation in employee satisfaction. Weak, moderate, and strong relationships for η^2 are .0099, .0588, and .1379 (roughly 1, 6, and 14 percent), respectively.

Although a significant and important F test indicates an important difference somewhere among the means, you cannot say exactly where that difference lies. To identify which training formats differed from one another, you must complete a second step. Upon finding a statistically significant F test, you complete a version of the t test on each pair of means. Because it is based on more information (s^2 from more than two groups), MS_W from the denominator of the F test is substituted in the denominator of the t test. In addition, df_D associated

Table 8.3
Summary of Analysis of Variance for Three Training Formats

Sources of Variation	***SS***	***df***	***MS***	***F***
Between Groups	19.5	2	9.75	14.03*
Within Groups	50.065	72	.695	

$^* p < .05$

with the denominator of the F test is used when obtaining the Table t value. This version of the t test has more power to detect small impacts because it more precisely estimates sampling error and has greater *df* for the test.

However, conducting multiple t tests inflates the significance level α. Several adaptations of the t test exist, each using a different strategy to control α. For example, the Bonferroni t test divides α among the t tests to be conducted. For α = .05, you would use the .05/3 ≈ .016 level for three tests. If computer results include the specific probability for each t test, only those beyond .016 would be considered significant. Otherwise, you could adopt the .01 level to locate the Table t value.[12] The formula for the Bonferroni t test is

$$t = \frac{\overline{X}_1 - \overline{X}_2}{\sqrt{\frac{MS_W}{n_1} + \frac{MS_W}{n_2}}}$$

where one of the means being tested is $\overline{X}_1$, and the other mean being tested is $\overline{X}_2$, and MS_W is the denominator of the F test.

Before conducting t tests in our example, let's refresh our memory. Following a significant F test, we are comparing the effects on employee satisfaction of three training formats. The sample sizes, means, and pertinent results of the F test reported in Table 8.3 are

Training Format	n	$\overline{X}$	
Full Interactive	25	4.20	
Video Conference	25	3.90	$MS_W = .695$
Video Playback	25	3.00	$df_D = 72$

We conduct three Bonferroni t tests and compare each result to the Table t value for *df* = 72 at the .05/3 ≈ .01 level. Dropping down to *df* = 60, the Table t value is 2.66. Using the above formula, I obtained the following results for each Bonferroni t test.

	Bonferroni t	$r_{\text{point-biserial}}$
Full Interactive vs. Video Conference	1.27 (ns)	—
Full Interactive vs. Video Playback	5.08	.51
Video Conference vs. Video Playback	3.81	.41

The first test was not significant, so we cannot conclude whether the full interactive format created higher employee satisfaction than video conference. Because each was significant, we can conclude that both the full interactive format and the video conference format created higher employee satisfaction than video playback. The *r* values indicate the presence of strong relationships. Thus it seems that the impersonalness of video playback detracts from its perceived value. The interesting finding, perhaps, is that video conference training may better serve those at a distance than video playback.[13]

Assumptions of the F Test. Three assumptions are required to ensure that a Program F value is derived on the same basis as the Table F values, that $F = MS_B/MS_W$ follows an F-distribution. Failure to meet the assumptions risks inflating the level of ∞ beyond its assumed level. First, the derivation of F assumes that a random process governed the selection of members of the program target group or their assignment to groups. This requirement will be satisfied by following the procedures for securing random samples or assigning employees to groups randomly, presented in Chapter 6. Second, the F test assumes that scores on the outcome measure are normally distributed. Among other things, a normally distributed measure assumes the form of a bell-shaped curve. Fortunately, the distribution of MS_B/MS_W seems little affected by departures from normality.[14] Concern over nonnormality arises only when samples sizes are very small, say less than five per group, and when populations differ markedly in form. Finally, the F test assumes that the spread of the scores is the same within all treatment populations. Violation of this assumption inflates α, but only to a nominal degree when sample sizes are equal and measures meet the normality assumption.[15] Greater concern arises when sample sizes are unequal. Most computer analyses include a test for equal spread. When sample sizes are unequal and this test is significant, alternative procedures may be used.[16]

We have found that testing the impacts of multiple programs entails two steps. First, the evaluator conducts an F test to determine if the spread of the means exceeds that expected by chance. The F test holds ∞ steady while testing for differences among any number of means. Following a significant F test, the evaluator conducts multiple t tests to identify where those differences lie. These are modified t tests, designed to hold α steady. In this section, we have just explored what to do when an evaluator wants to assess the impact of multiple programs. In the next section, we will consider what to do when the evaluator wants to explore a program's impact on multiple outcomes.

Multiple Program Outcomes

Evaluators sometimes want to assess a program's impact on multiple outcomes. For example, a manager may want to assess both employee learning and satisfaction with training. Alternatively, a manager may want to assess only employee satisfaction with training, but the questionnaire measures four separate components of satisfaction: The program content, the program presenter, the logistical arrangements, and the degree to which employees felt forced to attend. Each component of satisfaction is a separate program outcome.

Either example requires more than one t test. However, conducting multiple t tests inflates α. The solution is to conduct a more general test, one that holds α steady while assessing multiple program outcomes.

Hotellings T^2 is the appropriate statistic when testing for differences between two groups on multiple measures. Rather than computing the difference between two means, as does the t test, Hotellings T^2 computes Δ (delta), the difference between two sets of means, as shown here for the impact of two training formats on four dimensions of employee satisfaction.

Full Interactive | **Video Playback**

$$\Delta = \begin{bmatrix} \bar{X}_1 \\ \bar{X}_2 \\ \bar{X}_3 \\ \bar{X}_4 \end{bmatrix} - \begin{bmatrix} \bar{X}_1 \\ \bar{X}_2 \\ \bar{X}_3 \\ \bar{X}_4 \end{bmatrix}$$

The procedure uses matrix algebra to compute Δ^2, representing the influence of random sampling error and program impact combined, and to compute **S**, a matrix of values called the pooled covariance matrix, reflecting random sampling error only.[17] In effect, T^2 is equal to Δ^2 divided by **S** (although division in matrix algebra has unique rules). The logic of the T^2 test parallels that of the t test. A Program T^2, representing random sampling error and the program impact combined must exceed a Table T^2 value, representing random sampling error only. The Table T^2 value is obtained by first obtaining the Table F value with $df_N = p$ (where p is the number of program outcomes) and $df_D = n_1 + n_2 - p - 1$ from the Table of F values and then adjusting this Table F value as follows:

$$T^2 = m\,F$$

where $$m = \frac{(n_1 + n_2 - 2)p}{n_1 + n_2 - p - 1}$$

Calculations are performed by computer, producing a single program T^2 value to compare to a Table T^2 value. When the former exceeds the latter, you may conclude that the difference among the sets of means exceeds that expected by chance.[18]

When the T^2 test is not significant, you cannot conclude whether or not the effects of training format differ on these sets of measures. In contrast, a significant T^2 test indicates that a difference exists between the training formats somewhere among these measures. Where those differences lie isn't clear until a second step is taken. Following a significant T^2 test, the evaluator computes a modified t test on each measure to discover which outcomes differed. Each t test contains two means in the numerator and their corresponding element from the pooled covariance matrix in the denominator. Because multiple t tests are being conducted, the evaluator should take steps to prevent an inflated α level.[19] Thus, by a two-step procedure, we first discover whether a difference exists between the two training formats somewhere among the program outcomes. Followup t tests indicate which program outcomes differ. Analogous T^2 test procedures compare a set of outcome measures to a corresponding set of norms or quotas.[20]

Main Points of Chapter 8

- Conducting a t test without assigning employees randomly to groups is inappropriate, and conducting multiple t tests inflates ∞ the level of significance beyond that assumed in each test.
- Analysis of covariance, appropriate when assessment designs have a pretest, conducts an F test after the effects of initial differences between members of the program group and the control group are removed from the posttest measures. The F test compares a Program F value, which is enlarged by the program's impact, if any, to a Table F value, which represents random sampling error by itself.
- A series of observations before and after a program is cast as a system of random error generated by an ARIMA model, then the jump at the program is tested to see if it differs from jumps expected by a random process.
- The effectiveness of multiple programs is tested through analysis of variance, culminating in an F test, whereby a Program F value, enlarged by program impacts, is compared

to a Table F value, representing random sampling solely. A significant F test is followed by modified t tests designed to control α over all tests. One such test, the Bonferroni t test, conducts t tests after dividing α by the number of tests to be performed.

- Program impacts on multiple outcomes are assessed by Hotellings T^2, whereby a Program T^2 value, reflecting program impacts, if any, is compared to a Table T^2 value, reflecting random sampling error only. A significant T^2 test is followed by modified t tests to discover which program outcomes differ.

Chapter Notes

1. Generally, k number of programs generates $k(k - 1)/2$ comparisons.
2. Generally, k number of t tests increases α by $1 - (1 - \alpha)^k$. See Roger E. Kirk, *Experimental Design: Procedures for the Behavioral Sciences*. Belmont, CA: Brooks/Cole, 1968, p. 78.
3. Charles S. Reichardt, The statistical analysis of data from nonequivalent group designs. In Thomas D. Cook and Donald T. Campbell, *Quasi-Experimentation: Design and Analysis Issues for Field Settings*. Chicago: Rand McNally, 1979, p. 186.
4. Thomas D. Cook and Charles S. Reichardt, Statistical analysis of nonequivalent control group designs: A guide to some current literature. *Evaluation*, 1976, *3*, pp 136–138.
5. Charles S. Reichardt, p. 200.
6. David McDowall, Richard McCleary, Errol E. Meidinger, and Richard A. Hay, Jr., *Interrupted Time Series Analysis*. Newbury Park, CA: Sage, 1980; Leslie J. McCain and Richard McCleary, The statistical analysis of the simple interrupted time-series quasi-experiment. In Thomas D. Cook and Donald T. Campbell, *Quasi-Experimentation: Design and Analysis Issues for Field Settings*. Chicago: Rand McNally, 1979, pp 223–293.
7. Steps are also taken to remove any trend (departure from a straight line) and any cyclic influences that vary with the season, such as might arise in the holiday season each December.

8. Leslie J. McCain and Richard McCleary, The statistical analysis of the simple interrupted time-series quasi-experiment. In Thomas D. Cook and Donald T. Campbell, *Quasi-Experimentation: Design and Analysis Issues for Field Settings*. Chicago: Rand McNally, 1979, p. 237.
9. Time series data typical of the behavioral sciences usually contain either autocorrelation or a moving average. They rarely occur together and rarely reach higher order (i.e., dependence reaching two or more observations back in time). See McCain and McCleary, p. 247.
10. Richard McCleary, personal communication, February 17, 1998.
11. Jacob Cohen, *Statistical Power Analysis for the Behavioral Sciences.* NY: Academic, 1969, pp 277–281.
12. A procedure for obtaining a critical value for α spread among any number of means is presented in Roger E. Kirk, *Experimental Design: Procedures for the Behavioral Sciences.* Belmont, CA: Brooks/Cole, 1968, pp 79–80.
13. The Bonferroni test is one of several t tests you may encounter that are designed to control α for multiple comparisons. The most commonly used methods, listed in order of descending power, are LSD (least significant difference), N-K (Newman-Keuls), HSD (honestly significant difference, Tukey), Dunnett (test of multiple means to a control group mean), Bonferroni, and Scheffe (test for any linear combination of means). See Roger E. Kirk, *Experimental Design Procedures for the Behavioral Sciences*. Belmont, CA: Wadsworth, 1968, p. 96.
14. Jerome L. Myers, *Fundamentals of Experimental Design.* 2nd ed., Boston: Allyn and Bacon, 1972, p. 71.
15. Myers, p. 72.
16. This F test is described in Myers, p. 74. The approach is similar to the Behren's Fisher-Welch solution advocated for the t test for small and unequal sample sizes. A version of the Bonferroni test is also available for t tests following a significant F test, described in H. K. Ury and A. D. Wiggins, Large sample and other multiple comparisons among means. *British Journal of Mathematical and Statistical Psychology*. 1971, *24*, pp 174–194.

17. The pooled covariance matrix contains both variances and covariances. The variance is s^2, the square of the standard deviation. The covariance is the correlation between two measures before it has been standardized (i.e., the numerator of the correlation coefficient).
18. Donald F. Morrison, *Multivariate Statistical Methods*. NY: McGraw-Hill, 1967, pp 125–128.
19. B. J. Winer, *Statistical Principles in Experimental Design*. NY: McGraw-Hill, 1971, pp 54–57.
20. Morrison, pp 117–124.

9

Communicating Assessment Results and Making Program Decisions

Chapter Preview

This final chapter seeks to ensure that assessment results reach their intended audiences to further decision making. We will identify six communication goals for assessment reports and present guidelines to prepare both oral and written reports. Finally, we will discuss the several organizational arenas within which program decisions are made.

Learning Objectives

After reading Chapter 9, you should be able to:

- identify the main constituencies that receive assessment results
- identify the level of knowledge and interests of each constituency
- recall the communication goals common to all assessment reports
- recall the formats of oral and written assessment reports
- prepare and present effective oral assessment reports
- prepare effective written assessment reports
- identify the main organizational arenas within which program decisions are made and identify the effects they have on the decision process

The Focus of Chapter 9

The program assessment steps discussed in this chapter, along with their corresponding components in the Scientific Model, are highlighted below.

The Steps of Program Assessment

1. Involve stakeholders throughout the assessment.
2. Specify the expected program outcome.
3. Establish a measure of the program outcome.
4. Plan a method of gathering data.
5. Collect the data.
6. Analyze the data.
7. Communicate the results.
8. Make program decisions.

The Scientific Model of Program Assessment

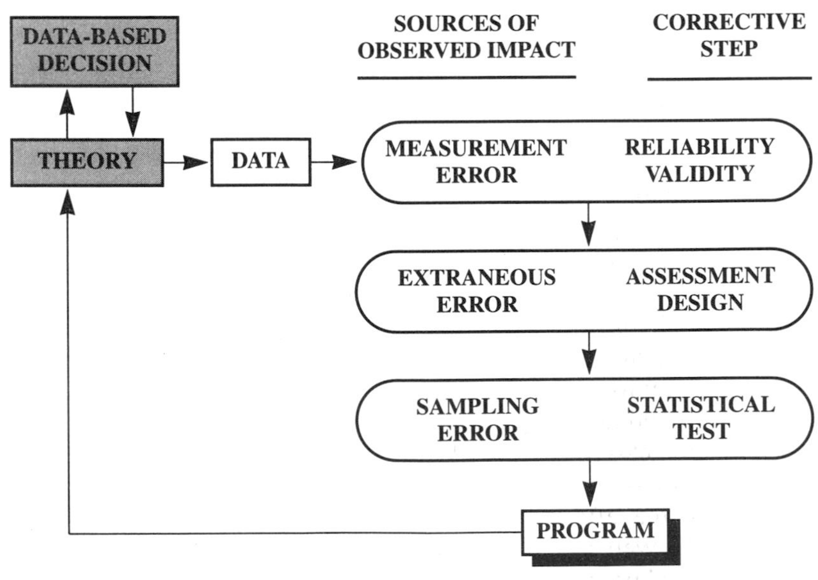

Program assessment aims to provide sound information for organizational decision making. In the process, program assessment tests the theory on which program expectations are based. Toward these ends, program assessment results must reach organizational stakeholders as well as those interested in building theory.

Communicating Assessment Results

After completing the analysis of the data, the results and recommendations need to be communicated to facilitate decision making. Stakeholders will be curious about the results—because they were involved in the program assessment, because program decisions will affect them, or because they need to make decisions about the fate of the program. Assessment reports should be tailored to the interests and knowledge of their audiences. Stakeholders value assessment results for a practical purpose, deciding whether the program should be continued, ended, modified, or expanded. Often unfamiliar with the vocabulary and methods of science, stakeholders benefit from plain talk, talk using the vocabulary of the organization. Consequently, assessment reports to stakeholders are usually oral and informal, allowing time for questions and discussion.

Assessment results may also interest constituencies outside the organization. Managers whose organizations operate within the public sphere sometimes ask their public relations department to communicate assessment results and decisions to the public through a press release. Managers typically do not communicate assessment results to one potential constituency: managers in other organizations who may have or plan to enact similar programs where they work. Knowing the effectiveness of programs in other organizations would facilitate decisions in their own organization. Managers who have completed a program assessment, however, hesitate to share the results with managers elsewhere. On one hand, communicating program ineffectiveness puts the organization's image at risk, but sharing a program's effectiveness risks putting information into the hands of the organization's competitors. We should not be surprised, therefore, that the World Wide Web and the Internet—two rich venues for the quick and informal exchange of information—contain few if any sites that routinely post assessment reports on the effectiveness of internal organizational programs. Whereas the Web contains evaluation reports of governmental, social, or educational programs, evaluations of internal programs such as employee orientations, diversity training, and production incentives are noticeably absent. Cyberspace does, however, provide valuable guidance on how to conduct evaluations. The home page of the American Evaluation Association (http://www.eval.org/) is a good resource. Anyone may use the EVALTALK Listserv, which is maintained by the association. Subscription is free. A Listserv allows you to pose a question about program assessment and receive replies, often from experts. Appendix 9 lists several World Wide Web sites that provide information or services of interest to evaluators.

Finally, if recast to emphasize the theory underlying the assessment and its testing, assessment results hold interest to members of the academic community. College professors and professional consultants read academic journals and attend professional conferences to stay current on theory and research on organizational effectiveness. Familiar with the vocabulary and methods of science, they expect reports to use this vocabulary and contain enough information for them to evaluate and replicate the study. To this end, the academic community has adopted a standard format for written reports, a description of which is presented in Appendix 10. Examples of academic journals that publish assessment results are contained in Appendix 7. In Chapter 3 of this book, we emphasized how common theories are, that managers hold a theory when they know what to expect from a program and why. The difference between such lay theories and those advanced in academia is the degree to which they are spelled out, shared with others, and tested. In this book you were encouraged to do just that, and the academic community would be interested in the result of a rigorous test of your theory. The report would simply emphasize the theory of your assessment, over its role for decision making.

Thus, assessment reports can be informal or formal, oral or written, to suit the knowledge and interests of the intended audience. Preparers of assessment reports should consider their specific communication goals and select strategies likely to achieve those goals.

Communication Goals

Although they address the interests and knowledge of varied audiences, all assessment reports seek the same communication goals. Table 9.1 lists these common goals.

You accomplish little without the listeners' favorable attention. Whether uninterested, distracted, or emotionally charged, an inattentive audience neither grasps nor remembers your message. More specifically, you need the listeners' *favorable* attention. While movement, novelty, suspense, and humor often gain attention, they must be congruent

Table 9.1
Six Communication Goals

1. Attain the listener's favorable attention.
2. Establish the topic's importance to the listener.
3. Enable the listener to understand the main points.
4. Enable the listener to remember the main points.
5. Enable the listener to believe the main points.
6. Enable the listener to act effectively.

with the nature of the occasion, the tastes and values of the listeners, and the credibility of the presenter to gain attention that is favorable.

Second, you need to convince your audience of the importance of the topic. Attention fades quickly when talk skirts what listeners value. Interest is highest when listeners recognize how the topic affects them personally, that they will lose or gain something of value by what is being said. When listeners hold marginal interest, or don't recognize the interest they actually have, it must be generated, brought to the fore. When listeners already hold interest in the topic, they need only be reminded of it.

Third, listeners should clearly understand the main ideas of the report. Essential main ideas include the purpose of the assessment and its conclusions and recommendations. Generally, you should describe the methods used to gather information only if interest is present and time allows. With this understanding, listeners will weigh the implications results have for enhancing organizational functioning. Using vocabulary familiar to listeners facilitates understanding, as does defining unfamiliar terms, presenting examples, and relating unfamiliar ideas to familiar ones. Definitions clarify, examples illustrate, the familiar resonates.

Fourth, listeners should remember the main ideas of the assessment report, especially the purpose, conclusions, and recommendations. They will need this information for effective decision making. Be aware that typically listeners recall less than 20 percent of a presentation. You must ensure that that 20 percent includes the essentials—your purpose, findings, and recommendations—rather than nonessentials, minor details, a story told to gain attention, or some minor difficulty you encountered and related.

Fifth, you want listeners to believe in the integrity of the assessment, in the soundness of the conclusions and recommendations. More specifically, listeners should believe that you did as you claim and found as you reported. They should believe that you knew what you were doing and that you know what you are talking about. Listeners will discount the results unless both you and what you did appear credible to them.

Finally, listeners should act on the information presented, incorporating the assessment's recommendations into their deliberations and future plans.

Attaining these communication goals will ensure effectiveness, whether reports are targeted to stakeholders in the organization, the public, managers at other organizations, or members of the academic community. While seeking the same communication goals, reports will emphasize different topics to tailor the report to its intended audience. Generally, reports tailored to organizational stakeholders are informal and oral.

Preparing Oral Assessment Reports

Reports of assessment results to stakeholders are usually informal and presented in a face-to-face meeting. Generally, oral reports present topics in the order listed in Table 9.2.

Table 9.2
Format for an Oral Assessment Report

I. Introduction
  Welcome
  Importance of the Program Outcome
  Overview of the Program
  Purpose of the Assessment

II. What Was Found?
  Conclusions
  Recommendations

III. Question and Answer Period
  Closure

You may adjust the emphasis you give each topic and even the sequence of topics as the audience or situation warrants. For example, you need not welcome listeners if someone has already done so, and you need not describe the program in detail if all are intimately familiar with it. We next consider each component of the oral report.

Introduction

The introduction should secure the listeners' favorable attention and arouse their interest. Listeners attend when you speak in an interesting way about a topic that interests them. Not that they require entertainment, although appropriate amusement entices. Speaking skill is not a prerequisite either, although a pleasant, versatile voice impresses, and eye contact engages. Rather, people listen attentively as long as they believe that what is being said affects them and that the speaker is informed and sincere. Toward this end, an introduction usually includes a welcome, a discussion of the link between the program outcome and organizational effectiveness, a description of the program, and a statement of the purpose of the program assessment. We will consider each briefly.

Most listeners find it helpful if the speaker begins with some sort of ice-breaker, especially when the listeners do not know each other well or if some tension or nervousness surrounds the anticipated results of the program assessment. Several options are available. The welcome can acknowledge the presence and importance of the listeners. The welcome can also express the speaker's pleasure in being present. A welcome can also refer to a positive aspect of the immediate situation, such as the presence of an important guest or the anniversary of the program. The welcome should address a negative aspect of the immediate situation that competes for the listener's attention, such as the crowdedness of the room or audible thunder from an approaching storm. The idea is to begin in a favorable way. Avoid beginning with a statement of your purpose. That is too serious and not what listeners want to hear first anyway. They prefer you to break the ice and then transition smoothly into your next remarks, gaining their attention and increasing their interest as you proceed.

To hold their attention, you will want to convince the listeners you are discussing something they want to know about, something that affects them. Thus, follow the welcome with a compelling discussion of the nature and importance of the program outcome at this organization (although avoid the term program outcome). Make clear how the program outcome is related to organizational effectiveness.

If the outcome is employee morale, for example, you could treat it several ways. You could document in an interesting way the importance of employee morale for all companies like yours, possibly by using a relevant quotation from someone your listeners respect. You could use a sobering statistic, say one that specifies a specific turnover rate associated with low morale. You could document the importance of employee morale in your company, possibly by quoting relevant results of an internal company survey. You could cite recent company experiences related to employee morale, or you could relate a hypothetical example that shows how morale is related to important company goals. Finally, you could illustrate how employee morale relates to these specific listeners—to their goals, their effectiveness, their daily experience.

For most listeners, what directly affects them provides the most compelling motivation to listen attentively. The emphasis you place on establishing the importance of the program outcome should match the listeners' interest in the program's effectiveness. The less interested they are, or the less clear it is to them how the program outcome relates to organizational success, the more emphasis this section deserves. Conversely, listeners familiar with the program and interested in its effectiveness may need only to be reminded of this in a brief but compelling way. Skip this step at your own peril, however, for it is your main way of securing listener interest. You may need that interest as you delve into details, as an afternoon wears on, or if other matters preoccupy listeners' attention.

To have a context for the results of the assessment, listeners need to be familiar with the nature of the program. The speaker should present an overview of the program commensurate with how familiar listeners are with the program. The less familiar with the program listeners are, the more orientation they need, perhaps to include the origin and history of the program, its purpose, its characteristics, and information about its previous impacts or concerns about its current impact. Conversely, the more familiar with the program listeners are, the less orientation they need, perhaps only a reminder of its existence and purpose. You must carefully equate the level of detail you present with the level of listeners' familiarity with the program or risk boring them.

Close the introduction with a succinct statement of the purpose of the program assessment. For example, a speaker might say, "This assessment sought to discover whether employees who receive safety awareness training have fewer accidents than employees who do not receive safety awareness training." Notice the statement of purpose contains three important elements of an assessment: the program (safety awareness training), the program outcome (number of accidents), and the comparison (trained versus untrained employees). The introduction prepares the audience to learn the results of the assessment.

What Was Found?

This section of the report presents the conclusions drawn from the data analysis and advances recommendations. Listeners will want to know the impact of the program and the implications of the findings for enhancing organizational effectiveness.

Begin by reporting any evidence of program effectiveness obtained from the analysis of the data. For example, if the program was safety awareness training, report the average number of accidents committed by employees who received safety awareness training and the average number of accidents committed by untrained employees. Here, you would remind listeners that a low average score reflects a good outcome, since it is desirable to have few accidents. Next, present a conclusion about the degree to which the results of the data analysis support the effectiveness of the program. Finally, interpret the importance to the organization of the size of the program impact that was observed.

Based on the conclusion drawn from the data analysis, advance a recommendation about whether the program should be ended, reduced, maintained, expanded, or whether its characteristics should be modified. When it is appropriate, you may withhold the recommendation so stakeholders can be involved in this important step. In this case, you could replace the recommendation with an invitation to stakeholders to become involved in the decision-making process.

Question and Answer Period

Be sure to reserve time to invite questions from stakeholders. This is a good opportunity to discover how clearly they understood your presentation and a chance to gauge their reactions to the report. If you will make available a formal written report, identify the type of information it contains and where it can be accessed.

You need to be prepared to address a range of questions. Stakeholders may want you to clarify a point you discussed or they may want additional information. Some may have concerns about how information was gathered or from whom. Others may question how you arrived at your recommendations. Clearly, some questions are easier to answer than others, while some may seem threatening. If there are no initial questions, it is not safe to assume this indicates acceptance of the report's recommendations. Instead, you might advance a topic or question of your own and begin discussing it. For example, you could say it might be useful for you to describe something in a little more detail. This usually gives participants time to formulate their own questions or overcome their initial hesitation to speak.

It is often helpful to paraphrase succinctly long, complex, or softly spoken questions so everyone knows what was asked. Restating the questions also allows you to divide a complex question into smaller questions that are easier for you to address and assures that you understood the question before attempting to answer it. You should attempt to address questions accurately. You want to be responsive without answering beyond your knowledge. If appropriate, you could offer to research the answer to a question you don't know. In formulating answers, it is helpful to be mindful of the type of organizational issues important to the asker. This helps you understand what they are asking and why they are asking it.

You may look at the asker as you begin your answer, but soon you will want to turn to address the group as a whole. Getting into a dialogue with one person often results in devoting excessive time to one issue and risks boring others. After answering an important question, you might want to inquire if the asker found the answer useful. If someone uses the opportunity to expound on a side issue or begins to dominate the session, you need to skillfully regain control so that all get a chance to speak. If the offender is your senior, considerable skill is required here. For instance, you might indicate that an important goal of the meeting is to identify issues just like the one raised by the speaker so they can be examined in detail and will be at another time. You could then summarize the speaker's issue in one sentence to show you understood it and will remember it. Finally, you could thank the speaker for identifying that issue and then either ask if anyone has another question or ask an easy but relevant question of another person to resume the discussion quickly.[1]

Observe the time allotted for your presentation. As their hearts—if not their minds—turn elsewhere, few listeners are swayed in overtime. When time is up or the questioning ends, conclude the question and answer period, and add closure to your presentation. If possible, conclude the presentation on an upbeat note, as it was begun in the welcome. Effective presenters often return to an important theme from their introduction. If in your introduction you used a quotation, quoted a statistic, or related a recent organizational incident, you could refer to it again in an interesting way, perhaps saying how things can be different. If you welcome additional questions after the meeting, you could indicate this. If appropriate, announce the next step of the decision process, a timeline for its completion, and indicate how stakeholders will be involved. To close, you could thank the stakeholders, although they may be about to thank you for your presentation. Alternatively, you could indicate what you hope happens next. If done well, the oral report provides stakeholders the information they need to reach an informed decision.

Preparing Written Assessment Reports

Most organizations are accustomed to putting important information in writing, and assessment information is no exception. A written report should be prepared for stakeholders, even if a report is presented orally. A written report describes the purpose and results of an assessment in detail and provides an accessible record. Because most readers will be unfamiliar with the vocabulary and methods of science, the written report should use the voculary of the organization as much as possible. As was the case for an oral report, the topics of a written report should be arranged to facilitate decision making: important information first, details last. Table 9.3 presents a typical format for a written report. Whereas this format works well in most settings, the topics and their sequencing should be adapted to the interests of the stakeholders and the writing customs of the organization. Elements I–VI are headings in the written report. Pages are numbered consecutively, beginning with the first page of the background section. The report should be written in the past tense. The finished product is usually bound in a folder or binder that contains an appropriate title and date on the front cover. We'll now examine each element of the written report.

Summary

The initial page of the report should present a concise summary of the program assessment, emphasizing its purpose, conclusions, and recommendations. This is important because the busy or marginally interested stakeholder who might not otherwise read the report may read this one page. To make them more prominent, you could indent and bullet sentences that contain the assessment's conclusions and recommendations. The summary need not describe the program, the

Table 9.3
Format for a Written Assessment Report

I. SUMMARY
   Table of Contents

II. BACKGROUND
   Importance of the Program Outcome
   Description of the Program
   Purpose of the Study

III. CONCLUSIONS AND RECOMMENDATIONS

IV. METHODS
   Description of the Measure
   Description of the Participants
   Description of the Procedures

V. ANALYSIS OF THE DATA
   Limitations of the Assessment

VI. APPENDIX
   Copy of the Questionnaire

methods used to gather data, or the data analysis—unless some mention is necessary for stakeholders to understand the assessment's purpose, conclusions, and recommendations. To invite reader attention, the summary should be succinct, easy to read, and contain only the essentials. Toward this end, use ample white space between margins and between paragraphs.

Table of Contents. The next page should contain a table of contents that lists each major topic and the page on which discussion begins. For lengthy reports, you might want to insert labeled tabs or divider pages for each section so stakeholders can find each section easily.

Background

The background section should secure the reader's favorable attention, increase the reader's interest in the topic area of the report, and provide a context for understanding the results. You should highlight the importance of the program outcome to the success of this organization, describe the program, and state the purpose of the study. If you look back, you will notice that these three components are also contained in the introduction section of an oral assessment report and were described earlier. Please consult those earlier descriptions as needed.

Conclusions and Recommendations

Present the conclusions and recommendations of the assessment, providing explanation and rationale for each conclusion and each recommendation. You can advance conclusions without recommendations if you plan to involve stakeholders in this task. If appropriate, recommendations can include guidelines and a timeline for implementation. Finally, this section can specify the anticipated benefits of adopting the recommendations or the possible dangers of not doing so.

Methods

The methods section details the procedures by which the data were collected. It describes how the program outcome was measured, specifies the nature and number of employees that participated in the assessment, and chronicles the participants' activity during the assessment.

Description of the Measures. Describe how the program outcome was measured. For a questionnaire, identify its origin, whether preexisting or developed for this study. Briefly describe the questionnaire's content, length, and format, and indicate that a copy is presented in the appendix to the report. If a low questionnaire score indicates a desired outcome, indicate this. For example, a low score is desirable if the outcome is number of accidents or level of employee turnover. For a preexisting questionnaire, present any information available about its measurement reliability and measurement validity. For a new questionnaire, describe the steps taken in its development and present any prestudy information about its reliability and validity. If this section becomes too long or too detailed for the average reader, shift the latter topics to the appendix and refer the interested reader there.

Description of the Participants. Identify the number of employees whose data was analyzed in the assessment and the percentage this number reflects of the total number of employees that participated in the program. Describe the nature of the employees, including their gender, age, tenure in the organization, position or rank within the organization, and other characteristics that seem relevant to the study. Finally, indicate how the subjects came to participate in the study—for example, whether they volunteered, were chosen by a manager, or were selected randomly.

Description of the Procedures. The procedures of an assessment are the steps taken to control the experiences of the assessment participants. These steps include assigning employees to the program group—and the control group if one was used—what happened to employees while they were in the groups, and the steps taken to gather data from them. First, identify whether subjects were assigned randomly to groups, and identify the number of subjects in each group. Summarize the activities of each group. For instance, one group may have participated in diversity training workshops and then completed a questionnaire, while another group did not participate but did complete the questionnaire. Identify how and by whom the questionnaires were administered and collected.

Analysis of the Data

This section addresses measurement error and sampling error, reporting evidence bearing on the reliability and validity of the measurement tool and the significance and importance of the observed program impact. To address measurement error, first identify the methods used to assess measurement reliability, report the results, and state any conclusions drawn about the measurement reliability of the questionnaire. Second, identify the methods used to assess measurement validity, report the results, and state any conclusions drawn about measurement validity. Finally, summarize the degree to which measurement error remains a concern in the study.

To address the issue of random sampling error, summarize the results of a statistical test in table format. For a t test, the table should contain the sample sizes (or degrees of freedom), the means, the standard deviations, and the Program t value. The table should also indicate whether the Program t value was statistically significant and at what level (e.g., $p < .05$). See Table 7.4 in Chapter 7 for an example of this type of table. Refer the reader to the table and highlight its main results. Finally, discuss the importance of the results. For a t test, discuss the size of its corresponding *r* value. If this information is too detailed for your stakeholders, you could shift it to the appendix and refer the interested reader there.

Limitations of the Assessment. Alert readers to major limitations of the assessment. Limitations are especially important when the assessment fails to provide evidence of program effectiveness. Failure to find program effectiveness suggests one of two possibilities: the program is ineffective, or the effectiveness of the program was not detected due to limitations of the assessment. Likely limita-

And in conclusion, I'm convinced that my theory that Dogs have Nine Lives is correct, except for the 47 possible errors in the study.

Report Page 19

tions include low measurement reliability or validity, the presence of extraneous influences associated with a poor assessment design or a good assessment design poorly implemented, and a statistical test of low power, such as occurs with small sample sizes. As you can see, we are back to the topics of measurement error, extraneous error, and sampling error.

Appendix

The appendix contains information pertinent to the assessment report but that was too detailed or specialized for the main discussion. Here you should present an uncompleted copy of the questionnaire used in the assessment. Normally you would not include employee scores on the questionnaire or computer printouts of the results of the data analysis. Additional information may be placed in separate appendices or in separate sections of one appendix but should only be included if it helps the reader understand the assessment.

That completes the topics usually contained in a written report. You will want to edit and revise the report to attain the communication goals listed in Table 9.1. You might ask a stakeholder to read the report and offer suggestions for improvement. Such feedback can assist revision immeasurably. Strive for clarity of thought and progression, spotlight the essential, and omit the tangential.

Making Program Decisions

Once assessment results are in the hands of stakeholders, the assessment enterprise can fulfill its main purpose—to serve decision making. Assessment results may warrant one of several options regarding the fate of the program: it may be retained as is, expanded, reduced, ended, or its content or characteristics modified. Our assumption has been that sound decision making requires sound information, and in turn, that information is more likely to be sound when we have addressed the types of error that accompany inquiry. We have taken steps so that decisions are not based on tradition, unquestioned authority, consensus, or intuition.

We know, however, that organizational decisions are not made in a vacuum. Rather, they are made in organizations, and thus are subject to a variety of influences. A program change can affect people, processes, even the structure of an organization. In this sense, a program change has a ripple effect, like a wave with height and distance. Sometimes the wave affects only those nearby and only in a small way, and sometimes the wave impacts those far removed from the program and sometimes in a big way. The latter catches people's attention if not their disdain.

The path from recommendation to decision can be complex, if it is even completed, for decisions sometimes become waylaid. We should remember that one decision that can be made is to not make a decision, in which case the program remains unchanged. As yet, we have not considered who makes the decision or how various organizational realities affect the decision making process. Fig. 9.1 portrays four influences on program decisions in addition to the assessment findings themselves. We'll consider these influences in turn.

Level of Approval

In many organizations, especially those where decision making is centralized, decision responsibility resides with a single decision maker, often one at much higher status than the realm in which the program exists. Whereas assessment results and recommendations often undergo group deliberation, say within an executive committee, ultimate decision responsibility often remains with a single person, usually the chair of the committee. That responsibility may appear to be exercised infrequently, because group deliberation, through the chair's influence, often coincides with the chair's view, and indeed, committee members may perceive that the decision was reached through consensus. In tall organizations, assessment recommendations may have to gain intermediate approvals before reaching the ultimate decision maker. That is, the evaluator may submit assessment recommendations to an immediate superior for approval, who upon approval, submits the recommendations to his or her superior for approval, until at some point, recommendations may reach an executive committee. Persons at each level may use different criteria for what constitutes a good recommendation, although this often goes unnoticed provided the recommendation moves along.

In flatter organizations, especially those facing rapidly changing environments, responsibility for program decisions often resides at a lower level, sometimes even at the program level, and sometimes, responsibility lies with a group rather than a single individual.

The implications are first that persons at different status levels may make different decisions and second, that influences exist within groups that do not impinge on a single decision maker. Status carries a perspective of organizational effectiveness, one that usually differs from the perspectives of those above and below. From research on small groups, we know that a group's level of cohesion and conformity produce differences in decision accuracy and risk taking compared to

Figure 9.1
Organizational Arenas Affecting Program Decisions

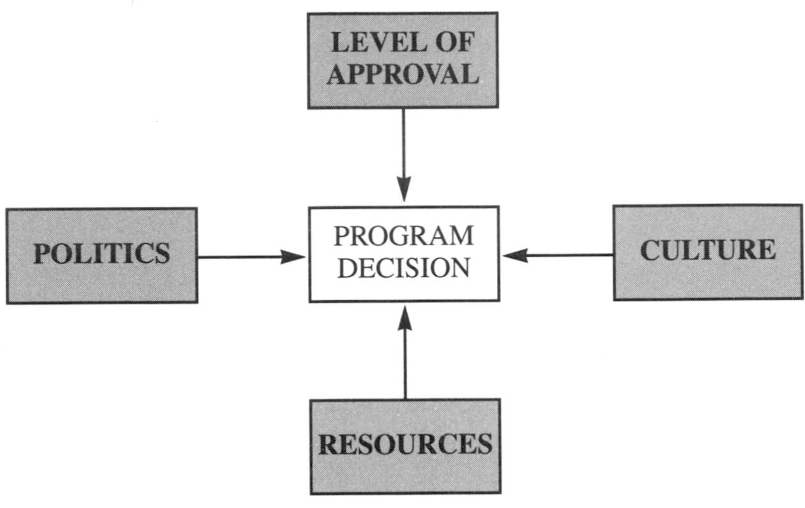

the decisions made by individuals and the risks taken by individuals. The fate of a program may turn on the organizational level of decision making and whether decisions are made by individuals or by groups.

Resources

Organizational success entails attaining not just bottom-line states such as profit, service, or growth but also entails attaining intermediate outcomes, such as efficiency, quality, and customer satisfaction. The list of sought outcomes for most organizations is often quite lengthy (e.g., attendance, promptness, employee morale, and so on). As you can see, some outcomes are more specific than others, some more central to success than others. Managers and administrators recognize that organizational success is comprised of an accumulation of interrelated, smaller successes and plan organizational activities accordingly. They generate goals for the organization and enact programs to produce many of these outcomes.

Programs require resources. Some require staff, facilities, and equipment. Some require technology and information. And generally, all programs welcome money, but just as generally, organizations have a limited amount of resources to allocate. Shortages force managers to distinguish between the essential and the desired. Not only is this distinction difficult to make, but the desired often contributes to the essential. What can we safely diminish? Safety? Employee morale? Facilities upkeep? Shortages also force managers to consider the desired level of each outcome. What amount of each outcome is required? The maximum? Enough to get by? Any is better than none? Finally, shortages may prompt managers to redirect resources from long-term goals to short-term goals.

The point is, a program recommendation—whether it is to continue, expand, restrict, or end a program—enters the financial arena. Continuing a program means continuing its current level of support. Expanding a program means additional support, perhaps denying support to other programs. Reducing or ending a program may free support for other programs. In short, the resources available to decision makers affect the level of support that can be allocated to organizational programs. The more essential to success a program's outcome is perceived to be, the more resources it usually draws.

The above discussion assumed that the decisions to allocate limited resources are genuine in spirit, aimed at what the organization needs to realize success. Additional complexity is added when decisions arise from struggles among subunits of the organization to maximize their own resources.

Politics

When organizational units draw from the same limited resources, influential members of those units often attempt to influence the decisions that allocate resources. When those units are highly interdependent, competition for resources can be intense, as concern within each unit for its own welfare or survival supplants concern for what will help the organization succeed. Prospective influencers do not limit themselves to established communication channels; they often approach decision makers informally in one-on-one encounters. Units that have garnered power and support often attain a disproportionate portion of resources. In turn, the added resources may increase their power. Members of less successful units may believe that decision makers "played favorites." The allocation of limited resources can easily become politicized. Many employees accept politics as simply an organizational reality, an unavoidable, inevitable process. In this light, they see political processes as a way to get needed resources, to get jobs done, to cut through red tape, to coordinate their efforts with others, to attain visibility, and so on.

The point is, a recommendation that emerges from a program assessment enters the political arena. A recommendation to continue a program means that resources already devoted to the program continue. Seeking the needed resources for their own units or programs, organizational members may use political channels and tactics to influence this decision. Expanding a program requires additional support, perhaps syphoning support from other programs. Expect political resistance, power struggles, and bargaining. In an extreme case, those who assessed the program may "fudge the data" to make the program look worthy of expansion. Restricting or ending a program may free support for other programs. Influential members of other units may hasten this decision. Expect a political scramble for the resources. In an extreme case, another unit may have sabotaged the program or its assessment to hasten its demise. Although political tactics often take a surreptitious route to retain the plausibility of denial, they usually stop short of such extremes as falsifying data or sabotage because the consequences of detection are too great. Political maneuvering requires skill, sometimes the very skill that is rewarded through promotion and advancement. Managers often apply those skills to vie for limited resources. In short, political processes can affect the decisions that govern the fate of organizational programs.

Occasionally, ineffective programs are retained, effective programs are dropped, or potentially effective programs are never begun. Reaching beyond the presence of limited resources or political maneuvering, such decisions are directed by the organization's sense of identity and its set of shared values.

Culture

When humans live interdependently for extended periods with common purpose, they develop a culture. They generate a shared sense of who they are and a shared set of values about what is important for the survival and well-being of the group. This identity and these values are promulgated and reinforced through organizational rites and rituals, stories of the organization's heros and villains, and metaphors and symbols. Each organization has its own philosophy: "Quality is job one," "We are family," "No challenge is insurmountable," "Nobody beats us to the punch."

A program's outcome will be measured against the organization's shared sense of identity and values. A program—even one competitors use effectively—may never see the light of day in the organization because "It's just not who we are." An otherwise ineffectual program may be supported because "It's the way we do things here." Program recommendations must jive with the organization's culture.

As described in Chapter 1, the metaphysical method of decision making consults tradition, unquestioned authority, consensus, or intuition. In the process, emphasis shifts from the merits of the program to what was done in the past, what the boss says, what all agree on, or what we simply *know* is true. In contrast, the scientific method focuses on the merits of the program and the types of errors that accompany inquiry. Managers can choose between these methods of decision making and are encouraged to adopt the latter.

Because limited resources, politics, and culture are organizational realities within which all decisions are made, managers cannot avoid them. Managers must operate as best they can within these arenas. The premise of this book is that program-related information should be sound as it enters these organizational realms, that sound decisions are more likely when based on sound information.

Conclusion to the Book

This book has two goals: to enable readers to help plan program assessments where they work and to equip readers to be educated consumers of program assessment reports that cross their desks. If the reader can ask pertinent questions during the planning or reporting of a program assessment, those goals will have been fulfilled. These questions, of course, would reflect the premise of this book, namely that sound decision making in the workplace requires sound information. Toward this end, the book advanced a model of program assessment centered on addressing the types of error that can accompany inquiry, lest the influence of mismeasurement, nonprogram factors, or sampling be mistaken for program impact. Sound decision making requires no less.

Main Points of Chapter 9

- Assessment results should be communicated to stakeholders to further decision making. Occasionally, results are shared with the organization's public and the academic community.
- The communication goals of an assessment report are to gain the listeners' attention, interest, understanding, belief, and action.
- Often unfamiliar with the research process, stakeholders benefit from an informal, oral report with opportunity for

questions and answers. A formal, written report should be available for stakeholders interested in more detail than presented in the oral report. In both oral and written reports, the vocabulary of the organization, the conclusions and recommendations are emphasized over the theory and the intricacies of data analysis.

- Members of the academic community want a formal report that uses the vocabulary of science and that emphasizes the theory that underlies the assessment and its testing over the program and its effectiveness.
- Program decisions can be made at different levels of the organization and by groups or by individuals. Different organizational levels often use different criteria of effectiveness, and groups are affected by influences that do not impinge on the individual.
- Administrators often allocate limited resources among organizational programs according to their perceived value to the success of the organization.
- Program decisions occur within, and thus are affected by, the financial, political, and cultural arenas of the organization.

Chapter Note

1. This discussion was drawn from Ronald L. Applbaum and Karl W.E. Anatol, *Effective Oral Communication for Business and the Professions.* Chicago: Science Research Associates, 1982, pp 240–243.

Appendix 1

Table of Random Numbers

Line \ Column	1	2	3	4	5	6	7	8	9	10
1	1368	9621	9151	2066	1208	2664	9822	6599	6911	5112
2	5953	5936	2541	4011	0408	3593	3679	1378	5936	2651
3	7226	9466	9553	7671	8599	2119	5337	5953	6355	6889
4	8883	3454	6773	8207	5576	6386	7487	0190	0867	1298
5	7022	5281	1168	4099	8069	8721	8353	9952	8006	9045
6	4576	1853	7884	2451	3488	1286	4842	7719	5795	3953
7	8715	1416	7028	4616	3470	9938	5703	0196	3465	0034
8	4011	0408	2224	7626	0643	1149	8834	6429	8691	0143
9	1400	3694	4482	3608	1238	8221	5129	6105	5314	8385
10	6370	1884	0820	4854	9161	6509	7123	4070	6759	6113
11	4522	5749	8084	3932	7678	3549	0051	6761	6952	7041
12	7195	6234	6426	7148	9945	0358	3242	0519	6550	1327
13	0054	0810	2937	2040	2299	4198	0846	3937	3986	1019
14	5166	5433	0381	9686	5670	5129	2103	1125	3404	8785
15	1247	3793	7415	7819	1783	0506	4878	7673	9840	6629
16	8529	7842	7203	1844	8619	7404	4215	9969	6948	5643
17	8973	3440	4366	9242	2151	0244	0922	5887	4883	1177
18	9307	2959	5904	9012	4951	3695	4529	7197	7179	3239
19	2923	4276	9467	9868	2257	1925	3382	7244	1781	8037
20	6372	2808	1238	8098	5509	4617	4099	6705	2386	2830
21	6922	1807	4900	5306	0411	1828	8634	2331	7247	3230
22	9862	8336	6453	0545	6127	2741	5967	8447	3017	5709
23	3371	1530	5104	3076	5506	3101	4143	5845	2095	6127
24	6712	9402	9588	7019	9248	9192	4223	6555	7947	2474
25	3071	8782	7157	5941	8830	8563	2252	8109	5880	9912

Line \ Column	1	2	3	4	5	6	7	8	9	10
26	4022	9734	7852	9096	0051	7387	7056	9331	1317	7833
27	9682	8892	3577	0326	5306	0050	8517	4376	0788	5443
28	6705	2175	9904	3743	1902	5393	3032	8432	0612	7972
29	1872	8292	2366	8603	4288	6809	4357	1072	6822	5611
30	2559	7534	2281	7351	2064	0611	9613	2000	0327	6145
31	4399	3751	9783	5399	5175	8894	0296	9483	0400	2272
32	6074	8827	2195	2532	7680	4288	6807	3101	6850	6410
33	5155	7186	4722	6721	0838	3632	5355	9369	2006	7681
34	3193	2800	6184	7891	9838	6123	9397	4019	8389	9508
35	8610	1880	7423	3384	4625	6653	2900	6290	9286	2396
36	4778	8818	2992	6300	4239	9595	4384	0611	7687	2088
37	3987	1619	4164	2542	4042	7799	9084	0278	8422	4330
38	2977	0248	2793	3351	4922	8878	5703	7421	2054	4391
39	1312	2919	8220	7285	5902	7882	1403	5354	9913	7109
40	3890	7193	7799	9190	3275	7840	1872	6232	5295	3148
41	2671	4690	1550	2262	2597	8034	0785	2978	4409	0237
42	9111	0250	3275	7519	9740	4577	2064	0286	3398	1348
43	0391	6035	9230	4999	3332	0608	6113	0391	5789	9926
44	2475	2144	1886	2079	3004	9686	5669	4367	9306	2595
45	5336	5845	2095	6446	5694	3641	1085	8705	5416	9066
46	6808	0423	0155	1652	7897	4335	3567	7109	9690	3739
47	8525	0577	8940	9451	6726	0876	3818	7607	8854	3566
48	0398	0741	8787	3043	5063	0617	1770	5048	7721	7032
49	3623	9636	3638	1406	5731	3978	8068	7238	9715	3363
50	0739	2644	4917	8866	3632	5399	5175	7422	2476	2607
51	6713	3041	8133	8749	8835	6745	3597	3476	3816	3455
52	7775	9315	0432	8327	0861	1515	2297	3375	3713	9174
53	8599	2122	6842	9202	0810	2936	1514	2090	3067	3574
54	7955	3759	5254	1126	5553	4713	9605	7909	1658	5490
55	4766	0070	7260	6033	7997	0109	5993	7592	5436	1727
56	5165	1670	2534	8811	8231	3721	7947	5719	2640	1394
57	9111	0513	2751	8256	2931	7783	1281	6531	7259	6993
58	1667	1084	7889	8963	7018	8617	6381	0723	4926	4551
59	2145	4587	8585	2412	5431	4667	1942	7238	9613	2212
60	2739	5528	1481	7528	9368	1823	6979	2547	7268	2467
61	8769	5480	9160	5354	9700	1362	2774	7980	9157	8788
62	6531	9435	3422	2474	1475	0159	3414	5224	8399	5820
63	2937	4134	7120	2206	5084	9473	3958	7320	9878	8609
64	1581	3285	3727	8924	6204	0797	0882	5945	9375	9153
65	6268	1045	7076	1436	4165	0143	0293	4190	7171	7932

Line \ Column	1	2	3	4	5	6	7	8	9	10
66	4293	0523	8625	1961	1039	2856	4889	4358	1492	3804
67	6936	4213	3212	7229	1230	0019	5998	9206	6753	3762
68	5334	7641	3258	3769	1362	2771	6124	9813	7915	8960
69	9373	1158	4418	8826	5665	5896	0358	4717	8232	4859
70	6968	9428	8950	5346	1741	2348	8143	5377	7695	0685
71	4229	0587	8794	4009	9691	4579	3302	7673	9629	5246
72	3807	7785	7097	5701	6639	0723	4819	0900	2713	7650
73	4891	8829	1642	2155	0796	0466	2946	2970	9143	6590
74	1055	2968	7911	7479	8199	9735	8271	5339	7058	2964
75	2983	2345	0568	4125	0894	8302	0506	6761	7706	4310
76	4026	3129	2968	8053	2797	4022	9838	9611	0975	2437
77	4075	0260	4256	0337	2355	9371	2954	6021	5783	2827
78	8488	5450	1327	7358	2034	8060	1788	6913	6123	9405
79	1976	1749	5742	4098	5887	4567	6064	2777	7830	5668
80	2793	4701	9466	9554	8294	2160	7486	1557	4769	2781
81	0916	6272	6825	7188	9611	1181	2301	5516	5451	6832
82	5961	1149	7946	1950	2010	0600	5655	0796	2569	4365
83	3222	4189	1891	8172	8731	4769	2782	1325	4238	9279
84	1176	7834	4600	9992	9449	5824	5344	1008	6678	1921
85	2369	8971	2314	4806	5071	8908	8274	4936	3357	4441

Appendix 2

Table of t Values

Probability Level

df	*.05*	*.01*	*df*	*.05*	*.01*
1	12.706	63.657	21	2.080	2.831
2	4.303	9.925	22	2.074	2.819
3	3.182	5.841	23	2.069	2.807
4	2.776	4.604	24	2.064	2.797
5	2.571	4.032	25	2.060	2.787
6	2.447	3.707	26	2.056	2.779
7	2.365	3.499	27	2.052	2.771
8	2.306	3.355	28	2.048	2.763
9	2.262	3.250	29	2.045	2.756
10	2.228	3.169	30	2.042	2.750
11	2.201	3.106	40	2.021	2.704
12	2.179	3.055	60	2.000	2.660
13	2.160	3.012	120	1.980	2.617
14	2.145	2.977	∞	1.960	2.576
15	2.131	2.947			
16	2.120	2.921			
17	2.110	2.898			
18	2.101	2.878			
19	2.093	2.861			
20	2.086	2.845			

Appendix 3

Survey Sample Sizes for 95 Percent (Boldfaced) and 99 Percent Confidence Levels

	MARGIN OF ERROR				
POPULATION	±1	±2	±3	±4	±5
Infinity	**9604** 16587	**2401** 4147	**1067** 1843	**600** 1037	**384** 663
100,000	**8762** 14227	**2345** 3982	**1056** 1810	**596** 1026	**383** 659
50,000	**8057** 12455	**2291** 3829	**1045** 1778	**593** 1016	**381** 654
10,000	**4899** 6239	**1936** 2931	**964** 1556	**566** 940	**370** 622
5,000	**3288** 3842	**1622** 2267	**879** 1347	**536** 859	**357** 585
3,000	**2286** 2541	**1334** 1741	**787** 1142	**500** 771	**340** 543
2,000	**1655** 1785	**1091** 1349	**696** 959	**462** 683	**322** 498
1,000	**906** 943	**706** 806	**516** 648	**375** 509	**278** 399
500	**475** 485	**414** 446	**340** 393	**273** 337	**217** 285

For a diverse population (50/50 split of opinion).

Appendix 4

Per Group Sample Sizes for **95 Percent (Boldfaced)** and 99 Percent Confidence Levels

	Program Impact		
Power	Small	Medium	Large
70%	**310** 482	**50** 79	**20** 32
80%	**393** 586	**64** 95	**26** 38
90%	**526** 746	**85** 120	**34** 48

For two-tailed t tests

Appendix 5

One-Group Sample Sizes for **95 Percent (Boldfaced)** and 99 Percent Confidence Levels

	PROGRAM IMPACT		
POWER	Small	Medium	Large
70%	**159** 247	**26** 40	**11** 17
80%	**201** 300	**32** 48	**13** 20
90%	**269** 381	**43** 61	**18** 25

For two-tailed t tests

Appendix 6

Compilations of Research Measures

Buros, Oscar K. *The Seventh Mental Measurements Yearbook.* Highland Park, NJ: Gryphon Press, 1972.

Dunham, R. B., and Smith, F. J. *Organizational Surveys.* Glenview, IL: Scott, Foresman, 1979.

Lake, Dale G., Miles, Mathew B., and Earle, Ralph B. Jr. *Measuring Human Behavior: Tools for the Assessment of Social Functioning.* NY: Teachers College Press, 1973.

Mahlar, W. R. *Diagnostic Studies.* Reading, MA: Addison-Wesley, 1974.

Miller, Delbert C. *Handbook of Research Design and Social Measurement.* 3rd ed. NY: David McKay Company, 1977.

Patchen, H. *Some Questionnaire Measures of Employee Motivation and Morale.* Ann Arbor, MI: Institute for Social Research, 1965.

Pfelffer, J. W., Haslin, R., and Jones, J. E. *Instrumentation in Human Relations Training.* 2nd ed. San Diego, CA: University Associates, 1976.

Price, James L., and Mueller, Charles W. *Handbook of Organizational Measurement.* Marshfield, MA: Pitman Publishing, 1986.

Reader, Leo G., Ramacher, Linda, and Gorelnik, Sally. *Handbook of Scales and Indices of Health Behavior.* Pacific Palisades, CA: Goodyear Publishing Co., 1976.

Robinson, John P., Athanasiou, Robert, and Head, Kendra B. *Measures of Occupational Attitudes and Occupational Characteristics.* Ann Arbor, MI: Institute for Social Research, University of Michigan, 1969.

Robinson, John P., and Shaver, Phillip R. *Measures of Social Psychological Attitudes.* Ann Arbor, MI: Institute for Social Research, University of Michigan, 1969.

Shaw, Marvin. E., and Wright, Jack M. *Scales for the Measurement of Social Attitudes.* NY: McGraw-Hill, 1967.

Appendix 7

Journals That Publish Assessment Reports

A. Journals in the Field of Evaluation

American Journal of Evaluation
Evaluation and Program Planning
Evaluation Review
New Directions for Evaluation

B. Journals in the Field of Management

Administrative Science Quarterly
Employee Assistance Quarterly
Journal of Management
Journal of Occupational and Organizational Psychology
Journal of Organizational Behavior
Journal of Organizational Behavior Management
The Academy of Management Executive

C. Journals in the Field of Health

Evaluation and the Health Professions
Health Education
Health Education and Behavior
Health Care Management Review
International Quarterly of Community Health Education
Journal of Alcohol and Drug Education
Journal of Applied Gerontology
Journal of Health and Human Services Administration

Journal of Health and Social Behavior
Journal of Substance Abuse Treatment

D. Journals in the Field of Education

Educational Evaluation and Policy Analysis
Journal of Educational Administration
Journal of Vocational Education and Training
Studies in Educational Evaluation
The Journal for Research on Learning in the Workplace

E. Journals in the Field of Business, Public Administration, and Government

American Journal of Police
Annals of Tourism Research
Criminal Justice and Behavior
Environment and Behavior
Environmental Impact Assessment Review
Human Factors
Journal of Labor Research
Journal of Retailing
Military Psychology
Public Administration Quarterly
Public Personnel Management
Review of Public Personnel Administration
State and Local Government Review
The American Review of Public Administration
The Logistics and Transportation Review
Tourism Management
Work and Stress

F. Journals in the Field of Communication

Business Communication Quarterly
International Journal of Advertising
Journal of Business Communication
Journal of Consumer Research
Journal of the Market Research Society
Management Communication Quarterly
Marketing Science
Psychology and Marketing
The Journal of Personal Selling and Sales Management

Appendix 8
Table of F Values

Probability .05

df_D \ df_N	1	2	3	4
1	161.45	199.50	215.71	224.58
2	18.51	19.00	19.16	19.25
3	10.13	9.55	9.28	9.12
4	7.71	6.94	6.59	6.39
5	6.61	5.79	5.41	5.19
6	5.99	5.14	4.76	4.53
7	5.59	4.74	4.35	4.12
8	5.32	4.46	4.07	3.84
9	5.12	4.26	3.86	3.63
10	4.96	4.10	3.71	3.48
11	4.84	3.98	3.59	3.36
12	4.75	3.89	3.49	3.26
13	4.67	3.81	3.41	3.18
14	4.60	3.74	3.34	3.11
15	4.54	3.68	3.29	3.06
16	4.49	3.63	3.24	3.01
17	4.45	3.59	3.20	2.96
18	4.41	3.55	3.16	2.93
19	4.38	3.52	3.13	2.90
20	4.35	3.49	3.10	2.87
21	4.32	3.47	2.07	2.84
22	4.30	3.44	3.05	2.82
23	4.28	3.42	3.03	2.80
24	4.26	3.40	3.01	2.78
25	4.24	3.39	2.99	2.76
26	4.23	3.37	2.98	2.74
27	4.21	3.35	2.96	2.73
28	4.20	3.34	2.95	2.71
29	4.18	3.33	2.93	2.70
30	4.17	3.32	2.92	2.69
40	4.08	3.23	2.84	2.61
48	4.04	3.19	2.80	2.57
60	4.00	3.15	2.76	2.53
120	3.92	3.07	2.68	2.45
∞	3.84	3.00	2.60	2.37

Where df_N = degrees of freedom for the numerator
and df_D = degrees of freedom for the denominator

Probability .01

df_D \ df_N	1	2	3	4
1	—	—	—	—
2	98.50	99.00	99.17	99.25
3	34.12	30.82	29.46	28.71
4	21.20	18.00	16.69	15.98
5	16.26	13.27	12.06	11.39
6	13.75	10.93	9.78	9.15
7	12.25	9.55	8.45	7.85
8	11.26	8.65	7.59	7.01
9	10.56	8.02	6.99	6.42
10	10.04	7.56	6.55	5.99
11	9.65	7.21	6.22	5.67
12	9.33	6.93	5.95	5.41
13	9.07	6.70	5.74	5.21
14	8.86	6.51	5.56	5.04
15	8.68	6.36	5.42	4.89
16	8.53	6.23	5.29	4.77
17	8.40	6.11	5.19	4.67
18	8.29	6.01	5.09	4.58
19	8.19	5.93	5.01	4.50
20	8.10	5.85	4.94	4.43
22	7.95	5.72	4.82	4.31
24	7.82	5.61	4.72	4.22
26	7.72	5.53	4.64	4.14
28	7.64	5.45	4.57	4.07
30	7.56	5.39	4.51	4.02
40	7.31	5.18	4.31	3.83
60	7.08	4.98	4.13	3.65
80	6.96	4.88	4.04	3.56
120	6.85	4.79	3.95	3.48
∞	6.63	4.61	3.78	3.32

Where df_N = degrees of freedom for the numerator
and df_D = degrees of freedom for the denominator

Appendix 9

World Wide Web Sites Related to Evaluation

http://www.eval.org/

The home page of the American Evaluation Association. This site provides instructions on subscribing to the Listserv called EVALTALK, a free means of posing questions to professionals in the field of evaluation. The site also posts dates and locations of upcoming association conferences. Finally, the site contains links to many other Web sites related to evaluation.

http://www.unites.uqam.ca/ces/ces-sce.html

The home page of the Canadian Evaluation Association.

http://www3.sympatico.ca/gpic/gpichome.htm

Sponsored by Government Performance Information Consultants. This site contains links to many Web resources about evaluation.

http:www.wmich.edu/evalctr/

This is the address of the Evaluation Center at Western Michigan University. The Center focuses on evaluation within the fields of education and human services.

http://www.unitedway.org/outcomes/

Location of the Resource Network on Outcome Measurement of United Way, Inc. The Network provides resources for measuring program outcomes for health and human services.

Appendix 10

Guidelines for Academic Reports

An academic report provides enough information for a reader familiar with the research process to evaluate and replicate the research. The reader will want to understand (1) the theory that was tested, (2) the method of testing, (3) the steps taken to minimize measurement error, extraneous error, and statistical error, and (4) how the theory fared. The written report emphasizes theory and its testing, for the purpose of evolving theory applicable to effectiveness at organizations generally.

The written report is submitted either for presentation at a professional conference such as the annual meeting of the American Evaluation Association, or for inclusion in an academic journal such as *Evaluation Review* or one of those listed in Appendix 7. Most journals ask preparers of reports to follow the publication manual of the American Psychological Association. The journal also indicates how to submit the report. Specific information about contacting specific professional organizations is available on the Internet. Submitted reports are usually reviewed by experts in the field, so the report should be sent for consideration at only one journal at a time. Obviously the written report should be carefully revised and rewritten for clarity before submission.

The written report follows a standard format to ensure that all important topics of the assessment are covered thoroughly and in logical order. For inclusion in an academic journal, the written report is submitted as typed pages, following the guidelines presented in the publication manual of the American Psychological Association or the publication manual of the Modern Language Association (available in most libraries and bookstores). Those guidelines will differ slightly from those presented in this chapter, and they will also be more detailed. You should consult the manual recommended by the academic journal for which you are preparing your report. Table A10.1 presents the standard format for a written report.

The report should be typed, double spaced, and use the uppercased (capitalized) elements in Table 8.3 as centered, uppercased section headings. Each page should have a number centered at page bottom, beginning with the second page of the introduction and continuing to the footnote, figure, table, and appendix pages. The writing

Table A10.1
The Standard Format for a Written Assessment Report

I. Title Page

II. Abstract

III. Introduction
  - Importance of the Program Outcome
  - The Theory of the Program Assessment
  - Purpose of the Study

IV. METHOD
  - Nature of the Program
  - Description of the Measure
  - Description of the Subjects
  - Description of the Procedures
  - Description of the Methods of Data Analysis

V. RESULTS
  - Measurement Error
  - Sampling Error

VI. DISCUSSION
  - Interpretation of the Results
  - Limitations of the Study
  - Conclusion

VII. FOOTNOTES

VIII. Figure Page

IX. Table Page

X. APPENDIX

should use the past tense. Each element of the written report is described below.

Title Page

The title page contains a title appropriate to the topic of the theory of the assessment. The title should be centered and one-third down the page. The first letter of each important word should be capitalized. The title page also includes the author's name and position or affiliation.

Abstract

The abstract appears on a separate page immediately following the title page. The heading *Abstract* should be centered and one-third down the page. Below its title, the abstract is a one-paragraph summary of the purpose, methods, findings, and conclusions of the study.

Introduction

The introduction begins on a new page with no heading. The introduction should capture the reader's favorable attention, increase the reader's interest in the topic area of the report, and provide a context for understanding the report. Readers are most likely to read the report if they believe it will present information in an interesting way about a topic of interest to them. The prospect of increased understanding of organizational effectiveness entices managers at other organizations and members of the academic community alike. Managers will look toward improving effectiveness in their own organization, and members of the academic community will look toward strengthening theories of organizational effectiveness. Toward these ends, the introduction should: (1) highlight the importance of the program outcome to organizational success, (2) advance a theory of organizational effectiveness, and (3) state the purpose of the study.

Importance of the Program Outcome. Begin the report by establishing the program outcome as a component of organizational success (although avoid the term *program outcome* here). For example, if your program outcome is employee morale, you may refer to the conclusions of previous research or to the provisions of existing theory that advance employee morale as a component of organizational success. In the absence of relevant research or theory, anecdotal evidence may suffice. For example, you may cite several large companies that place high value on achieving and maintaining high employee morale. The task in this part of the report is to alert the reader that this report will focus on an important dimension of organizational effectiveness.

The Theory of the Program Assessment. Next you should identify how and why the program affects the program outcome; however, avoid the terms *program* and *program outcome*. That is, identify organizational activity (the program) that affects an important dimension of organizational success (the program outcome). More specifically, present your theory using the methods in Chapter 3 of this text. For example, your theory may explain why employee participation in decision making increases employee morale. You may present an existing theory or an original theory. In either case, describe the theory, defining important terms you use. Also, highlight any previous research that supports the propositions of the theory. A diagram of the theory can be included (usually on a separate page at the back of the report). The diagram should be labeled and numbered. For example, the diagram may be labeled *Figure 1: Theory of Employee Morale.* Use the figure number to refer the reader to the diagram. Finally, you may clarify the theory and how it works, by using an example.

Purpose of the Study. Conclude the introduction with a statement of the purpose of the study. For example, you may state that the purpose of your study is to discover whether the presence of employee participation in decision making produces higher employee morale than the absence of employee participation in decision making.

Method

The Method section of the written report details the procedures by which the data was collected and analyzed. The description should include: the nature of the program, the measure of the program outcome, the nature and number of employees who were studied, the activity of the researcher and the employees during the study, and the methods used to analyze the data. You need to present enough detail for the reader to evaluate and replicate the study.

Nature of the Program. Briefly explain the nature of the program, including its goals and implementation. The program's implementation includes who administered the program, who participated in the program, what administrators and participants did, where they did it, when they did it, and for how long they did it. This description should be thorough but succinct—perhaps one paragraph—because the reader's interest lies more in theory and its testing than in the effects of a program in a specific organization.

Description of the Measure. Define the measure of the program outcome. For a questionnaire, identify its origin—whether preexisting or developed for this study. Describe the questionnaire's content, length, and format; and give examples of typical questions. Indicate whether a good outcome is indicated by a high score or a low score. For example, a high score usually reflects an outcome, such as employee morale, for which a high level is desired; a low score usually reflects an outcome such as number of accidents or level of employee turnover, for which a low level is desired. For a preexisting questionnaire, present any available information about its measurement reliability and measurement validity. For a new questionnaire, describe the steps taken in its development and present any prestudy information about its measurement reliability and measurement validity.

Description of the Subjects. The term *subjects* refers to the participants in the study, usually employees. Identify the number of subjects whose data was analyzed in the study and the percentage this number reflects of the total number of subjects who began the program. Some participants may have dropped out of the program, transferred departments, or returned unusable questionnaires, thereby lowering the rate of return. Describe the subjects, including their gender, age, tenure in the organization, position or rank within the organization, and other characteristics that seem relevant to the study. Finally, indicate how the subjects came to participate in the study—for example, whether they were volunteers, were chosen by a manager, or were selected randomly.

Description of the Procedures. *Procedures* refer to the steps used to gather data prescribed by a program assessment design. First, identify or describe the program assessment design of your study. The description would follow the explanation of program assessment designs presented in Chapter 5 of this text, although a diagram of the assessment design is usually not presented. Identify whether or not subjects were assigned to each group randomly, and identify the number of subjects in each group. Summarize the activities of each group. For example, one group may have participated in decision making and then completed a questionnaire, while another group may not have participated in decision making but did complete a questionnaire.

Identify how and by whom the questionnaire was administered and collected.

Description of the Data Analysis Methods. Name the methods you plan to use in analyzing the data for measurement error and sampling error. For example, you may plan to assess measurement reliability with the test-retest method and plan to assess sampling error with a t test. Identify the significance level of the t test to be used, usually .05 or .01.

Results

The Results section presents the results of the data analysis and advances any conclusions drawn from it. With extraneous error already addressed by the assessment design, the data analysis addresses measurement error and sampling error. Thus the results section includes an assessment of the reliability and validity of the measurement tool, as well as the significance and importance of an observed program impact.

Measurement Error. Identify the methods used to assess measurement reliability, report the results, and state any conclusions about measurement reliability that are warranted by the data analysis. Similarly, identify the methods used to assess measurement validity, report the results, and state any conclusions about measurement validity that are warranted by the data analysis. Finally, summarize the degree to which measurement error remains a concern in the study.

Sampling Error. Summarize the results of a t test (usually in a table on a separate page at the end of the report). Label and number the table. For example, you may label the table, *Table 1. Effects of Participation in Decision Making on Employee Morale.* The table should contain the sample sizes (or degrees of freedom), the means, the standard deviations, and the Program t value. The table should also indicate whether the Program t value was statistically significant and at what level (e.g., $p < .05$). (See Table 7.2 for an example of this type of table.) In the report, refer the reader to the table and highlight its main results, including the conclusions about the statistical significance of the results. Finally, present evidence about the importance of the results and state any warranted conclusions about their importance.

Discussion

The Discussion section evaluates the theory in light of the results of the data analysis, it identifies major limitations of the study, and it concludes the report.

Interpretation of the Results. Succinctly restate the purpose of the study and the data-analysis findings about the significance and importance of the program impact. Discuss the degree to which those findings support the theory of the study—remembering that theories can be supported, not proven. Conversely, unsupported theories are wrong in either whole or part, or they were tested inadequately due to limitations of the study. In the first case, you may suggest modifications to the theory. In the second case, you may suspend judgment of the theory until it is tested more adequately.

Limitations of the Study. Describe major limitations of the study. This is especially important when the data analysis does not support the theory. Limitations of the study arise from inadequate control of the sources of measurement error, extraneous error, or sampling error.

Conclusion. Close the report with one or more of the following: a restatement of the soundness of the theory in light of the findings, a call for further theoretical work, a call for additional research, or a restatement of the importance of the program outcome to organizational success. The conclusion completes the body of the report.

Footnotes

Sources that are quoted or cited in the report should be fully identified on the footnote page. Give the footnote page the title Footnote, or Footnotes if there are two or more. Make the title all uppercase letters, one inch from the top of the page, and centered in the page width. Below the title, give the footnote number, and list the full information for the reference. You can use the notes at the end of the chapters in this book as a guide for an appropriate format for footnotes.

Figure Page

Place each figure on a separate page following the footnote page. Each figure should be numbered and titled. You can use the figures in Chapter 1 of this book as a guide to numbering and naming your figures.

Table Page

Place each table on a separate page following the figure page. Each table should be numbered and titled. You can use Table 6.1 in Chapter 6 of this book as a guide to numbering and naming your tables.

Appendix

Include a copy of an original questionnaire developed specifically for this study as an appendix. The report should not include a copy of a preexisting or adapted preexisting questionnaire, original scores on the questionnaires, or standard formulas or computations.

For all parts of a report, keep in mind that writing benefits from thoughtful revision. The written report should always be carefully reread, revised, and rewritten for clarity.

Index

Academic journals, *Appendix 7*
Academic reports, *Appendix 10*
Analysis of covariance. *See F test*
Analysis of variance. *See F test*
ARIMA model, 227–230
Assessment design
  deficient assessment designs, 119–126
  description of, 117–119
  quasi-assessment designs, 129–136
  strengths and weaknesses of, 231
  summary of, 136
  true assessment designs, 126–129
Assessment reports
  academic reports, *Appendix 10*
  oral reports, 248–253
  written reports, 253–257
Autocorrelation, 227–230

Boundary, 60–62

Chronbach's alpha, 95–96
Communication goals, 246–248
Content validation, 97–98
Convergent validity, 99–102
Correlation, 89–91

Decision making, 5, 7, 24, 36, 257–263
Deficient assessment designs
  one-group observation design, 120–121
  one-group pre- and postobservation design, 121–124
  nonequivalent groups observation design, 124–125
Degrees of freedom, 186–188

Empirical method of decision making, 13–21
Expectations, 56–57
Explanations, 57–59
Extraneous error
  definition of, 115
  effects of, 116–117
  protection against, 231
  sources of, 115–116

F test
  assumptions of, 237
  follow-up t tests, 235–237
  for analysis of covariance, 224–226
  for analysis of variance, 233–236
  importance of result, 234–235

Hotelling's T^2, 238–239

Known-groups validity, 99

Mean, 182–183
Measurement error
  effects of, 85
  forms of, 82–83
  sources of, 83–85
Metaphysical method of decision making, 7–13
Moderators, 59–60
Moving average, 227–230

Oral assessment reports, 248–253

Predictive validation, 102
Program
  expectations, 56–57
  explanations, 57–59
Program assessment
  definition of, 4–5
  model of, 37

pressure for, 3–4
purpose of, 4
scope of, 6–7
steps of, 30–37
Program target group, 143

Quasi-assessment designs
nonequivalent groups pre- and postobservation design, 129–130, 226
one-group multiobservation design, 130–132, 227–230
two-group multiobservation design, 132–134, 230
Questionnaires
Likert-type, 33–34
scoring, 33
sources of, *Apendix 6*

r^1, 95
Random sampling. *See Sampling*
Reliability (measurement)
definition of, 19
internal consistency
split-half method, 23–24
Cronbach's alpha, 24–26
stability
equivalent forms method, 93–94
test-retest method, 92–93
to increase, 96

Sample size
descriptive surveys, 164–167
program versus control group, 168–171
program versus norm, 171–172
summary of, 164
Sampling
generalizing results, 162–164
nonrandom, 161–162
random
assignment to groups, 157–161
definition of, 148
how to form, 150–157
reasons for, 144–146
Sampling error
definition of, 178
effects of, 180–182
sources of, 178–179
visualizing, 179–180
Scientific method of decision making, 21–25
Scientific model of program assessment
components of, 38–42
logic of, 42–47
model, 37
Split-half reliability, 94–95
Stakeholders, 31
Standard deviation, 183–186
Steps of program assessment, 30–37

Test-retest reliability, 92–93
Theory
defining concepts, 62–66
definition of, 52
components of, 52–62
constructing, 66–69
qualities of, 70–73
True assessment designs
equivalent groups observation design, 126–128, 223
equivalent groups pre- and postobservation design, 128–129, 223–225
t test
assumptions of, 212–213, 215
multiple t tests, 221–222, 235–237
program versus control group, 189–208, 223
program versus norm, 213–215
significant versus important, 208–210
table of t Values, *Appendix 2*
the comparison, 196–201
t^1, 212–213
time-series data, 227–230

Validity (measurement)
construct validation
convergent method, 99–102
known-groups method, 99
content validation, 97–98
definition of, 96
predictive validation, 102

World Wide Web, 245–246, *Appendix 9*
Written assessment reports, 253–257